BEN JONSON'S
BASIC COMIC CHARACTERS
and Other Essays

BEN JONSON'S
BASIC COMIC CHARACTERS
and Other Essays

JAMES E. SAVAGE

UNIVERSITY AND COLLEGE PRESS OF MISSISSIPPI

ACKNOWLEDGMENTS

Of noteworthy help to me in the preparation of this manuscript has been my former graduate assistant Virginia Morgan. My colleague Professor John Pilkington has pointed out inconsistencies and corrected lapses in construction. My former student, now Professor Martha L. Adams, who also read the manuscript, offered many useful suggestions.

To the Committee on Research of the Graduate Council of the University of Mississippi I am indebted for a grant that enabled me to complete the essay that gives the book its title. And to the editorial staff of *Studies in English*, a journal published by the University of Mississippi, my thanks are expressed for permission to reprint the four essays that form the remainder of the text.

Perhaps greatest of all is my debt to students who over the years have been in my courses in the work of Jonson. Their questions, their suggestions, have prompted many of the observations in these essays, and their urging has moved me to organize the material.

TABLE OF CONTENTS

BEN JONSON'S
BASIC COMIC CHARACTERS
and Other Essays

I.
BEN JONSON'S
BASIC COMIC CHARACTERS

INTRODUCTION

Of all men, perhaps the most arrogant is the comic poet. He has answers. The tragic poet, generally, can ask the great questions, but his answers are tentative. His questions need not stop at the threshold of the gods, but his answers must.

But the comic poet, asking only how man should act in relation to man, can show through his creations both how a man should not act and, by implication, how he should; he can supply models for correct conduct; and he can through many voices comment on the consequences among men of conduct ranging from the greedy and hypocritical, through the mistaken, to the selfless and the magnanimous.

The comic poet may look, as does Shakespeare generally, at those persons of goodwill who are under illusions about their own natures and motives and those of their fellows. He may say with Shakespeare's melancholy Jaques in *As You Like It*: "Give me leave / To speak my mind, and I will through and through / Cleanse the foul body of th' infected world, / If they will patiently receive my medicine" (II.vii.58–61).

Or he may, as Ben Jonson does, work on a wider canvas and include those so devoid of intelligence, so possessed by greed, or so lost in self-deception that there is no hope of their redemption. Even with reference to these hopeless ones, Jonson has the answer —exposure and ridicule which will render them innocuous. Says his Asper in *Every Man Out of His Humour*: "(with an armed, and resolued hand) / Ile strip the ragged follies of the time, / Naked, as at their birth" (Intro. Grex, ll. 16–18).[1] Even a Jonson, however, recognizes that his severe didacticism must be tempered—"not to please the cookes tastes, but the guests" (*Epicoene*, Prol., l. 9). And, as a consequence, he involves his victims in complex actions, in many cases not theirs, but the poet's. The wideness of his canvas and the concentrated quality of his attack render such persons as Shakespeare uses impractical. Instead, types, almost stock characters, differentiated by humours—a technique by which the poet achieves invective, choric judgment, or satiric self-revelation—take postures of those wrought on and those manipulating them.

These puppets of Jonson fall into three broad categories of character: a Humourous Group, in which lie the basic vices—greed, hypocrisy, and folly[2]—as well as the lesser foibles of self-deception and the more extreme manifestations of the humours, concentrated for the therapeutic attention of those whom I shall call the Choric Group; and a third group, largely outside the poet's serious consideration, who serve as a sort of well-oiled machinery for arranging the interaction of the other two groups. These I shall designate as the Broker Group. Differences in definition, in function, or in fate among the groups will be described. The groups will be broken down into types, with each type discussed and exemplified through one or more prototypes.[3]

In the group to be considered first, the Choric Group, there seem to be three persons with distinct functions: the *Wit*, the *Chorus*, and the *Deity*. In the second major group there are two members, the *Broker* and the *Plyant Woman*. The persons in the third group, the humourous characters, are individuals of three basic types, the

---

[1] The source for all excerpts from the work of Jonson is *Ben Jonson*, ed. C. H. Herford and Percy and Evelyn Simpson (11 vols.; Oxford: Oxford University Press, 1925–1952). Citations are in the body of the text.

[2] Helena Watts Baum, in *The Satiric and Didactic in Ben Jonson's Comedy* (Chapel Hill: University of North Carolina Press, 1947), lists five objects of comic satire: avarice, lust, drunkenness, witchcraft, and the Puritans.

[3] C. G. Thayer, in *Ben Jonson: Studies in the Plays* (Norman: University of Oklahoma Press, 1963), pp. 157 and 158, divides Jonson's characters into two groups, the "Poet-figures" and "another group of characters whose quintessence they oppose."

basis of distinction being awareness of character and situation. The *Mistaken Man* knows himself, but is deceived about circumstances outside himself; for example, the man is not a cuckold, but fears that he may be one. The *Hypocritical Man* knows what he is, but presents to the world a contrary picture of himself. Lastly, the *Would-Be Man* firmly believes himself to *be* what he is *not*— poet, statesman, courtier.

Such an analysis as I am making is, of course oversimplified; and it certainly does not allow of sufficient nuances to envision fully the workings of the comic spirit; but it may serve to remove from Jonson a part of the burden of the humours with which he has been weighted down by generations of critics.

THE CHORIC GROUP

THE WIT

Much of the weaving of Jonson's intricate patterns must be done by that one of the Choric group designated as the Wit. He may be either the urbane young gentleman who, when some of his conventional morality has been eroded, will become the hero of the comedy of manners of the Restoration; or he may be a sort of reincarnation of the witty slave of the comedies of Plautus.

As a prototype for the first of these young men-about-town, Wellbred of *Every Man in His Humour* will do nicely. He is of the class that Jonson chooses almost exclusively for this function, the London gentry. In general, Jonson's representatives of the country, the landed gentry, are the unhappy recipients of what one might call the professional attentions of the Wellbreds. As an educated man, Wellbred can use his own Latin on occasion and can correct Bobadil's false Latin; he can detect Matthew's plagiarisms from Marlowe and render a sound critical judgment on Stephen's insipid verse. Although he has not been designated as soldier, he is, on behalf of his proteges, prepared to engage in sword-play with the redoubtable Squire Downright. He has no humour, unless it is to wind up the members of the Humourous Group into full manifestations of their follies.

The uses to which Jonson puts Wellbred are typical of those to which he puts others of this class. In terms of the action in *Every Man in His Humour*, Jonson's purpose is to bring all offenders against comic decorum to the attention of Justice Clement. It is Wellbred who, together with his counterpart, Edward Knowell, assembles the Bobadils and Matthews to manifest their folly in unison at Kitely's house; it is he who conceives the marriage of Edward Knowell to Bridget and, to further the project, sends those guilty of the lesser follies of jealousy and suspicion to Cob's house—to see themselves.

But a far more important service than his contribution to the action, one in which he is ably assisted by young Knowell, is performed by Wellbred. He says of the fools, "Ile wind 'hem vp" (III.i.62). That winding-up is the process by which each of the fools manifests his own folly. Matthew, being wound up, can say: "Oh, it's your only fine humour, sir, your true melancholy breeds your perfect fine wit, sir: I am melancholy my selfe diuers times, sir, and then doe I no more but take pen, and paper presently, and ouerflow you halfe a score, or a dozen sonnets, at a sitting" (III.i.89–93). Or a wound-up Bobadil can describe imaginary exploits worthy of his ancestor Pyrgopolynices.

This winding-up process is of course preparation for the comic *coup-de-grace*, which almost in a phrase defines and mocks the folly. To Mistress Bridget, of Matthew's verses addressed to her, says Wellbred: "Nay, you lampe of virginitie, that take it in snuffe so! come, and cherish this tame *poeticall furie*, in your seruant, you'll be begg'd else, shortly, for a concealement: goe to, reward his muse. You cannot giue him lesse then a shilling, in conscience, for the booke, he had it out of, cost him a teston, at least. How now, gallants? Mʳ· MATTHEW? Captayne? What? all sonnes of silence? no spirit?" (IV.ii.99–106). Or on Bobadil's slaughters full comment is achieved by Edward Knowell: "But did you all this, Captaine, without hurting your blade?" (III.i.150–51).

A third, more generalized function is also performed by the Wellbreds. They are the examples, the reality not only by which the foolish and mistaken characters can measure themselves, but they also constitute a standard against which the audience can measure the follies or vices on which Jonson is expending scorn or invective. Master Stephen would be a gallant, a gentleman; but he takes for his model not Knowell and Wellbred, who *are* gentlemen, but the braggart Bobadil. The Stephens, the Bobadils, the Matthews cannot learn. From the Wellbreds, and from Justice Clement, Kitely *does* learn to dispense with suspicion; Downright, with unreasonable anger; and Cob, with intolerance.

In *Every Man Out of His Humour, Cynthia's Revels*, and *Poetaster*, Jonson dispenses with the Wit of the Wellbred type. Some close counterparts, however, appear under the classifications of Chorus and Deity. The type returns, however, in Peregrine of *Volpone*, though his activities are confined to the lesser segments of the action. He is the winder-up of the two Would-bes, Lady and Sir Politic, the former to her perjured testimony about Celia, and the latter to the ridiculous episode of the tortoise shell. To Peregrine is given the appropriate comic comment about each of them. He serves also, in the third function of the Wit, as the proper traveller, the model on which a wiser man than Sir Politic might pattern himself. If he has a humour, it is the very slight one of taking pleasure in winding up the fools.

In *The Silent Woman* Jonson gives his Wits freest rein in all their aspects. Dauphine, Clerimont, and Truewit share in the winding-up process, Truewit largely for sheer joy. Their commentary is continuous throughout the play, with perhaps a little more salt in it than in that of *Every Man Out of His Humour*, as for example Truewit's analysis of the perils of marriage (II.ii), or Clerimont's assessment of Daw and La Foole: "Yes, but this [La Foole] feares the brauest: the other a whiniling dastard, IACK DAW! But LA-FOOLE, a braue heroique coward! and is afraid in a great looke, and a stout accent" (IV.v.233–36). All three are in a general way models for what the humourous characters, male and female, would be.

The next Wits who resemble the Wellbred type are those of *Bartholomew Fair*, Winwife and Quarlous, but they are not of the pure breed. Their social origin and their education are appropriate. But they have little winding-up to do, for such creations as Zeal-of-the-Land Busy are self-winding. And such winding-up as they do is self-serving, for it leads each of them to a marriage of his liking. Their commentary on follies is less pervasive than that of the Wits in *The Silent Woman*. The eloquence of Busy and Justice Overdoo generates its own devastating self-comment, and certainly no Wit could trace the ubiquitous Bartholomew Cokes. But the Wits find occasions to help the spectator toward a proper perspective, in this case with reference to Justice Overdoo: "I would faine see the carefull foole deluded! of all Beasts, I loue the serious Asse. He that takes paines to be one, and playes the foole, with the greatest diligence that can be" (III.v.264–67). Their function as standards of judgment for the audience, and as models for the characters in the play itself, is limited. The Matthews and Stephens and the Captain Otters would be seen as something they are not, cannot become, and that something is usually an approximation to what the Wits are. In *Bartholomew Fair* only John Littlewit wishes to be thought something different from what he is, and his aspiration extends only to greater prosperity as proctor. And, insofar as both are self-serving in the matter of marriage, Quarlous and Winwife lack the wholesomeness of, for example, an Edward Knowell.

Of this group of urbane young gentlemen who are winders-up, commentators, and models, only two exemplars remain—the pair in *The Devil Is an Ass*, Wittipol and Manly. They too are of impeccable social status, are educated and travelled. They lead Fitz-dottrell into the full statement of his folly and analyze it fully, in his presence, to his wife; their gulling of the master broker, Meer-craft, is masterful; and, once they have been reformed in the fashion of sentimental comedy, they would be models for conduct, were there any characters in the play to profit by example.

The second class of Wits is probably descended from the witty slaves or servants of Plautus. Members of this class are not so numerous as those of the gentleman class, but they are on the whole of more interest, for they in general have much more of Jonson's work to do. Not scholars, not brave men, not poets or critics, they are merely repositories of common sense who can manipulate their betters and skillfully point up their follies. Unfortunately, they are only three: Brainworm of *Every Man in His Humour*, Mosca of *Volpone*, and Face of *The Alchemist*. Like their gentlemen counterparts, they enjoy greatly the game of winding-up; but they are not disinterested players and commentators—some degree of greed or desire for profit is always apparent.

As prototype, Brainworm of *Every Man in His Humour* is best, for he alone is interested primarily, as is his gentleman counterpart, in the game itself rather than in its rewards. Two among the functions of the other Wits he has: he is winder-up and commentator. His performance in deceiving his master, as the soldier Fitz-sword, is masterful. His handling of the supposed warrant from Justice Clement undoubtedly contributes to the display of the folly of Captain Bobadil and Master Stephen. He can easily relieve Justice Clement's clerk, Formall, of his garments; and he can even wind himself into the very good graces of the redoubtable Justice Clement.

These performances are on his own initiative. He can with equal facility, on orders, deceive the Kitelys and the Elder Knowell, so as to produce the hilarious confrontation at the house of Cob. Although he has few opportunities to act as commentator, he makes the most of them, as, for example, in the following:

> BRAY. You haue an excellent good legge, master STEPHEN, but I cannot stay, to praise it longer now, and I am very sorie for't.
> STEP. Another time wil serue, BRAYNE-WORME. Gramercie for this.
>
> (I.iii.51–55)

He can say of his master, who has just hired him as Fitz-sword, "S'lid, was there euer seene a foxe in yeeres to betray himselfe thus?" (II.v.135–36). He is the first to introduce a similitude to be much used in Jonson's later work: "one of the deuil's neere kinsmen, a broker" (III.v.31–32).

Though not of the stature in Jonson's comic scheme of his more gentlemanly counterparts, Brainworm is certainly what Wellbred calls him—"a successful merry knaue" (IV.viii.61).

Mosca of *Volpone* and Face of *The Alchemist* are by any measure more cogent commentators and more skillful winders-up than Brainworm, but since their activities are essentially motivated by greed, they are best reserved for consideration among the Brokers.

THE CHORUS

The comic character to be examined next has some functions in common with the Wit just discussed; but "Chorus" is certainly not the urbane young gentleman-about-London. He is frequently a lean scholar; he may be a jolly justice; he may be a detached commentator, entirely outside the action; he may even be a group, formally designated as chorus and used for explication or for enrichment of a central theme in the play. Whatever his status in the play, he will carry much of Jonson's didactic burden. Since the Chorus has this marked lack of homogeneity, I shall look at several members of the group in some detail, with a view to implementing my remark above that the Chorus carries much of Jonson's commentary.

The functions of this choric personage, as an individual and as a direct participant in the action, seem to be fourfold: he will in many cases be the dispenser, at the end of the play, of suitable comic fates, whether reward or punishment or cure; he may be the primary commentator, as the play progresses, on characters and actions which he observes; he may be a spokesman for Jonson himself, through analysis or invective, on matters almost completely outside the specific sequence of incidents. In one case at least he is the prime mover in such action as the play contains.

Lovewit, in *The Alchemist*, is an excellent example as the dispenser of comic justice, though he illustrates none of the other roles given to choric characters. He appears, unexpectedly, only in the last act. Having learned as much of the circumstances as Face chooses to tell him, and having been bribed with the hand of Dame Plyant, he makes several important dispositions. Sir Epicure Mammon must lose his household goods unless he will prove in court that he has been duped. Surly, who would not be cheated, has lost the widow to him. Tribulation Wholesome and Ananias, the Puritans, lose their investment, and Lovewit's threat to use the cudgel is an appropriate comic assessment. When he accepts the challenge of Kastril, the youth who would learn to quarrel, he effects a cure of the young man's humour. In acknowledgment of the wit of Face, he closes his eyes to the iniquities of a scoundrel, allows Face to keep his ill-gotten gains, and restores him to his place. In Jonson's comic world, justice has been done, with Lovewit as the instrument.

Peni-Boy Canter, in *The Staple of News*, offers an excellent example of a choric character, combining two of our functions: he is a dispenser of comic fates at the play's end; and, along the way, though not himself seriously involved in the action, he has had pithy commentary on the follies about him.

His role as dispenser of fates is deliberately heightened by Jonson, for his arrival in the last scene is thus announced by Lickfinger, the cook: "Arme, arme you, Gentlemen Ieerers, th'old *Canter* / Is comming in vpon you, with his forces" (V.v.51–52). The "jeerers," a group of fairly standard characters of the humourous type—Cymbal, Fitton, Shunfield, Madrigal—"conscious to themselues / Of their no-wit, or honesty, ranne routed" (V.vi.4–5) with the mere word of the Canter's appearance. Within a dozen lines he has restored to Peni-Boy Senior his Mortgage, Statute, Waxe, and Band, but has withheld his Broker, so that Peni-Boy Senior's career as "money-baud" is ended. And he has united the Lady Pecunia to the repentant "Prodigall," Peni-Boy Junior. Even Picklock, the treacherous man of law, he has "safe enough in a wooden collar" (V.vi.50).

The Canter's posture throughout *The Staple of News* has been that of assessor of other men's actions. Of his Prodigal's purchase of a new wardrobe he says: "I say 'tis nobly done, to cherish Shop-keepers, / And pay their Bills, without examining, thus" (I.iii.44–45). Of the many suitors of the Lady Pecunia he remarks:

> You shall haue stall-fed *Doctors*, cram'd *Diuines*
> Make loue to her, and with those studied
> And perfum'd flatteries, as no rome can stinke
> More elegant, then where they are. . . . . .
> . . . . And (by your leaue)
> Good *Masters worship* [the man of law], some of your
>   veluet coate
> Make corpulent curt'sies to her, till they cracke for't.
>   (I.vi.67–70; 71–73)

Such passages throughout *The Staple of News* are given to the Canter, but his noblest choric effort comes when he mocks the canting of those in the professions—poet, doctor, soldier, courtier, and man of law. His proof against the Doctor is damning:

> P.C.A. The *Doctor* here, I will proceed with the
>   *learned*.
> When he discourseth of *dissection*,
> Or any point of *Anatomy*: that hee tells you,
> Of *Vena caua*, and of *vena porta*,
> The *Meseraicks*, and the *Mesenterium*.
> What does hee else but *cant*? Or if he runne
> To his *Iudiciall Astrologie*,
> And trowle the *Trine*, the *Quartile* and the *Sextile*,
> *Platicke* aspect, and *Partile*, with his *Hyleq*
> Or *Alchochoden*, *Cuspes*, and *Horoscope*.
> Does not he *cant*? Who here does vnderstand him?
>   (IV.iv.37–47)

In such a passage Peni-Boy Canter of course speaks for Ben Jonson. But this massive condemnation by the "canter" has a function in the movement of this play: Peni-Boy Junior decides to found a "*Canters Colledge*." This prodigality forces the Canter to drop his disguise and appear as the father of Peni-Boy Junior, and this deed occasions the later chicanery of Picklock. Even though he is not a prime mover in the action, the Canter does not qualify as a disinterested spokesman for the comic poet himself.

In fact, no one of the so-called choric characters remains at all times outside the movement of Jonson's comic actions. But there are long speeches assigned, for example, to Crites in *Cynthia's Revels* and Horace in *Poetaster* which move neither the speaker nor any other of the characters directly to action. Such a speech, for instance, is that of Crites in the first act of *Cynthia's Revels* in which, alone on the stage, he offers these observations on the vanities of Amorphus and Asotus:

> O how despisde and base a thing is a man,
> If he not striue t'erect his groueling thoughts
> Aboue the straine of flesh? But how more cheape
> When, euen his best and vnderstanding part,
> (The crowne, and strength of all his faculties)
> Floates like a dead drown'd bodie, on the streame
> Of vulgar humour, mixt with commonst dregs?
> . . . .
> Well, checke thy passion, lest it grow too lowd:
> "While fooles are pittied, they waxe fat, and proud.
> (I.v.33–39; 65–66)

An utterance of this sort characterizes the action which has preceded it and predicts like action to follow. In a Greek tragedy, or even a comedy, it would have been given to a full Chorus.

In *Poetaster* the fifth scene of Act Three is an extended debate between Horace and Trebatius on the nature and function of satire. The audience, if it can stay awake, may hear some sound critical dogma, but it will learn little of use in digesting the remainder of the play. Neither Horace nor Trebatius makes any decision affecting the action, unless when Horace says, "I will write *satyres* still, in spight of feare" (III.v.100) he speaks not only for himself in the play, but also for Jonson in *Poetaster* and its successors. The two speakers do, however, arrive at sound, if not revolutionary, conclusions about the nature of satire:

> [HORA.] . . . But if they shall be sharp, yet modest rimes

That spare mens persons, and but taxe their crimes,
Such, shall in open court, find currant passe;
Were CAESAR iudge, and with the makers grace.
    TREB. Nay, I'le adde more; if thou thy selfe
        being cleare,
Shalt taxe in person a man, fit to beare
Shame, and reproch; his sute shall quickly bee
Dissolu'd in laughter, and thou thence sit free.
                                    (III.iv.133–40)

The discussion of this most versatile character, Chorus, has led us to examine Lovewit of *The Alchemist* as dispenser of comic justice; Peni-Boy Canter of *The Staple of News* as both dispenser and commentator throughout the play; and Crites and Horace as spokesmen directly for the comic poet. The most massive of these figures, however, is Macilente of *Every Man Out of His Humour*. Not only does he perform all the functions already examined, but he also is actually the prime mover of almost all that occurs in the play: he leads the objects of his envy into the manifestation of their follies and then leads them to their punishment or their cure.

The assertion that Macilente is a prime mover and a dispenser of comic fates in much of the action may be documented by analysis of his participation in certain events near the end of the play. He effectively terminates Sir Puntarvolo's project to journey to Constantinople and return with his dog and cat. He poisons the dog. He urges the scurrilous Carlo Buffone to "needle" Puntarvolo about the failure of his project, with the result that Carlo's beard and mustache are sealed by Puntarvolo with candle wax. Two humours have been moved, as it were, to the point where they are "out." The ensuing commotion causes the arrest of Fastidius Briske and the holding of the unhappy Fungoso at Macilente's suggestion as "pawn" for the bill in the tavern. Fungoso, as a result, is "out" of his humour of emulating the dress of the brightshining gallant, Fastidius. Similar machinations bring the uxorious Deliro and his erring wife Fallace into such situations that they too are "out" of their humours. But Macilente's crowning achievement is that by purging his victims of their follies he has rendered them worthy of their good fortunes—and so has purged *himself* of envy.

While bringing about these, and several other purgations, Macilente has, of course, spoken—largely with invective—for himself,
and frequently for Jonson. From the lordly Puntarvolo to the
groveling Shift he has, fearing "no mood stampt in a priuate brow,"
stripped "the ragged follies of the time, naked, as at their birth."

But even a Justice Clement, or a Crites, or a Macilente, with or
without the help of a Wellbred or a Truewit, cannot carry all of
Jonson's didactic burden. Occasionally a group, conceived in something of the Aristophanic manner, helps the "auditory" through
the mazes of the action, or justifies the comic procedures. Such a
group is the "Grex" (Mitis and Cordatus) of *Every Man Out of
His Humour*. Having a somewhat different function is the "Intermeane" (the Gossips Mirth, Tatle, Expectation, and Censure)
of *The Staple of News*. Only in *The Magnetic Lady* does Jonson
give this group the formal name of "Chorus" (Mr. Probee, Mr.
Damplay, and A Boy).[4]

These groups are not in the strict sense "characters," for they
are not concerned in the sequence of events. But, as part of comic
apparatus by which Jonson achieves his effects they should be
examined, if only for the reason that in some instances they themselves are impaled among Jonson's more prominent victims.

It has been noted that the members of the "Grex" of *Every Man
Out of His Humour* are not in a strict sense part of the *dramatis
personae*, since they do not enter into the action which moves
Jonson's comic creations toward their comic fates. But they are
most obviously part of the "play," for the artistic entity which is
a "play" is composite: a poem—spoken by actors—on a stage—before
an audience. Even costume and gesture are a part of the "play." The
ultimate effect of a Jonson play upon an audience will include, perhaps, scorn—for one cannot countenance a Bobadil; complacency—
for one is not, of course, a Bartholomew Cokes; and self-recognition
—for there may be in all of us a little of Fastidius Briske. To help
the audience in arriving at the proper comic assessment of action,

---

⁴ Portions of this segment of the study have appeared, in slightly different
form, as an article in *Studies in English*, XI (1971), 11–21. The title of the
article is "The Formal Choruses in the Comedies of Ben Jonson."

of motive, of character, and ultimately of itself, a "Grex" is a valuable tool in the hand of the author.

A second observation about Grex, and the other choric groups, is necessary. They *are* the audience: not in all the manifold humours of *Every Man Out of His Humour*, but in the simple category of the wise and learned, in contrast with the ignorant and foolish. Says Cordatus in the final word of the Grex at the end of *Every Man Out of His Humour*: "Besides, here are those (round about you) of more abilitie in censure then wee, whose iudgements can giue it a more satisfying allowance: wee'le refer you to them" (V.xi.71–74).

The two members of the Grex in *Every Man Out of His Humour* are Cordatus and Mitis. These are Jonson's formal "characters" for them:

CORDATVS.

THe Authors friend; A man inly acquainted with the scope and drift of his Plot: Of a discreet, and vnderstanding iudgement; and has the place of a Moderator.

MITIS.

IS a person of no action, and therefore we haue reason to affoord him no Character.

(Intro. Grex, ll. 110–16)

One questions, of course, whether Jonson would find many of his auditory to have "a discreet and understanding iudgement." The fiction, though, that there is in the audience a Cordatus to correct the misapprehensions and enlighten the ignorance of a Mitis gives the poet an opportunity to achieve many effects, not only intellectual but also mechanical.

The functions of the Grex, listed below in the ascending order of their importance, require brief examinations. At perhaps the lowest level, Cordatus and Mitis provide stage directions: "behold, the translated gallant" (Fungoso has entered wearing a new suit). Or they announce the entry of Sir Puntarvolo: "Stay, here comes the knight aduenturer. . . . I, and his scriuener with him." In a slightly different function they are of immense help, at least to the reader of *Every Man Out of His Humour*, for they announce changes of scene: "the *Scene* is the country still, remember"; "we must desire you to presuppose the stage, the middle isle in *Paules*"; "O, this is to be imagined the *Counter*, belike?"

Cordatus and Mitis have the responsibility, on a somewhat higher level, of adumbrating character. Though Jonson had, in the introductory material, given a thumbnail "character" of each of his actors, those descriptions were only for the reader, not for the auditory. It is therefore a help to the playgoer to have Cordatus describe Buffone: "He is one, the Author calls him CARLO BVF-FONE, an impudent common iester, a violent rayler, and an incomprehensible *Epicure*; one, whose company is desir'd of all men, but belou'd of none; hee will sooner lose his soule then a iest, and prophane euen the most holy things, to excite laughter: no honorable or reuerend personage whatsoeuer, can come within the reach of his eye, but is turn'd into all manner of varietie, by his adult'rate *simile's*" (Prol., 356–64). On the appearance of Clove and Orange—"meere strangers to the whole scope of our play"—Cordatus pinpoints both for the audience in what is almost a formal "character":

> I, and they are well met, for 'tis as drie an ORANGE as euer grew: nothing, but *Salutation*; and, *O god, sir*; and, *It pleases you to say so, Sir*; one that can laugh at a iest for company with a most plausible, and extemporall grace; and some houre after, in priuate, aske you what it was: the other, monsieur CLOVE, is a more spic't youth: he will sit you a whole afternoone sometimes, in a booke-sellers shop, reading the *Greeke, Italian,* and *Spanish*; when he vnderstands not a word of either: if he had the tongues, to his sutes, he were an excellent linguist.
>
> (III.i.23–33)

Much more important, however, to both reader and auditory is Cordatus' explication of Macilente's humour of envy:

> COR. . . . Why, you mistake his Humour vtterly then.
> MIT. How? doe I mistake it? is't not enuie?
> COR. Yes, but you must vnderstand, Signior, he enuies him not as he is a villaine, a wolfe i' the common-wealth, but as he is rich, and fortunate; for the true condition of enuie is, *Dolor alienae*

faelicitatis, to haue our eyes continually fixt vpon another mans prosperitie, that is, his chiefe happinesse, and to grieue at that. Whereas, if we make his monstrous, and abhord actions our obiect, the griefe (we take then) comes neerer the nature of hate, then enuie, as being bred out of a kinde of contempt and lothing, in our selues.

(I.iii.159–71)

Mitis, as the uninformed half of the Grex, and of the audience, has an occasional cavil which must be corrected. Scene three of Act II is unusually long, but the objection of Mitis is neatly spiked in this passage:

> MIT. Me thinkes, CORDATVS, he dwelt somewhat too long on this *Scene*; it hung i' the hand.
> COR. I see not where he could haue insisted lesse, and t'haue made the humours perspicuous enough.
> MIT. True, as his subiect lies: but hee might haue altered the shape of his argument, and explicated 'hem better in single *Scenes*.
> COR. That had been single indeed: why? be they not the same persons in this, as they would haue beene in those? and is not an obiect of more state, to behold the *Scene* full, and relieu'd with varietie of speakers to the end, then to see a vast emptie stage, and the actors come in (one by one) as if they were dropt downe with a feather, into the eye of the spectators?
>
> (II.iii.288–301)

Two other cavils of Mitis are put to even more effective use in educating the auditory. After the end of Act II, says Mitis, "Well, I doubt, this last *Scene* will endure some grieuous torture." Cordatus must again put him right. In the process he enunciates the essential theory of satire and offers the standard disclaimer of any personal portraiture:

> COR. No, in good faith: vnlesse mine eyes could light mee beyond sense. I see no reason, why this should be more liable to the racke, then the rest: you'le say, perhaps, the city will not take it well, that the marchant is made here to dote so perfectly vpon his wife; and shee againe, to bee so *Fastidiously* affected, as shee is?
> MIT. You haue vtter'd my thought, sir, indeed.
> COR. Why (by that proportion) the court might as wel take

offence at him we call the courtier, and with much more pretext, by how much the place transcends, and goes before in dignitie and vertue: but can you imagine that any noble, or true spirit in court (whose sinowie, and altogether vn-affected graces, very worthily expresse him a courtier) will make any exception at the opening of such an emptie trunke, as this BRISKE is! or thinke his owne worth empeacht, by beholding his motley inside?

MIT. No sir, I doe not.

COR. No more, assure you, will any graue, wise citizen, or mod-est matron, take the obiect of this folly in DELIRO, and his wife: but rather apply it as the foile to their owne vertues. For that were to affirme, that a man, writing of NERO, should meane all Em-perors: or speaking of MACHIAVEL, comprehend all States-men; or in our SORDIDO, all Farmars; and so of the rest: then which, nothing can be vtter'd more malicious, or absurd. Indeed, there are a sort of these narrow-ey'd decypherers, I confesse, that will extort strange, and abstruse meanings out of any subiect, be it neuer so conspicuous and innocently deliuer'd. But to such (where e're they sit conceal'd) let them know, the author defies them, and their writing-tables; and hopes, no sound or safe iudgement will infect it selfe with their contagious comments, who (indeed) come here only to peruert, and poison the sense of what they heare, and for nought else.

(II.vi.146–79)

The unhappy Mitis again at the end of the sixth scene of Act III falls into a trap, thereby allowing Cordatus to state for Jonson a sort of capsule Poetics on the nature of comedy:

MIT. I trauell with another obiection, signior, which I feare will bee enforc'd against the author, ere I can be deliuer'd of it.

COR. What's that, sir?

MIT. That the argument of his *Comoedie* might haue beene of some other nature, as of a duke to be in loue with a countesse, and that countesse to bee in loue with the dukes sonne, and the sonne to loue the ladies waiting maid: some such crosse wooing, with a clowne to their seruingman, better then to be thus neere, and familiarly allied to the time.

COR. You say well, but I would faine heare one of these *autumne*-judgements define once, *Quid sit Comoedia?* if he cannot, let him content himselfe with CICEROS definition, (till hee haue strength to propose to himselfe a better) who would haue a *Comoedie* to be *Imitatio vitae, Speculum consuetudinis, Imago veritatis;* a thing throughout pleasant, and ridiculous, and accommodated to the correction of manners: if the maker haue fail'd in any particle of this, they may worthily taxe him.

(III.vi.191–210)

Finally, Cordatus and Mitis serve as a sounding board for the formal statement of the humours concept by Asper-Macilente-Jonson:

As when some one peculiar quality
Doth so possesse a man, that it doth draw
All his affects, his spirits, and his powers,
In their confluctions, all to runne one way,
This may be truly said to be a Humour.

(Intro. Grex, ll. 105–09)

They applaud the statement of his satiric purpose: "And therefore I would giue them pills to purge, / And make 'hem fit for faire societies" (ll. 175–76). They also concur with his comic method:

To please, but whom? attentiue auditors,
Such as will ioyne their profit with their pleasure,
And come to feed their vnderstanding parts:
For these, Ile prodigally spend my selfe,
And speake away my spirit into ayre;
For these, Ile melt my braine into inuention,
Coine new conceits, and hang my richest words
As polisht jewels in their bounteous eares.

(ll. 201–08)

When Asper has gone to become the envious Macilente, Cordatus and Mitis remain "as censors to sit here" and explain why Jonson has not in this play observed the "lawes of *Comedie*." Cordatus points out that Aristophanes, Plautus, and others felt free to alter the conventions handed down to them and proceeds thus: "I see not then, but we should enioy the same licence, or free power, to illustrate and heighten our inuention as they did; and not bee tyed to those strict and regular formes, which the nicenesse of a few (who are nothing but forme) would thrust vpon us" (ll. 266–70). Apparently that "licence" was to be for this play only; for in prologues to his later plays Jonson insists on those same "lawes," and in general, in his comedies, he conforms strictly to the "unities."

Jonson did not introduce another formal chorus into a comedy for twenty-six years. In *The Staple of News* (1625) he has the "Intermeane" of the Gossips—Mirth, Tatle, Censure, and Expectation. But their presence is not to instruct reader or auditory in Jonson's poetic dogma; they in no way assist the poet in presenting the action, or the audience in understanding it. Though they are seated on the stage, they speak only as prologue and between acts.

But they are, I suspect, the audience. If so, however, the audience has degenerated since the days of Cordatus and Mitis. Even Mitis had some knowledge, and Cordatus possessed all the wisdom of Jonson himself. These four Gossips understand nothing. They praise the foolish (Peni-Boy Junior as prodigal) and condemn the wise (Peni-Boy Canter as the true Chorus). They constitute, at best, another object of the poet's satire. In part of that satire they have a sort of mirror function, for they are the avid consumers of the ridiculous news collected and disseminated by the Staple. A measure of their discernment, as representatives of the audience, and perhaps of all *London*, is provided in the Third Intermeane:

> MIRTH. . . . *But how like you the newes? you are gone from that.*
> CEN. *O, they are monstrous! scuruy! and stale! and too exotick! ill cook'd! and ill dish'd!*
> EXP. *They were as good, yet, as butter[5] could make them!*
> TAT. *In a word, they were beastly buttered! he shall neuer come o' my bread more, nor in my mouth, if I can helpe it. I haue had better newes from the bake-house, by ten thousand parts, in a morning: or the conduicts in* Westminster! *all the newes of* Tutle-street, *and both the* Alm'ries! *the two* Sanctuaries! *long, and round* Wool-staple! *with* Kings-street, *and* Chanon-row *to boot!*

[5] A reference to Nathaniel Butter, printer and disseminator of news, whose first newspaper, *Newes from most parts of Christendom*, appeared in 1622.

MIRTH. *I, my Gossip* Tatle *knew what fine slips grew in* Gar-
diners-lane; *who kist the Butchers wife with the Cowes-breath;
what matches were made in the* bowling-Alley, *and what bettes
wonne and lost; how much griest went to the* Mill, *and what besides: who coniur'd in* Tutle-fields, *and how many? when they
neuer came there. And which Boy rode vpon* Doctor Lambe, *in
the likenesse of a roaring* Lyon, *that runne away with him in his
teeth, and ha's not deuour'd him yet.*

(ll. 12–32)

In a second function they are Jonson's old enemy: the audience
which cannot understand a play, but would censure it. Jonson
makes that point abundantly clear in a "To the Readers" appended
to the Second Intermeane (This "To the Readers" is, of course, not
part of the "play"): "IN this following *Act*, the *Office* is open'd,
and shew'n to the *Prodigall*, and his *Princesse Pecunia*, wherein the
allegory, and purpose of the *Author* hath hitherto beene wholly
mistaken, and so sinister an interpretation beene made, as if the
soules of most of the *Spectators* had liu'd in the eyes and eares of
these ridiculous Gossips that tattle betweene the *Acts*" (ll. 1–7).

A sample of their censure, taken from the Fourth Intermeane,
shows the bitterness of Jonson's attack:

MIR. *I wonder they would suffer it, a foolish old fornicating*
Father, *to rauish away his sonnes* Mistresse.
CEN. *And all her women, at once as hee did!*
TAT. *I would ha' flyen in his* gypsies *face i' faith.*
MIRTH. *It was a plaine piece of* politicall *incest, and worthy to
be brought afore the* high Commission *of wit. Suppose we were to
censure him, you are the youngest voyce,* Gossip Tatle, *beginne.*
TATLE. *Mary, I would ha' the old* conicatcher *coozen'd of all
he has, i'the young heyres defence, by his learn'd* Counsell, *Mr*
Picklocke!
CENSVRE. *I would rather the* Courtier *had found out some
tricke to begge him, from his estate!*
EXP. *Or the* Captaine *had courage enough to beat him.*
CEN. *Or the fine* Madrigall-*man, in rime, to haue runne him
out o' the Countrey, like an* Irish *rat.*
TAT. *No, I would haue* Master Pyed-mantle, *her* Graces

Herald, *to pluck downe his* hatchments, *reuerse his* coat-armour, *and nullifie him for no* Gentleman.
EXP. *Nay, then let Master* Doctor *dissect him, haue him open'd, and his tripes translated to* Lickfinger, *to make a* probation dish *of.*
CEN. TAT. *Agreed! Agreed!*
MIRTH. *Faith, I would haue him flat disinherited, by a decree of* Court, *bound to make restitution of the* Lady Pecunia, *and the vse of her body to his* sonne.
EXP. *And her traine, to the* Gentlemen.
CEN. *And both the* Poet, *and himselfe, to aske them all forgiueness!*

(ll. 40–68)

The third of Jonson's semi-formal comic choruses is in *The Magnetic Lady* (1632). It consists of Mr. Probee, in an attitude very similar to that of Cordatus in *Every Man Out of His Humour*; of Mr. Damplay, who is both more uninformed and more censorious than Mitis; and of a Boy of the House, who "had the dominion of the shop, for this time under him [the poet]," and who speaks for Jonson.

Probee and Damplay, as heretofore, are the audience—but only the "Plush and Velvet-outsides." The Boy fears, however, that this description fits only "clothes, not understandings." These three members of the Choric Group serve not only for the functions previously suggested in this paper, but also in one or two not observed earlier. They provide a sort of "argument" for the play, explaining that the Magnetic Lady herself and her marriageable niece are the poet's "Center attractive," with "persons of different humours to make up his *Perimeter*." The Boy explains to the auditory the proper procedure for hearing a play: "A good *Play*, is like a skeene of silke: which, if you take by the right end, you may wind off, at pleasure, on the bottome, or card of your discourse, in a tale, or so; how you will: But if you light on the wrong end, you will pull all into a knot, or elfe-locke; which nothing but the sheers, or a candle will undoe, or separate" (Induction, 136–41). Probee offers the standard disclaimer of any personal intent in the satire, and mounts a severe attack on all those who undertake the "civill murder" of a play through "the solemne vice of interpretation."

Probee and the Boy enlarge the auditory to include Charles I himself, for on behalf of "an overgrowne Poët," they very neatly beg for Jonson a gratuity:

> PRO. Why doe you maintaine your Poëts quarrell so with velvet, and good clothes, *Boy?* Wee have seene him in indifferent good clothes, ere now.
> BOY. And may doe in better, if it please the King (his Master) to say Amen to it, and allow it, to whom hee acknowledgeth all. But his clothes shall never be the best thing about him, though; hee will have somewhat beside, either of humane letters, or severe honesty, shall speak him a man though he went naked.
> (I.Chor., 49–57)

Cordatus and Mitis, Tatle and Expectation, and Probee and Damplay should, along with the Wits, the individuals with primarily choric functions, the Brokers, and the unfortunate ones possessed of the humours, be admitted to the list of Jonson's comic *dramatis personae*. But such is the thrust of the formalized choric groups toward the follies and ignorance of the audience, that one is disposed to feel that, not only in *Every Man Out of His Humour*, *The Staple of News*, and *The Magnetic Lady*, but perhaps in all the plays, an additional name should be admitted to the cast of characters—"Auditory."

THE DEITY

The final comic tool in the group of Jonson's characters that have been designated as choric is the Deity. Of these there are few, and their function is slight. It is most closely allied to that of a Macilente or a Peni-Boy Canter, but the differences are worth noting.

In this group are Cynthia of *Cynthia's Revels*; Mercury and Cupid of the same play; Augustus and Virgil of *Poetaster*; Satan and the unfortunate Pug of *The Devil Is an Ass*; Pecunia of *The Staple of News*; and Lady Loadstone of *The Magnetic Lady*.

Cynthia, of course, is Elizabeth, and can take part in the action only insofar as becomes a goddess. Cupid's design to introduce wantonness to her court cannot succeed, for his arrows are powerless in the presence of her chastity. But, as Mercury points out, the waters of the Fountain of Self-Love help to make his shafts innocuous. Nor can the "deformities" (the courtiers male and female) conceal their true character in her presence. She can do no injustice, though she is constrained to defend herself against calumnies because of the justice lately done Actaeon (Essex, 1600): "A Goddesse did it, therefore it was good" (V.xi.26). The resolution of the difficulties can come only as a result of her decree—"Th' incurable cut off, the rest reforme" (l. 97). This instruction is delivered to Arete (Virtue), also "diuine," and administered at her request by Crites ("who aspires to be so"). Cupid and Mercury have been of importance, not in their identities as deities, but only in their assumed identities as pages. Elizabeth the *Queen* has been of far more importance to Jonson the aspirant than has been Cynthia the comic character to Jonson the poet. In fact, Justice Clement of *Every Man in His Humour* took care of the resolution of the play much more efficiently than the combined deities of Cynthia, Arete, and Crites.

Augustus Caesar in *Poetaster* is a more satisfactory Deity than Cynthia, for Jonson did not find it necessary in him to placate an irascible old queen. In fact, though his status among the gods is given lip-service, he is remarkably fallible. He misjudges the Heavenly Banquet and reverses his doom against Gallus and Tibullus, though not that against the unfortunate Ovid. Before he receives that other deity, Virgil, to read his divine poetry, he conducts a seminar on Virgil's genius and opens the discussion with an unjust thought—that Horace might be envious. Again he must recant. Thereafter, however, in the hearing of Virgil's verses, in decreeing the trial of the poetasters, and in entrusting their dooms to Virgil and Horace, he conducts himself like himself. But, again, one feels that Augustus is not an extremely useful comic tool.

Our next Deity is *"the great diuell,"* Satan, of *The Devil Is an*

Ass. In the action he has only two functions: to arrange the appearance in London of Pug, "*the lesse diuell*," in the body of a cutpurse and the garments of a gentleman usher, and to rescue Pug from Newgate and send him again to Hell on the back of Old Iniquity, the Vice. He has no part in assigning comic fates to the *men* and *women* of the play.

Satan does, however, serve the poet in a choric function, for it is he who points out that the vices in London in the year 1616 very nearly exceed those of Hell. A few lines will serve to illustrate this duty of Satan:

> They haue their *Vices*, there, most like to *Vertues*;
> You cannot know 'hem, apart, by any difference:
> They weare the same clothes, eate [o'] the same
>   meate,
> Sleepe i' the selfe-same beds, ride i' those coaches,
> Or very like, foure horses in a coach,
> As the best men and women.
>   (I.i.121–26)
>   . . . they are other things
> That are receiu'd now vpon earth, for Vices;
> Stranger, and newer: and chang'd euery houre.
> They ride 'hem like their horses off their legges.
>   (ll. 100–103)
> And it is fear'd they haue a stud o' their owne
> Will put downe ours. Both our breed, and trade
> Will suddenly decay, if we preuent not.
> Vnlesse it be a *Vice* of quality,
> Or fashion, now, they take none from vs.
>   (ll. 108–12)

His final assessment of Pug's efforts has a similar thrust:

>   Out vpon thee,
> The hurt th' hast don, to let men know their strength,
> And that the[y]'are able to out-doe a *diuel*
> Put in a body, will for euer be
> A scarre vpon our Name! whom hast thou dealt with,
> Woman or man, this day, but haue out-gone thee
> Some way, and most haue prou'd the better fiendes?
>   (V.vi.56–62)

Pug, as "the lesse diuell," has likewise had little to do with the action, beyond failing in a few minor undertakings. He has in London exercised no supernatural powers, but he has one or two choric utterances which reinforce those of Satan: "You talke of a *Vniuersity*! why, *Hell* is / A Grammar-schoole to this!" (IV.iv.170–71); "Who, / Comming from *Hell*, could looke for such Catechising? / The *Diuell* is an *Asse*. I doe acknowledge it" (ll.242–43).

The Lady Pecunia of *The Staple of News* is technically a Deity. She has impeccable credentials, as reported by Picklock:

> A great *Lady*,
> Indeede, shee is, and not of mortall race,
> *Infanta* of the *Mines*; her Graces Grandfather,
> Was *Duke*, and Cousin to the *King* of *Ophyr*,
> The *Subterranean*, let that passe. Her name is
> Or rather, her three names are (for such shee is)
> *Aurelia Clara Pecunia*. . . .
>
> (I.vi.40–46)

In reality, however, she is an almost completely allegorical representation of wealth. Possession of her favors is the goal of all lines of action in the play, but she pursues no actions of her own. She does, however, pass with docility from one to another of the *dramatis personae*—finally to reside with the reformed Prodigal. She has no hand in dealing out comic fates, nor does she, as did Cynthia and Caesar, order them to be imposed.

One person who, though mortal, is placed in the attitude of a Deity should be examined. She is Lady Loadstone of *The Magnetic Lady*. She, like Pecunia, is the goal of all lines of action; she is protected from all knowledge of ill; her presence is almost as sacred as that of Cynthia. She makes two decisions that help in the resolution of the play: to award her niece to Mr. Compasse and herself to Captain Ironside. But the comic dispositions of the humourous characters are made, not by her, but by Compasse.

The Deities are manifestly not a major tool in Jonson's dramatic technique. They do not have the vital winding-up function of the Wits, nor do they provide a comic representation of proper, normal, human conduct, for they cannot be of the audience, as could all of Jonson's other characters. They utter much less of Jonson's satire and invective than do the Wits and the Choruses. Perhaps most important, as Deities they cannot exercise what is probably Jonson's most powerful weapon: satiric self-portraiture. Finally, they are of less importance than those of the other groups in meting out comic fates to the most numerous of our major groups—the humourous characters.

It will have become apparent by this point in the discussion that the Choric Group is not conceived in terms of the humours. Of not one may it be said that "all his affects, his spirits, and his powers, in their confluctions . . . runne one way." It is true that Justice Clement loved a wit and loved to make the punishment fit the crime, but there were to him also many more sides—poet, soldier, critic. Truewit partook slightly of the humourous flavor, for he sought to appear as a witty contriver. But even here there is a difference. He *was* a witty contriver. Perhaps, of all the group only Macilente, who is powerfully possessed by envy, conforms to Jonson's definition given above. Even he, however, has many attitudes other than his humour: scholar, soldier, contriver, disposer of fates. The humour, for Jonson, is not a characteristic of the group which utters the poet's thought, but rather of the group against which that thought is directed. Humour is the mark not of the witty man, but of the fool; not of the soldier, but of the coward; not of the scholar, but of the hypocrite.

The redoubtable group of characters explored under the appellation of "Choric" does much of Jonson's work, speaks most of his mind. As a group, they express his indignation at the workings of greed, of hypocrisy, of folly. The Wit is particularly agile in leading the fool into manifestations of his folly; his comments frequently, as it were in a quip, attain to the very nature of the comic itself. The Chorus may generalize by looking beyond the individual fool to folly itself, beyond the individual Puritan to hypocrisy itself, beyond the "money-baud" to all ramifications of greed. The choric individual frequently uses invective or satire, but seldom rises to the comic perfection of the Wit. If there is a somewhat formalized choric group, it may well enunciate Jonson's critical theories; it may be a sort of mirror of the audience itself, possibly in matters of "censure," possibly in a basic folly characterized in the play. The Deity has little more to do than give his or her blessing to punishments, rewards, or cures as prescribed by Wit or Chorus.

THE BROKER GROUP

In the foregoing assessment of the group of characters designated as Choric, three distinct functions have appeared: 1) the winding-up of the victims of Jonson's satiric attention; 2) commenting on character and conduct; 3) dispensing of comic fates. In the earlier plays the winding-up process was largely in the hands of the Wits. In the later plays, however, much of this function is taken up by that member of the cast whom I have chosen to call the Broker.

THE BROKER

An extremely useful tool for Jonson, the Broker can skillfully take advantage of at least two of Jonson's major objects of attack, greed and folly. He is *not* in himself a primary object of Jonson's corrective measures. He exists—he *can* exist—only as greed and folly unite in the *personae* of the Humourous Group to permit the exercise of his talents. In fact, frequently the gains resulting from his skillful manipulations are left with him—as part of the punishment Jonson contrives for his true victims. He may, particularly in the case of Mosca in *Volpone*, be given the most significant choric commentary.

But the Broker is an essentially different man from the Wit. The Broker's purpose is ordinarily not fun at the expense of fools, but gain. He is seldom of the gentry. On those occasions when he is, he is decayed, disgraced, bankrupt; unlike those of the Choric

Group, he is neither critic nor poet, neither scholar nor soldier. But he is clever, resourceful, optimistic. He may occupy almost any station in life—from that of Cutberd the barber in *Epicoene* to that of Sir Moath Interest of *The Magnetic Lady*, who might well be an alderman. To Jonson, however, the Broker is always "bawd"— whether it be of flesh or money. Seldom is he subject to a humourous analysis, for he knows himself. Master Matthew of *Every Man in His Humour* is not a poet, would be thought a poet, is too ignorant to know he is *not* a poet, has no existence outside his humourous facade. Not so the brokers. They know themselves; if they would appear to be what they are not, it is for professional purposes; their ultimate end is always gain. If in one of them a humourous trait appears, it may very well be the key to the failure— or success—of his projects. More of that specifically will appear, however, in looking at Mosca and Volpone of *Volpone*. Whatever his qualities, the Broker is, for Jonson—as he has Satan say in *The Devil Is an Ass*—of "our tribe of brokers."

Of this group of Satan's tribe one who would be quite at home in Hell is Mosca of *Volpone*. It is hardly safe to call him a prototype, for the membership of this group is hardly homogeneous. But he will serve nicely as an example of the use Jonson makes of the Broker. For, next to the Wit, he is Jonson's most useful tool in setting up fool or glutton or coward for exposure, either through self-revelation or through the choric utterances of others.

In five of Jonson's comedies, the Broker does not appear in any significant capacity: *The Case Is Altered, Every Man in His Humour, Cynthia's Revels, Poetaster*, and *The New Inn*. One reason is not far to seek, since greed is not a major theme in these comedies. There are also other reasons. *The Case Is Altered* is essentially a romantic comedy, and the miserliness of Jacques de Prie is merely a circumstance of plot, not an object of attack. *Every Man in His Humour* is dominated by the Wits Knowell and Wellbred, whose effects are attained by manipulation of folly, not of greed. *Cynthia's Revels* is dominated by the massive choric figure, Crites, whose victims are essentially allegorical; the closest the play comes to treatment of greed is perhaps in the prodigal, Asotus, almost at the opposite extreme from greed. *Poetaster* also is dominated by the choric figure, Horace, the object of whose efforts is not greedy men but bad poets. *The New Inn* is essentially a return to romantic comedy. The minor figures—Shift of *Every Man Out of His Humour* and Cutberd of *Epicoene*—do little more than run errands. In the plays of Jonson's maturity, in which romance has been abandoned and in which his massive attack on greed, folly, and hypocrisy has attained its full power, the Broker becomes a necessary tool. His schemes can give vent to the greed and folly in the greedy and to the greed and hypocrisy in the hypocrite. And, usually, in his comments on the follies of his victims, the Broker carries the principal burden of choric commentary. Of this Devil's tribe Mosca in *Volpone* is the first, and perhaps the greatest.

Mosca's picture of himself is perhaps a bit romanticized; still it reflects not only his qualities, but also those of two of his great colleagues, Face of *The Alchemist* and Meercraft of *The Devil Is an Ass*. He sees himself as

> . . . your fine, elegant rascall, that can rise,
> And stoope (almost together) like an arrow;
> Shoot through the aire, as nimbly as a starre;
> Turne short, as doth a swallow; and be here,
> And there, and here, and yonder, all at once;
> Present to any humour, all occasion;
> And change a visor, swifter, then a thought!
> (III.i.23–29)

But this virtuosity of Mosca is put, by him, only to the service of greed; by Jonson, however, it is put to use in the massive condemnation of greed and folly—in men worse than Mosca. It is a pleasure to watch Mosca at work, as "winder-up" and as spokesman for the comic poet.

His first manipulation of Volpone, his master, is typical:

> You are not like the thresher, that doth stand
> With a huge flaile, watching a heape of corne,
> And, hungrie, dares not taste the smallest graine,

> But feeds on mallowes, and such bitter herbs;
> Nor like the merchant, who hath fill'd his vaults
> With *Romagnia*, and rich *Candian* wines,
> Yet drinkes the lees of *Lombards* vineger:
> You will not lie in straw, whilst moths, and wormes
> Feed on your sumptuous hangings, and soft beds.
> You know the vse of riches, and dare giue, now,
> From that bright heape, to me, your poore obseruer.
>
> (I.i.53–63)

In a single skillful passage Jonson has had Mosca flatter his master, satirize misers in general, and obtain a gift for himself.

The first of the legacy-hunters to visit the supposed deathbed of Volpone is Voltore, the advocate. Because there is not yet occasion for the use of Voltore, Mosca sends him on his way—"when will you haue your inuentorie brought, sir?" But he has also exercised his powerful choric function by flattering Voltore thus:

> He euer lik'd your course, sir, that first tooke him.
> I, oft, haue heard him say, how he admir'd
> Men of your large profession, that could speake
> To euery cause, and things mere contraries,
> Till they were hoarse againe, yet all be law;
> That, with most quick agilitie, could turne,
> And re-turne; make knots, and vndoe them;
> Giue forked counsell; take prouoking gold
> On either hand, and put it vp: these men,
> He knew, would thriue, with their humilitie.
> And (for his part) he thought, he should be blest
> To haue his heire of such a suffering spirit,
> So wise, so graue, of so perplex'd a tongue,
> And loud withall, that would not wag, nor scarce
> Lie still, without a fee.
>
> (I.iii.51–65)

The next object of Mosca's attention is the senile Corbaccio, also a legacy-hunter. Corbaccio's greed makes him accede to Mosca's instruction to go home and make a will, disinheriting his son in favor of Volpone. Mosca dismisses Corbaccio, who is deaf, with "Your knowledge is no better then your eares, sir," and

"Rooke goe with you, rauen." But it is to Volpone rather than to Mosca that Jonson gives the definitive comic statement about Corbaccio: "What a rare punishment / Is auarice, to it selfe?" (I.iv. 142–43).

The winding-up of the next of the visitants, Corvino, is even more sophisticated. Assuring Corvino that Volpone can hear nothing, Mosca says: "Those filthy eyes of yours, that flow with slime, / Like two frog-pits; and those same hanging cheeks, / Couer'd with hide, in stead of skin: (nay, helpe, sir) / That looke like frozen dish-clouts, set on end" (I.v.57–60). Corvino, catching the spirit, responds: "His nose is like a common sewre, still running" (l. 65). In the same vein, Mosca suggests, "Faith, I could stifle him, rarely, with a pillow, / As well, as any woman, that should keepe him" (ll. 68–69). This is said, of course, to evoke Corvino's response: "I pray you, vse no violence.... Nay, at your discretion" (ll. 72, 74); Corvino, moved by so great a show of friendship, declares, "Thou art my friend, my fellow, my companion, / My partner, and shall share in all my fortunes" (ll. 80–81). Mosca's response winds up not only Volpone to lust after Corvino's wife, but also, in due time, Corvino himself to bring her to Volpone. When later Corvino does indeed bring the innocent Celia, too early, Mosca is given perhaps the best single comic utterance in the play: "Did man ere haste so, for his hornes?" (III.vii.4).

One more circumstance will be sufficient to demonstrate Mosca's virtuosity. After Corbaccio has brought the will, after Corvino has brought his wife, after Mosca has brought Corbaccio's son Bonario in the hope that he will slay his father, after Bonario has rescued Celia, and after they have brought charges before the Avocatori, Mosca arms the advocate Voltore with the lines which will release the scoundrels, and condemn the innocent Celia and Bonario. Mosca then winds up Volpone, who wishes to gloat over the discomfited suitors, to put Mosca's name in a will as heir, to have himself reported dead, and to leave the house in disguise.

Enough has been said to indicate the usefulness of the Broker, Mosca, to the poet, Jonson. Through Mosca's machinations, greedy and foolish men have been led to show the depths of degradation to which their greed may drive them. And through his mouth the poet has achieved biting commentary on their follies.

Before we leave *Volpone*, however, we should look at the other Broker, Volpone himself. He has much of the skill of Mosca in the ordering of gulling plots, and in uttering the poet's own comic assessments. He and Mosca must work in unison to achieve the massive satiric effects of the play.

But there is another aspect of Volpone's role which should be noted, for he is an almost perfect representation of the opposite face of the Aristotelian tragic hero. Aristotle's hero must be, not a "virtuous man" nor an "utter villain," but "the character between these two extremes—that of a man not eminently good and just, yet whose misfortune is brought about, not by vice or depravity, but by some error or frailty." Volpone approaches the "utter villain," but he alone of the major characters misses the level of utter depravity. Voltore, because of his greed, will betray his profession and perjure himself; Corbaccio will not only disinherit his son, but also in court declare him a bastard; Corvino will send his wife to Volpone and will in court falsely declare her a known whore. But Volpone, even though he dupes the Corbaccios and the Corvinos, has one redeeming feature, one quality, perhaps a sort of humourous trait, which lightens his character to the extent that he is not utterly possessed by greed. These lines are stressed very early in the play: "Yet, I glory / More in the cunning purchase of my wealth, / Then in the glad possession" (I.i.30–32).

We have earlier seen our Wits thoroughly enjoying the game of making the gulls expose their own follies. In Wellbred, in Truewit, this game was admirable rather than reprehensible. In them, of course, it was not a means toward any personal gain. In Volpone it is. But one should take at face value his statement of "glorying more" in the "cunning purchase" than in the "glad possession." It becomes clear that Volpone, the villain, is betrayed to his destruction by the one *good* trait—essentially a humourous characteristic—which he possesses.

A fairly extensive passage must be quoted to establish the implementation of this inverted "tragic flaw" in Volpone:

[VOLP.] I will beginne, eu'n now, to vexe 'hem all:
This very instant. MOS. Good, sir. VOLP. Call
  the dwarfe,
And eunuch, forth. MOS.CASTRONE, NANO. NAN.
  Here.
  VOLP. Shal we haue a jig, now? MOS. What you
  please sir. VOLP. Go,
Streight, giue out, about the streetes, you two,
That I am dead; doe it with constancy,
Sadly, doe you heare? impute it to the griefe
Of this late slander. MOS. What doe you meane, sir?
  VOLP. O,
I shall haue, instantly, my vulture, crow,
Rauen, come flying hither (on the newes)
To peck for carrion, my shee-wolfe, and all,
Greedy, and full of expectation—
  MOS. And then to haue it rauish'd from their
  mouthes?
  VOLP. 'Tis true, I will ha' thee put on a gowne,
And take vpon thee, as thou wert mine heire;
Shew 'hem a will: open that chest, and reach
Forth one of those, that has the blankes. I'le
  straight
Put in thy name. MOS. It will be rare, sir. VOLP. I,
When they e'ene gape, and finde themselues deluded—
  MOS. Yes. VOLP. And thou vse them skiruily.
  Dispatch,
Get on thy gowne. MOS. But, what, sir, if they
  aske
After the body? VOLP. Say, it was corrupted.
  MOS. I'le say, it stunke, sir; and was faine
  t'haue it
Coffin'd vp instantly, and sent away.
  VOLP. Any thing, what thou wilt. Hold, here's
  my will.
Get thee a cap, a count-booke, pen and inke,
Papers afore thee; sit, as thou wert taking
An inuentory of parcels: I'le get vp,

Behind the cortine, on a stoole, and harken;
Sometime, peepe ouer; see, how they doe looke;
With what degrees, their bloud doth leaue their faces!
O, 'twill afford me a rare meale of laughter.

(V.ii.56–87)

The playing of this "game" continues as Volpone assumes the disguise of "one o' the *Commandadori*" and goes out of his house to taunt his victims.

Thanks to the eloquence with which Voltore lied and the skill with which the witnesses Corvino, Corbaccio, and Lady Politic Would-be perjured themselves, the gulling plot has been an eminent success, apparently for both Mosca and Volpone. But Volpone is out of his house and his identity—reported dead—and Mosca is now the heir, the "*Clarissimo.*" At the hearing for the sentencing of Celia and Bonario, Volpone must reveal all—or lose all. He chooses the former. His sentence at the hands of the Avocatori is severe enough that it will lead to his death. Quite as much as an Oedipus— or an Othello—he has been betrayed by a specific quality of character. But it has been the one *good* trait, conceived in the manner of the humours, in a character otherwise possessed by that which to Jonson is the most massive of evils—greed.

The "indenture tripartite" of *The Alchemist*, between Face and Subtle and Dol Common, is in general terms much like the gulling operation conducted by Volpone and Mosca in *Volpone*. The bait is different—the philosopher's stone instead of a legacy. The basic appeal, as in *Volpone*, is to human greed. It is not, however, the searing, corrosive greed of that play, but a lesser sort, which will provide, at its worst, a sybaritic existence for Sir Epicure Mammon and, at its least harmful, a successful career for Drugger as shopkeeper.

But the techniques by which Face and Subtle and Dol work are similar to those in *Volpone*; and the uses to which Jonson puts them—the winding-up of victims, both to action and to self-revelation—are essentially like those in the earlier play. There is one notable difference between the two plays, however, for almost

no choric commentary is given to any one of the three Brokers in
The Alchemist.

Face is in reality Jeremy the butler, in charge of the house of his
master Lovewit, while Lovewit is absent from London because of
the plague. Face, Subtle, and Dol have no humours. True, they
assume many identities, but for professional purposes only. Like
Mosca and Volpone, they know themselves.

The winding-up process should be briefly examined from two
points of view: the prompting to action and the prompting to self-
revelation. In most cases, the former is a cooperative affair, with
Face pushing the victim, a Dapper or a Drugger or a Kastril, toward Subtle's wonderful gifts, with Subtle feigning reluctance,
and Dol functioning as bait—the Queen of Faery for Dapper, or
the mad sister to "lord WHATS'-HVM" for Sir Epicure Mammon.

The primary object of Jonson's indignation in *The Alchemist* is
probably the Puritans, represented by Tribulation Wholesome
and Ananias. A few excerpts from Scene 2 of Act III will show the
skill with which the Broker can lead the greedy and hypocritical
Puritan into full revelation of himself:

> [SVB.] ... Wicked ANANIAS!
> Art thou return'd? Nay then, it goes downe, yet.
>   TRI. Sir, be appeased, he is come to humble
> Himselfe in spirit, and to aske your patience,
> If too much zeale hath carried him, aside,
> From the due path.
>   .   .   .   .
>   SVB. And, then, the turning of this Lawyers pewter
> To plate, at *Christ-masse*— ANA. *Christ-tide*, I pray you.
>   SVB. Yet, ANANIAS? ANA. I haue done. SVB. Or changing
> His parcell guilt, to massie gold. You cannot
> But raise you friends. Withall, to be of power
> To pay an armie, in the field, to buy
> The king of *France*, out of his realmes; or *Spaine*,
> Out of his *Indies*: What can you not doe,
> Against lords spirituall, or temporall,
> That shall oppone you? TRI. Verily, 'tis true.

We may be temporall lords, our selues, I take it.

. . . .

   TRI. What will the orphanes goods arise to, thinke you?
   SVB. Some hundred markes; as much as fill'd three carres,
Vnladed now: you'll make six millions of 'hem.
But I must ha' more coales laid in. TRI. How!
   SVB. Another load,
And then we ha' finish'd. We must now encrease
Our fire to *ignis ardens*, we are past
Fimus equinus, Balnei, Cineris,
And all those lenter heats. If the holy purse
Should, with this draught, fall low, and that the
   Saints
Doe need a present summe, I haue [a] trick
To melt the pewter, you shall buy now, instantly,
And, with a tincture, make you as good *Dutch* dollers,
As any are in *Holland*. TRI. Can you so?
   SVB. I, and shall bide the third examination.
   ANA. It will be ioyfull tidings to the *Brethren*.
   SVB. But you must carry it, secret. TRI. I, but stay,
This act of coyning, is it lawfull? ANA. Lawfull?
We know no Magistrate. Or, if we did,
This's forraine coyne. SVB. It is no coyning, sir.
It is but casting. TRI. Ha? you distinguish well.
Casting of money may be lawfull. ANA. 'Tis, sir.

              (ll. 5–10, 42–52, 133–53)

The Alchemist has remarkably few of the somewhat detached choric utterances that have appeared in other plays— "what a punishment is avarice to itself." In fact, only one seems entirely divorced from both action and characterization: "[FAC.] A wench is a rare bait, with which a man / No sooner's taken, but he straight firkes mad" (II.iv.4–5). Perhaps part of the greatness of the play lies in that very fact. Certainly *The Alchemist* carries a great didactic burden, but carries it as a necessary part of the action.

    The third of Jonson's great Brokers is Meercraft of *The Devil Is an Ass*. He is of less interest to reader or auditor than either Mosca or Face, for he is given few lines of powerful comic force. But the fertility with which he can conceive projects and the dexterity with which he can put them into effect are most impressive. The conception of the play itself, *The Devil Is an Ass*, is notably different from, and less effective than, that of *Volpone* or *The Alchemist*. In those plays a small Broker group wrought their effects on a large group of gulls—of varying, and perhaps ascending, degrees of greed, folly, hypocrisy. In *The Devil Is an Ass*, however, all the efforts of a considerably larger Broker group are directed primarily to the gulling of one man who is a massive representation of both greed and folly, Fitz-dottrell.

Meercraft himself is different in conception from Mosca and Face. He pretends that he has access to court, and does wear the garments of a gentleman. To Wittipol he describes both himself and his projects: "... wee poore Gentlemen, that want acres, / Must for our needs, turne fooles vp, and plough *Ladies* / Some- times, to try what glebe they are" (III.iv.45–47). But he takes no pleasure in the game, as do Volpone and Face. Greed is paramount.

Meercraft has an impressive list of associates: Everill, Ingine (the technical broker), Traines, Guilthead, Plutarchus. He uses as tools Lady Tail-bush, who is gulled by Meercraft into believing she may be a Broker; Lady Either-side; and the redoubtable Sir Poule Either-side, the Puritan man-of-law. He undertakes to use Wit- tipol, by whom he is himself gulled. Even the inept little devil, Pug, is wrought into his schemes.

But Meercraft's and Jonson's efforts are focussed primarily on Fitz-dottrell—Meercraft seeking to relieve him of his estate, and Jonson to present perhaps his most damning portrait of the mar- riage of greed and folly. A presentation of the winding-up process— both toward action and self-revelation—will be found in my essay "The Cloaks of *The Devil is an Asse*."[6]

Humour is of as little importance in the work of the Broker group in *The Devil Is an Ass* as it has been in *Volpone* and *The Alchemist*. Meercraft is deadly serious, taking no pleasure in the outwitting of fools; if he appears to be what he is not, it is merely for professional purposes and is in no sense self-deception.

[6] *Studies in English*, VI (1965), 5–14. Reprinted here as Chapter IV.

The associates of Meercraft, though they have names of the humourous type, are also conceived for the most part without the obsessions of the true humourous characters. Ingine turns a dishonest penny on secondhand clothes. Everill does not assume to be, but *is*, what his name implies. Guilthead is almost obsessed with the idea of gulling the country gentry, but he is fully qualified to do so. That he would see his son a country gentleman may be a suggestion of self-deception of the humourous type. While the portrait of Sir Poule Either-side is that of a vicious Puritan, he is what he is—believes what he believes—"It is the diuell, by his severall languages." Pug, however, even though he is on leave from Hell, displays some of the qualities of Jonson's humours. He believes himself to be a worthy operator for his Commonwealth, even in London; and believes himself to have a talent for "venery." Yet, of all this unsavory group, none is punished by Jonson, unless the slight warning by Manly to mend their ways can be construed as punishment. They, like others of their kind, are for Jonson the tools of castigation, not the objects.

Having examined the three full-dress portraits of Brokers, we should perhaps point out representatives of the class in other plays where they assume importance. If we accept the chronology of Herford and Simpson, we must mention first Canon Hugh of *A Tale of a Tub*. He is not a major figure in the play but merely one who seeks small gratuities through minor deceptions. Though associated with the Church, he is not used as a vehicle for satire and is not a Puritan.

The Broker does not appear in *The Case Is Altered*, or in *Every Man in His Humour*. He reappears, briefly, in Shift in *Every Man Out of His Humour*. Again, he is a minor character, one employed by Sogliardo to teach him to be a gentleman, *i.e.*, to take tobacco. Though he is a bully, a coward, and a liar, he is not a primary object of Jonson's attention but is merely the instrument by which Macilente, and Jonson, can cure the humour of Sogliardo.

Aside from those in *Volpone* and *The Alchemist*, at whom we have already looked, the type does not reappear until 1614, in

Bartholomew Fair. All the people of the Fair are Brokers. But they are not the object of Jonson's attack; they are rather a sort of microcosm of the real world, against which Jonson tests his exemplars of greed and folly and hypocrisy.[7] There are eleven of them, thus listed in "The Persons of the Play":

LANT. LEATHERHEAD.	*A Hobbi-horse seller.*
IOANE TRASH.	*A Ginger-bread woman.*
EZECHIEL EDGWORTH.	*A Cutpurse.*
NIGHTINGALE.	*A Ballad-singer.*
VRSLA.	*A Pigge-woman.*
MOON-CALFE.	*Her Tapster.*
IORDAN KNOCK-HVM.	*A Horse-courser, and ranger o' Turnbull.*
VAL. CVTTING.	*A Roarer.*
CAPTAINE WHIT.	*A Bawd.*
PVNQVE ALICE.	*Mistresse o' the Game.*
TROUBLE-ALL.	*A Madman.*

Among these eleven there is very little that might be classed as Jonsonian humour. Jordan Knock-hum, and his subordinate, Cutting, "A Roarer," impose their quarrelsomeness, and particularly their game of "Vapours," on the customers at Ursula's booth as a Matthew might impose his verses on any who would hear. But their exercise of this humour is for Jonson a plot device, not a manifestation of folly to be castigated. Trouble-all, "A Madman," is mad of what is essentially a humour. Justice Overdoo's "warrant" is to him the only valid occasion for any action, the only source of authority.[8] But Trouble-all is also outside Jonson's customary practice with regard to the humours. Treatment of him is sympathetic, for all his numerous actions are directed toward the solution of problems concerning visitors to this "Vanity Fair," not toward either the punishment or cure of Trouble-all.

---

[7] For additional development of this idea, see my essay "Some Antecedents of the Puppet Play in *Bartholomew Fair*," *Studies in English*, VII (1966), 43–64. Reprinted here as Chapter III.

[8] The thematic significance of the "warrant" is explored by Ray L. Hefner, Jr., in his study "Unifying Symbols in the Comedy of Ben Jonson," *English Institute Essays 1954* (New York: Columbia University Press, 1955), 74–97.

The two other dramatic functions in which the Brokers partake, the winding-up of Jonson's victims to the display of their follies, and the choric commentary thereon, are sparsely represented in *Bartholomew Fair*. The two are frequently intertwined, and seldom do they go beyond the individual victim to a generalized assessment. A very few passages will serve to illustrate methods and results. There is probably a generalization behind Edgworth's (the Cutpurse's) assessment of Winwife and Quarlous: "These fellowes are too fine to carry money." Perhaps many Puritans lie behind Knock-hum's observation about Zeal-of-the-Land Busy and his disciples: "... good guests, I say right hypocrites, good gluttons. In, and set a couple o' pigs o' the board, and halfe a dozen of the biggest bottles afore'hem, and call *Whit*, I doe not loue to heare Innocents abus'd: Fine ambling hypocrites! and a stone-puritane, with a sorrell head, and beard, good-mouth'd gluttons: two to a pigge, away" (III.ii.116–22). Perhaps in the following passages Bristle and Haggise, the Watchmen, contemplate members of the Quorum in addition to Justice Overdoo:

> HAG. Before me, Neighbour *Bristle* (and now I thinke on't better) Iustice *Ouerdoo*, is a very parantory person.
> BRI. O! are you aduis'd of that? and a seuere Iusticer, by your leaue.
> IVS. Doe I heare ill o' that side, too?
> BRI. He will sit as vpright o' the bench, an' you marke him, as a candle i' the socket, and giue light to the whole Court in euery businesse.
> HAG. But he will burne blew, and swell like a bile (God blesse vs) an' he be angry.
> BRI. I, and hee will be angry too, when him list, that's more: and when hee is angry, be it right or wrong; hee has the Law on's side, euer. I marke that too.
>
> (IV.i.69–81)

One fairly lengthy example will serve to show Jonson's skillful union of winding-up and satirical commentary. Knock-hum, the Horse Courser, is undertaking to assist Whit, the Bawd, in alluring Mistress Overdoo and Win-the-Fight Littlewit into Whit's "employment." Needless to say, both ladies have partaken a little too freely of Ursula's ale. Knock-hum initiates the persuasion with flattery of Win-the-Fight in the imagery of his profession:

> KNO. I conceiue thee, VRS! goe thy waies, doest thou heare, *Whit?* is't not pitty, my delicate darke chestnut here, with the fine leane head, large fore-head, round eyes, euen mouth, sharpe eares, long necke, thinne crest, close withers, plaine backe, deepe sides, short fillets, and full flankes: with a round belly, a plumpe buttocke, large thighes, knit knees, streight legges, short pasternes, smooth hoofes, and short heeles; should lead a dull honest womans life, that might liue the life of a Lady?
>
> WHI. Yes, by my fait, and trot, it is, Captaine: de honesht womans life is a scuruy dull life, indeed, la.
>
> WIN. How, Sir? is an honest womans life a scuruy life?
>
> WHI. Yes fait, shweet heart, beleeue him, de leefe of a Bond-woman! but if dou vilt harken to me, I vill make tee a free-woman, and a Lady: dou shalt liue like a Lady, as te Captaine saish.
>
> KNO. I, and be honest too sometimes: haue her wiers, and her tires, her greene gownes, and veluet petticoates.
>
> WHI. I, and ride to *Ware* and *Rumford* i' dy Coach, shee de Players, be in loue vit 'hem; sup vit gallantsh, be drunke, and cost de noting.
>
> KNO. Braue vapours!
>
> WHI. And lye by twenty on 'hem, if dou pleash, shweet heart.
>
> WIN. What, and be honest still, that were fine sport.
>
> WHI. Tish common, shweet heart, tou may'st doe it, by my hand: it shall be iustified to ty husbands faish, now: tou shalt be as honesht as the skinne betweene his hornsh, la!
>
> KNO. Yes, and weare a dressing, top, and top-gallant, to compare with ere a husband on 'hem all, for a fore-top: it is the vapour of spirit in the wife, to cuckold, now adaies; as it is the vapour of fashion, in the husband, not to suspect. Your prying cat-eyed-citizen, is an abominable vapour.
>
> (IV.v.20–52)

Ramping Alice, the "Mistresse o' the Game," assumes the recruitment has been successful, and perhaps her assessment of the situation includes ladies other than those attending the Fair: "ALE. A mischiefe on you, they are such as you are, that vndoe vs, and take our trade from vs, with your tuft-taffata hanches. KNO. How now, *Alice*! ALE. The poore common whores can ha' no traffique, for the priuy rich ones; your caps and hoods of veluet, call away our customers, and lick the fat from vs" (ll. 65–71).

Though these Brokers, who are Fair-folk, escape Jonson's retribution, even to Edgworth, the cutpurse, as does the similar group in *The Devil Is an Ass*, those of *The Staple of News* will not be so fortunate.

The reason is, at least in part, that many of the Brokers are also possessed of humours. *The Staple of News* is actually in many ways a departure from the pattern of the earlier plays. No character in the category of Wits appears; the play has an allegorical flavor not evident since *Cynthia's Revels*; in Peni-Boy Canter, Jonson has almost revived the largely choric figure of Horace or Crites. But certainly here the almost complete intermingling of tool—the Broker—and subject material—the humourous man—is Jonson's most important departure.

In *The Staple of News* only three of the characters, Peni-Boy Junior, the prodigal, Peni-Boy Canter, the choric figure, and the Deity, Lady Pecunia, are entirely free of the qualities which make the Broker. Of the remaining characters, three should be noted briefly. Peni-Boy Senior is the usurer, the "money-baud." But he is atypical insofar as the standard career of the Broker goes. He takes a very slight part in the action; he is given no choric commentary, except possibly a little satire, out of his own mouth, on himself and his kind; he has humourous traits, such as his obsession with the fact that the Lady Pecunia has "falne off two in the hundred" (a reference to the fact that in 1624 Parliament reduced the maximum rate of interest from ten per cent to eight) and his preoccupation with his two dogs, Blocke and Lollard (Calvinist and Puritan?); and, finally, he is cured, as so many of Jonson's humourous characters are cured, rather than merely dismissed, as are most of the members of the Broker group.

The master of the Staple of News, Cymbal ("tinkling," with mouth of "sounding brasse"), is the second of the Brokers in the play, which takes its name, though not its major action, from his activities. He is almost of the true breed: he is altogether motivated by greed; he has no humourous traits; but he departs from the image of the typical Jonson Broker in that he is punished at the end, metaphorically, by the powerful denunciation of Peni-Boy Canter. The third member of the Broker group in *The Staple of News* is Lickfinger, the Cook. But, like Peni-Boy Senior and, to a lesser extent, Cymbal, he is atypical. He is not very greedy, though he may cheat a little on the quality of food he dispenses; he has a humour, his marvelous preoccupation with the oneness of poetry and cooking; and in one very important aspect of the play he is primarily choric, speaking for Jonson himself, in what I take to be a carefully wrought tribute to Shakespeare.[9]

In Jonson's next play, *The New Inn* (1629), there is no character properly in our category of Brokers. This play is clearly one of Jonson's "dotages," a sort of sentimental comedy of humours. The characters of the humourous group are negligible, while the principal characters are merely under illusions, after the Shakespearian manner, and require no measuring against the powerful test of the Brokers.

In *The Magnetic Lady* the Broker reappears. Sir Moath Interest looks remarkably like Peni-Boy Senior; in fact he too is a "money-baud." He is in possession of the dowry of the Magnetic Lady's niece and will sell her to the highest bidder. In terms of seeking the niece, two or three of the humourous characters manifest themselves. But essentially, Sir Moath is merely a hurdle to be overrun in the action, not a significant part as tool, or as object, of Jonson's didactic apparatus. But unlike most of the Brokers, he is punished: he must disgorge the dowry, with accrued interest.

This brief examination of the Broker in Jonson's plays, leads, I believe, to one fairly safe generalization. The function of the Broker is greatest in the plays of Jonson's maturity, in the plays universally regarded as his best, *Volpone, The Alchemist, Bar-*

---

[9] For discussion of this suggestion, see my article "Ben Jonson and Shakespeare: 1623-1626," *Studies in English*, X (1970), 25-48. Reprinted here as Chapter V.

tholomew Fair. The Broker is also very important in *The Devil Is an Ass*, of the same period, but not of the same excellence. He is absent from *Epicoene*, also, which is of the maturity, but, in spite of Dryden's observation that "the intrigue of it is the greatest in any pure unmixed comedy in any language,"[10] it is considerably inferior to its great companions.

Part of the excellence of the three plays named lies, I believe, in the very presence of the Moscas, the Faces, the professional folk of Bartholomew Fair. They in themselves are not the primary objects of Jonson's didactic thrust, but they provide an admirable background against which he can make manifest the greed, the folly, the hypocrisy in his Everyman, who to a greater or lesser extent, falls within the scope of the Humourous Group. The Broker, though greedy, sees himself clearly and sees also clearly the qualities in his victims. Jonson's comedies reach their greatest heights when his Broker is kept clearly separate from his humourous characters but is given much of the commentary reserved in the earlier and later plays to members of the Choric Group.

THE PLYANT WOMAN

This Broker, to do his work, purports to have something that will be of great value to his victim: the legacy in *Volpone*; the philosopher's stone in *The Alchemist*; or the varied delights of Bartholomew Fair. He often has, however, a more luscious bait, the Plyant Woman. She takes her name, of course, from Dame Plyant of *The Alchemist*, who will do well as a prototype. Dame Plyant, a rich young widow, has been brought to London from the country by her brother, who seeks a suitable husband for her. Using her as bait, Face and Subtle extract tobacco and damask from Drugger. With her unwitting help, they achieve a masterwork, the gulling of the Gamester, Surly, who knows what they

---

[10] This observation is part of the "examen of *The Silent Woman*" in *The Essay of Dramatic Poesy*. See W. P. Ker, *Essays of John Dryden* (New York: Russell and Russell, 1961), 81–82.

are. When at the beginning of Act V Lovewit, Face's master, comes home, Face escapes punishment by bribing his master with the luscious widow. Throughout the play she has, without questioning, believed everything told her, and done anything asked of her. Her immediate usefulness has been to the Brokers, who have been in *The Alchemist* Jonson's primary tools in his powerful indictments of the Mammons and the Tribulation Wholesomes.

A second manifestation of the Plyant Woman in *The Alchemist* is Dol Common. She is in reality precisely the opposite of pliant, for she is the dominant force in the whole gulling operation of Face, Subtle, and herself. But she is bait, as Queen of Fairies, to Dapper and, as the Lord's sister, to Sir Epicure Mammon. Dol appears to be, but is not, pliant.

With the type and its variant set forth, the remaining members of the group may be enumerated briefly. Awdrey of *A Tale of a Tub* is affianced, unofficially, to Squire Tub. That arrangement is agreeable to her. She is almost abducted, again willingly, as a wife for Justice Preamble. She is promised as bride by her father to John Clay, Tile-maker. He is acceptable, for all she wants is a husband. In the final confusion, she is secretly married to Polmartin, gentleman usher to Lady Tub, again willingly. Awdrey has been not the tool of Brokers, but a unifying device for the poet; almost all action in the play directs itself toward the goal of Awdrey for bride. She has in no sense been the object of the poet's satire, nor a medium for his choric commentary.

The three young ladies of *The Case Is Altered* are anything but pliant; in fact, they resist much pressure in order to achieve ends entirely determined by themselves. But the type reappears in Bridget of *Every Man in His Humour*. She meets Edward Knowell, a most eligible young man, on the day of the play. He is proposed to her as a husband by Wellbred, and she accepts, though she demonstrates a little spirit when she suggests that Wellbred is to some extent in the attitude of a bawd. She, like Awdrey, is not a tool of any Brokers but a convenience in plotting for the poet. The only women of importance in *Every Man Out of His Humour*,

Fallace and Saviolina, belong in the group whose humours are to be cured or punished. In *Cynthia's Revels* there are no women actually. A few are completely virtuous, placed on the level already discussed as Deities, and several others are almost allegórical representations of vice and folly. In *Poetaster*, also, Jonson finds no occasion to use a Plyant Woman. Julia, the mistress of Ovid, can defy even her father, Augustus, who is a god. Chloe, wife to the citizen Albius, is an object of biting satire and belongs among the Humourous Group.

Celia of *Volpone* is, up to a point, very pliant. She throws her handkerchief to Volpone, disguised as the mountebank; she consents to go with her husband Corvino to a "feast" at Volpone's house; but she refuses utterly to approach the "death bed" of Volpone or to yield to the glittering proposals of the revived Volpone. As bait, she serves in a curious double role. Her husband Corvino in effect barters her for his place in the will of the dying Volpone. On the other hand, Mosca, one of the Brokers, uses her as bait for his master, the other of the Brokers. For Jonson himself she is somewhat unique, since Celia is almost the only woman in his comedies not subjected to a satirical thrust or two.

The bait in *Epicoene* looks like a Plyant Woman. But there are differences. Epicoene is a boy disguised as a woman; "she" is used, not by a Broker, but by one of the Wits, Dauphine, who himself displays no greed in using her. "She" is taken to wife by Morose, who sees her not only as pliant but silent as well. After the ceremony she becomes a scold, but in compliance with the restrictions of Dauphine. Epicoene is not herself an object of Jonson's satiric thrusts, but she does become after the marriage an excellent vehicle for satire on shrewish wives in general.

Though there are Plyant Women of sorts in *The Devil Is an Ass* and in *The Magnetic Lady*, and even in the tragedy *Catiline*, there is only one more of major stature. She is Win-the-Fight Littlewit of *Bartholomew Fair*. She is of use directly to Jonson in weaving his vast tapestry, and indirectly as bait used by his Brokers. As *Bartholomew Fair* opens, we see her as answerable to

her husband's wishes, accepting at his bidding the kisses of Quarlous. Win is governed largely by her mother, Dame Purecraft,
who is in turn governed by Rabbi Zeal-of-the-Land Busy, and
Win accedes to that government. Jonson, having introduced all
his characters except the Fair-folk at Dame Purecraft's house, needs
to get them all to the Fair. Win, being pregnant, easily succumbs to
her husband's request that she long for the roast pig of the Fair.
Though he finds roast pig an abomination, the gluttonous Busy,
smelling the pig afar off, consents to the visit—with the result that
everybody goes to the Fair. After using the "jordan" in Ursula's
booth, to which Mistress Overdoo also is courteously escorted by
Whit, the bawd, and Knock-hum, the horse-courser, Win-the-
Fight easily succumbs to their persuasions that, in order to be a lady
of fashion, one must have cuckolded her husband. Equipped, along
with Mistress Overdoo, with the promise of a coach expressly for
that purpose, in the garments of a prostitute, "green-gowns, crim-
son petticoats," she is ready for her next service as Plyant Woman.
    Whit, the bawd, expecting to find customers for the services of
his recruits at the puppet-play, takes them in their new finery (supplied by Ursula) to the booth where "The ancient moderne history
of *Hero* and *Leander*" is to be performed.
    The husbands of these two estimable women, John Littlewit,
the proctor, and Justice Overdoo, the disguised seeker of enormities at the Fair, are among the subjects of Jonson's comic justice.
It is a part of their correction and punishment that they find their
wives in the custody of Whit, the bawd, dressed as whores.
    The two groups of Jonsonian characters at which we have looked
thus far, the Choric group and the group of Brokers, are not the
primary objects of Jonson's didactic intent. The Chorus himself,
a Crites or a Macilente, usually has the poet's admiration and con-
currence, and the task of speaking much of Jonson's thought about
the human condition. The Wit, of the Choric group, also is beloved of the poet: he is frequently an admirable model for what
the humourous characters would be, or would seem to be. He is
valuable in setting the stage for the manifestation of those things

Jonson wishes to castigate; to him are given many of the most in-
cisive comic utterances. The third member of the Choric group,
the Deity, holds little interest for Jonson, but she, or he, is a useful
source of authority for implementing the judgments made by Wit
or Chorus.

Even though the members of his other major group of useful
people, the Brokers, are normally moved by what is for Jonson
the most contemptible of human motives, greed, they largely escape
his castigation. They are for him a secondary manifestation, in
that they can exist only if there are men more greedy than themselves on whom they can prey. Their primary function, like that
of the Wits, is as winders-up of the humourous characters to manifestations of their greed, their hypocrisy, or their utter foolishness.

The Macilentes, the Truewits, the Moscas, and their peers constitute a massive machinery for achieving Jonson's therapeutic effects. The unhappy objects of their efforts, those of the group of
humourous characters, are equally necessary for the accomplishment of Jonson's purpose. That he is able to direct these diverse
characters through actions both skillfully constructed and highly
entertaining toward ends conceived with conscious didactic intent is indeed a mark of genius. It would, however, have been
genius of a higher order if, like Shakespeare, he had used *men*—not
characters.

THE HUMOUROUS GROUP

The group of Jonson's creations to be discussed under the general
heading "The Humourous Group" will not be treated with reference to any psychological or physiological standards. They are
merely that group among the vast array of Jonsonian characters
who, as Jonson says in the first "Grex" in *Every Man Out of His
Humour*, are under the spell of "some peculiar quality" which
"Doth so possesse a man, that it doth draw / All his affects, his
spirits, and his powers, / In their confluctions, all to runne one

way" (ll. 106–108). Such people are offenders against decorum, against judgment, against the mores of the community. In the fifth act of *Cynthia's Revels*, the divine Cynthia, to whose attention the "deformities," male and female, have come, gives this solemn charge: "Deare ARETE [Virtue], and CRITES, to you two / We giue the charge; impose what paines you please: / Th' incurable cut off, the rest reforme" (V.xi.95–97). Arete, in turn, delegates her power to Crites, who decrees that all shall "passe" to "the well of knowledge, *Helicon*; / Where purged of your present maladies, / (Which are not few, nor slender) you become / Such as you faine would seeme" (ll. 153–56). This Crites of *Cynthia's Revels* was a poet, a critic, a scholar, a soldier. These are qualities which Jonson arrogated to himself, and one feels that he took to himself the charge given by Cynthia to Crites, for cutting off and reforming become the processes by which he handles his creations in the Humourous Group.

The means by which Jonson seeks to work out their correction or their castigation have been discussed in the pages above. What remains is to show how they are sorted out one from another and what determines whether they are "cut off" or are subject to "reforme."

The process of achieving at once a differentiation among these people and a comprehensive view of human follies or minor crimes is an extremely complicated one. There are three postures from which most of the Jonsonian humourous characters are treated: (1) the character's awareness, or lack thereof, of himself and his circumstances; (2) his possession by one or more of the great faults which Jonson castigates, greed, hypocrisy, and folly—"foolness," to coin a word; and (3) a trait of humours superimposed on the more basic qualities, such as hatred of noise (Morose), pursuit of a suit (Fungoso), the misuse of heroic oaths (Bobadil).

The Jonsonian characters of the humourous group are not to be looked at, as in Shakespeare, as *men* and *women*, of many hopes and fears, loves and hates, pettiness and grandeur. They are rather to be the products of analysis in some combination of the three ap-

proaches mentioned above. Sufficient elucidation of items two
and three will come with discussion of individual characters or
groups of characters. The first item, however, stated as a character's
"awareness, or lack thereof, of himself and his circumstances,"
needs further discussion, for it will be the basis of organization for
subsequent pages.

There are, among Jonson's array of posturing figures, three
basic distinctions with reference to a character's "awareness." The
first one is the individual whom I have chosen to call "The Mistaken
Man." But he is *not* mistaken about himself. Allowing, of course,
for a little human vanity, he knows his abilities and limitations, his
successes and failures in achieving what he must do. What he is
mistaken about is the posture of things outside himself—his wife,
society in general, the price of corn, the qualities that make up a
gentleman. Jonson in general provides, in the manner of a Shakespeare, for the removal of his misapprehensions, so that he can be,
not "cut off," but reformed. He may be but usually is not possessed
by one of the great faults, greed, or hypocrisy, or folly. Superimposed on this basic structure of personality is usually a quality
that is of the humourous type: Sir Puntarvolo has his "*puntilios*";
Justice Overdoo his "enormities"; Knowell his mistrust of poetry.
Obviously, for such a man the humour and the misapprehension
may be all one.

The next category, in terms of this analysis of "awareness," is
that which may be designated "The Hypocritical Man." He, too,
knows something of himself: that, like Bobadil, he is in reality a
coward; or that, like Zeal-of-the-Land Busy, he uses his piety to
cover peculation; or that, like Lady Politic Would-be, he parades
knowledge to cover ignorance. But he chooses to present to the
world a character, an identity, which is entirely different from
what he probably knows himself to be, brave rather than cowardly,
learned rather than ignorant, saintly rather than dishonest. Of the
three great objects of Jonson's attack, this man certainly is possessed
by hypocrisy; perhaps he is also greedy, or perhaps he is a fool.
His assumption of an identity such as saint or wise man or brave

man may also be his humour. But more likely, the humourous quality may be an additional technique superimposed on the hypo-critical posture, Bobadil's oaths, Captain Otter's Bull and Bear and Horse, the stuttering of Captain Tucca. This Hypocritical Man's fate at the hands of Jonson is inevitable: he is "cut off," usually in terms of the nature he strives to present. Captain Otter is beaten by his wife; Fastidius Briske is jailed for debts he incurred to buy the suits that made him appear a courtier.

The word "awareness" has been used as a starting point for discussion of the two groups of humourous characters analyzed above. The man in the third category—"The Would-Be Man," after Sir Politic Would-be of *Volpone*—may be measured in terms of an utter lack of awareness of what he is. Perhaps Jonson's array of Poetasters—Matthew, Crispinus, Daw, Madrigal—will provide the best exposition. These men are not poets; they have not the slightest idea what a poet is; because he has the gown, or the beard, or the book from which to plagiarize, the Poetaster believes, sin-cerely, that he *is* a poet. Whatever posture he believes to be appro-priate for a poet is his humour, though Jonson may embellish the humours a little: Matthew will be melancholy; Daw is the "only talking Sir"; Crispinus wishes to be entreated to sing. This Would-Be Man has little hypocrisy; he believes himself to be what he presents. In most instances, he is not greedy. In most instances, he is a fool. Other than one or two rather contrived exceptions, he is, like the Hypocritical Man, "cut off."

Since he is, in Jonson's pattern of offenders against decorum, the most innocuous, the Mistaken Man should be the first of the group of humourous characters to be examined in terms of his character, his conduct, and his fate.

THE MISTAKEN MAN

Perhaps the most fully developed portrait among this group of Jonson's characters is that of Justice Overdoo of *Bartholomew Fair*. His official position is Justice of the Peace, and problems of the Fair are a part of his jurisdiction. He is renowned among the Fair-folk as a severe and arbitrary judge. Fearing that, because of the inefficiency or veniality of his officers, not all abuses are brought to his attention, he comes to the Fair disguised as the mad Arthur of Bradley to seek out "enormities."

The first "enormity" that the Justice discovers is that Joan Trash's gingerbread cakes are made of "stale bread, rotten egges, musty ginger, and dead honey"; about them he does nothing. His second "enormity" is Ursula, the Pig-woman, whom he has known as *"Punke, Pinnace,* and *Bawd"* for two-and-twenty years. He notes also that she mixes a quarter pound of *"Coltsfoot"* with a half-pound of tobacco to "itch it out," and that she has half-a-dozen other similar cheats. But again he takes no action. Justice Overdoo's third "enormity" is that cutpurses frequent the Fair. He fears the influence of such disreputable characters as Ursula and Nightingale, the ballad-singer, who has "a terrible taint, *Poetry,"* on a fine youth named Edgworth. He makes it a major project throughout the play to save Edgworth from this dangerous company. That Edgworth is the cutpurse he learns only in his final purgation. Still happily mistaken, the Justice joins a crowd assembled to hear Nightingale sing a ballad warning the crowd against cutpurses, and those cutpurses of the consequences of their evil ways. Since the ballad discovers "enormity," the Justice relaxes a little in his condemnation of poetry. He does not see Nightingale receive the purse Edgworth passes to him, for delivery to Ursula, the purse he has filched from Bartholomew Cokes.

But the next "enormity" the Justice discovers is himself. He has a fellow madman at the Fair, this one not pretending as is Justice Overdoo, but mad in reality. Trouble-all's madness takes a unique form. He firmly believes, as a consequence of his own unfortunate experiences, that no action of any sort is permissible at the Fair without Justice Overdoo's "warrant." To cure Trouble-all is the second project of our Mistaken Man, and the process is to give Trouble-all his "warrant," his signature, on a blank sheet of paper, with his seal as Justice, and the signature of a witness, Dame Purecraft. In keeping with his course of mistakes, however, the Justice gives this "bond," not to the real madman, Trouble-all, but to Quarlous, disguised as Trouble-all. This mistake costs him his purchased ward, Grace Welborne, or rather, the profit he expected for "selling" her to Bartholomew Cokes.

In association with the Puppet Play, but not as a consequence of it, these mistakes come to light, the real enormities of the Fair-folk are forgotten, and Justice Overdoo sees himself as but "*Adam, flesh and blood.*" As the symbol of his reformation, he refrains from hanging the cutpurse and invites the company home to dinner. His intents have become, as he says, "*Ad correctionem, non ad destructionem; ad aedificandum, non ad diruendum*" (V.vi.112–13). The good Justice is not strictly a humourous character, except for the one day of the play itself. On that day, his preoccupation with his identity as the mad Arthur of Bradley and his search for enormities govern his conduct. Until almost the final moment of the play he fully believes himself to be a noteworthy magistrate, taking laudable measures for the good of the commonwealth.

This Mistaken Man is an important device in Jonson's early comedies. In *Every Man in His Humour* he appears five times. In that play, the mistake is a quality of humours, imposed on a character of reasonably good sense and devoid of the great vices of greed, hypocrisy, and foolishness. The elder Knowell believes his son Edward has fallen into bad company, which is untrue; he believes that his personal intervention will remedy the situation; and he believes that "idle *poetrie*" is a "fruitlesse, and vnprofitable art." As a consequence of the events in the play, plus the admonishment of Justice Clement, Knowell gives up his misapprehensions, and Jonson is able to "reforme" him. Kitely the merchant is possessed by an unfounded suspicion that he is, or will be, a cuckold, to the extent that he neglects his business and stoops to spying on his wife, in person and by deputy. Mistress Kitely is, to a lesser extent, affected with the same taint of suspicion. They, too, learn from events, *and* from Justice Clement, that "Hornes i' the mind are worse then o' the head." The redoubtable Squire Downright forsakes his "anger." And even Cob, the humble "water-bearer," relinquishes jealousy and animadversions on poetry and the taking of tobacco.

In *Every Man Out of His Humour* Jonson sets up an elaborate apparatus by which he can in some manner minister to the aberrations, defined in terms of the humours, of a very large group of almost one-dimensional characters. All are affected by the masterful manipulations of Macilente. Some are, in terms of Cynthia's instructions in *Cynthia's Revels*, "cut off." Some few Macilente is able to "reforme." The first of these men who come to see themselves as mistaken is Sordido, who, like the Porter's fancied customer in *Macbeth*, "hanged himself on th' expectation of plenty." Sordido's humour is the continual reading of the almanac seeking the prediction of bad weather that would make his hoard of buried grain more valuable. He does indeed hang himself. Observed by a group of "Rustici," one of whom cuts him down, he is saved from death. When he is recognized by them as "the catterpiller SORDIDO," the other Rustici curse the man who cut the rope. Their curses move Sordido to a view of himself: "What curses breathe these men! how haue my deeds / Made my lookes differ from another mans, / That they should thus detest, and lothe my life! / Out on my wretched humour, it is that / Makes me thus monstrous in true humane eyes" (III.viii.37–41). He has been cured not only of his humour, but has been purged of his inordinate greed.

The second of the Mistaken Men who profits by Macilente's ministrations is Sogliardo, who wishes to be a gentleman. He buys himself a coat of arms, with the motto "*Not without mustard*." For his tutor in the manners of gentlemen, he engages Shift, whose instructions lie entirely in the realm of taking tobacco properly. Sogliardo believes Shift's lies about dangerous exploits, and when Shift, threatened by Sir Puntarvolo, kneels for mercy, he is "dishumour'd." He certainly perceives that he has chosen the wrong tutor, but whether he sees himself, as did Sordido, is debatable.

Fungoso, also of *Every Man Out of His Humour*, is taught a

lesson not to be found in the law books of the Inns of Court. His particular humour is that of imitating the dress of the gallants, Fastidius Briske in particular. He is, unfortunately, always one suit behind Fastidius. As a consequence of his seeking out the company of his betters, he is left as "pawne" for a large bill at the tavern. He almost learns something: "I haue done imitating any more gallants either in purse or apparell, but as shall become a gentleman, for good carriage, or so" (V.ix.3–5).

In the same play Deliro is at the opposite pole from Master Kitely of the previous play. His uxoriousness rises to the quality of a humour: "O, MACILENTE, I haue such a wife! / So passing faire, so passing farre vnkind, / But of such worth, and right to be vnkind, / (Since no man can be worthy of her kindnesse)" (II.iv.28–31). His wife Fallace spits on him, strives vigorously to cuckold him with Fastidius Briske, steals from him. Fallace visits Fastidius, who is in prison, and recalls her "passion" to him. Deliro overhears the conversation, and his eyes are opened: "Out lasciuious strumpet" (V.xi.17).

The concept of the Mistaken Man is in a sense irrelevant to *Cynthia's Revels*, Jonson's next play. There are eight characters, called "deformities" by Crites, who earn comic castigation. They are not, however, humourous characters, since they are not, like Kitely, identifiable as, for example, merchant, whose conduct is governed almost completely by the one fear that he may be made cuckold. They are merely allegorical in that they are only manifestations, male or female, of the qualities they imply—self-love, prodigality, impudence. They confess their errors, but any saving grace for them comes not from a process of arriving at some knowledge of self, but from merely being in the presence of the divine Cynthia-Elizabeth.

Augustus Caesar of *Poetaster* has already been mentioned among the Deities. But even a Deity may be subject to misapprehensions. Caesar labors under one almost unforgivable mistake—that a true poet, even though poor, might stoop to envy or a malicious judgment. At a sharp rebuke from Horace even a Caesar is reformed, is no longer mistaken. Nor has his bad judgment been in any way associated with a humour.

The Mistaken Man does not manifest himself in *Volpone*, but he reappears in *Epicoene*. Morose of that play is the shining example of the technique of the humours. He can tolerate no noise. His manner of life, his place of residence, the servants he employs, the standard by which he judges the conduct of others, all these are governed by his aversion to noise. He is not under misapprehension about what he is, but he is sadly mistaken in believing that the world and his nephew Dauphine in particular are engaged in a conspiracy to torment him; and in retaliation he seeks to deprive Dauphine of his rightful heritage. A conspiracy of noise does follow, but, once Morose has provided for Dauphine, he is left alone to seek his quiet. Jonson has in his case violated the mandate of Cynthia, for Morose has been neither cut off nor reformed.

Only one of the characters in *The Alchemist* falls into our grouping of Mistaken Men. Kastril, the Angry Boy, is reformed rather than cut off. He is of the country gentry, and he comes to London to find a knight for Dame Plyant, his widowed sister, to marry, and to learn quarreling for himself, as a means of improving his gentility. Lovewit, not a knight, marries Dame Plyant and, in a subsequent confrontation, frightens Kastril out of his quarreling humour. Kastril is not cut off, but is, through greater knowledge of circumstances outside himself, reformed.

Only one of this breed of Jonsonian humourous characters remains, Peni-Boy, the Usurer, in *The Staple of News*. He labors under the misapprehension that the only function of the Lady Pecunia (wealth) is to bring him *"ten i' the hundred."* After fear of losing Pecunia leads him through a "short madnesse," he can say: "And lastly, to my *Nephew*, / I giue my house, goods, lands, all but my vices, / And those I goe to cleanse" (V.vi.54–56).

The Mistaken Man has gotten off lightly. He has suffered slightly, perhaps while he imagined himself to wear horns, perhaps when his opinions are challenged by wiser men than he. But he has been rewarded in that his misapprehensions have been removed.

THE HYPOCRITICAL MAN

But the next group, "The Hypocritical Man," does not escape lightly. At one extreme, where his greed is sufficiently great, as in *Volpone*, death outside the comedy is projected. At the other extreme, Surly of *The Alchemist* merely loses his prospect of marrying a rich wife. In between, these characters are generally punished, perhaps only metaphorically, by exposure, of their real, as against their assumed, identities. This Hypocritical Man has several faces—man of war, liberated woman, saint or prophet, professional man. But under these faces there lurks the real man—coward, woman who is ignorant or lascivious or both, precisian, charlatan.

It will be well to examine in some detail, as we look at the Hypocritical Man, representatives of each of these postures. The first, that of man of war, is of course our old friend from Plautus, the Braggart Soldier. But Jonson, largely by the embroidery of the humour, puts new life into a well-worn convention. For examination Captain Tucca of *Poetaster* is suggested. The reality of Captain Tucca, as stated by Gallus, a "souldier of renowne," to Caesar, is "one that hath had the mustring, or conuoy of a companie, now, and then." He is one whom Horace knew only for a "motion." His sword is taken away by Lictors, who also trip up his heels. Says Tucca of Horace, "I'le cudgell the rascall . . . I'le blow him into aire." When told that Horace is a man of the sword, he greets Horace as "my noble *prophet*; my little fat HORACE." When there is greater danger, as when he is faced with Caesar's wrath, his Page can say, "Pray IUPITER, we be not follow'd by the sent, Master." Finally, this great man of war needs *"eringo's"* (aphrodisiacs).

The facade of Tucca—accepted by all the humourous characters in *Poetaster*, but not by the Choric group—is exemplified by what he expects of Histrio, the player: "will he saile by, and not once strike, or vaile to a *Man of Warre?*" He to Luscus is a "madde skeldring captaine." In the "Heauenly Banquet" he is automatically assigned the part of "Mars." He can introduce himself to Caesar with these words: "I am one of thy Commanders, CAESAR; A man of seruice, and action; My name is PANTILIVS TVCCA: I haue seru'd i' thy warres against MARKE ANTONY, I" (V.iii. 196–99).

The hypocrisy of Tucca is abundantly evident in the contrast between the reality and the facade he presents. It is manifest also at the trial of the Poetasters, his protégés, in which he abandons them to their fates. He has employed them to malign Horace, yet he gets himself appointed one of the panel of judges which condemns them.

Less emphasized, but not less apparent, is the greed of Tucca. In the presence of Caesar, Horace, who has been accompanied by Mecoenas, is accused of creating a libel against Caesar. Tucca seizes the "flaggon chaine" of Mecoenas, with the words, "the law ha's made it mine now." And he cautions Lupus to "begge their land betimes; before some of these hungrie court-hounds sent it out" (V.iii.52–53).

The Captain gets six drachmas from Ovid Senior and twenty from Histrio. His technique in these borrowings is the use of a unique sort of language, so unusual in fact that, in conjunction with his tendency to stutter, it constitutes Tucca's humour. In its combination of rhythms, invective, and personifications, Tucca's language verges on eloquence. This passage, for instance, elicits the drachmas from Ovid Senior:

> Why, what should I say? or what can I say, my flowre o' the order? Should I say, thou art rich? or that thou art honorable? or wise? or valiant? or learned? or liberall? Why, thou art all these, and thou knowest it (my noble LVCVLLVS) thou knowest it: come, bee not ashamed of thy vertues, old stumpe. Honour's a good brooch to weare in a mans hat, at all times. Thou art the *man of warres* MECOENAS, old boy. Why shouldst not thou bee grac't then by them, as well as hee is by his *poets*?
>
> (I.ii.156–65)

Tucca's skill in language is equally well illustrated in his meeting with Albius, the citizen, and his beautiful wife Chloe, who would cuckold Albius if given opportunity:

TVCC. Giue me thy hand, AGAMEMNON: we heare abroad, thou art the HECTOR of citizens: what sayest thou? are we welcome to thee, noble NEOPTOLEMVS?
ALBI. Welcome, Captaine? by IOVE, and all the Gods i' the capitoll—
TVCC. No more, we conceiue thee. Which of these is thy wedlocke, MENELAVS? thy HELLEN? thy LVCRECE? that wee may doe her honor; mad boy?
CRIS. Shee i' the little fine dressing, sir, is my Mistris.
ALBI. For fault of a better, sir.
TVCC. A better, prophane rascall? I crie thee mercy (my good scroile) was't thou?
ALBI. No harme, Captaine.
TVCC. Shee is a VENVS, a VESTA, a MELPOMENE: Come hither, PENELOPE: what's thy name, IRIS?
CHLO. My name is CHLOE, sir; I am a gentlewoman.
TVCC. Thou art in merit to be an empresse (CHLOE) for an eye, and a lip; thou hast an emperors nose: kisse me again: 'tis a vertuous punke; So. Before IOVE, the gods were a sort of goslings, when they suffred so sweet a breath, to perfume the bed of a stinkard: thou hadst ill fortune, THISBE; the fates were infatuate; they were, punke; they were.

(IV.iii.22–44)

The fate of Tucca is predictable; Caesar pronounces it, in words perhaps a little influenced by Tucca's eloquence: "*Lictors*, gag him: doe. / And put a case of vizards o're his head, / That he may looke *bi-fronted*, as he speakes" (V.iii.433–35). That Tucca is not reformed is clearly indicated by his response to his sentence: "Gods, and fiends! CAESAR! thou wilt not, CAESAR? wilt thou? Away, you whorson vultures; away. You thinke I am a dead *corps* now, because CAESAR is dispos'd to iest with a man of marke, or so. Hold your hook't talons out of my flesh, you inhumane *Harpies*.

Goe to, do't. What? will the royall AVGVSTVS cast away a gent'man of worship, a Captaine, and a Commander, for a couple of condemn'd caitiue calumnious *Cargo's?*" (ll. 436–43).

Jonson's first venture with the Hypocritical Man of the Captain Tucca variety is Bobadil of *Every Man in His Humour*. Bobadil's essential cowardice is more emphasized than that of Tucca, for he refuses to draw his sword when challenged by Squire Downright, and as a consequence suffers a severe beating. His boasts about his imagined exploits are so frequent and so unbelievable as to constitute a humour in themselves. Needless to say, they deceive only those as foolish as himself. The more technical quality of Bobadil's humour is what he himself condemns as "prolixitie," and a tendency to the heroic oath: "By S. George"; "by the foot of Pharaoh"; "By Hercules"; "Body o' Caesar." The cutting-off of Bobadil is handled in terms of his pretensions. He appears before Justice Clement to request a peace bond. It is announced to the Justice that a "souldier" wishes to see him. In deference to the soldier, Justice Clement dons his own armor. When Bobadil's cowardice becomes evident, says the Justice: "take my armour of quickly, 'twill make him swoune" (V.ii.16).

Of these unheroic men of war who present facades of prowess, only three more appear. There is Shift, of *Every Man Out of His Humour*, who, except that his supposed valor is that of a highwayman, resembles Tucca and Bobadil. He receives the same punishment by way of exposure. There is Shunfield of *The Staple of News*, who, though he claims to have commanded both by sea and by land, does not deceive even his own peers in hypocrisy.

And then there is Captain Otter, also "amphibious," of *Epicoene*. He is worthy of more attention. Thomas Otter, a "land and sea-Captaine," a coward at heart, like Tucca and Bobadil puts on a facade of bravery. Those two quailed before swords. But Otter faces a far more redoubtable adversary, Mrs. Otter. His bravery, in her absence, verges on daring: "Wife! Buz. *Titiuilitium*. There's no such thing in nature. I confesse, gentlemen, I haue a cook, a laundresse, a house-drudge, that serues my necessary turnes, and goes vnder that title: But hee's an asse that will be so *vxorious*, to tie his affections to one circle. Come, the name dulls appetite. Here, replenish againe: another bout. Wiues are nasty sluttish *animalls*" (IV.ii.50–56). After Mistress Otter has soundly beaten him, he can only say, "O, hold, good Princesse" and "Vnder correction, deare Princesse." That he is greedy to a degree is unquestionable— "I married with sixe thousand pound, I. I was in loue with that." But he is not altogether a fool, for toward the end of the play he will sustain with skill the part of a Doctor of Divinity .

In the matter of his humour, Captain Otter is handled much more skillfully than are any of the other braggarts. Part of his humourous quality is a love for tags of Latin. They will in due time go into the making of the Doctor of Divinity. The other part is his devotion to his "bull, beare, and horse." They are drinking cups, to be employed in convivial bouts, and will be used in such a manner that Sir John Daw and Sir Amorous La Foole will become so drunk, and so frightened of each other, that they will swear to having known Epicoene "*carnaliter*." Otter has performed yeoman service for Jonson, if for no other purpose than to prompt the immortal line of Morose: "Marry a whore! and so much noise!" (V.iv.150).

Jonson, perhaps in appreciation, lets Otter off lightly. True, he has suffered his beating at the hands of Mistress Otter, but at the end of the play Dauphine promises "TOM OTTER, your Princesse shall be reconciled to you."

Jonson's earlier, and later, manifestations of the essentially hypocritical braggart soldier were present in their plays largely for display and as objects for castigation. Bobadil, and even Tucca, shared in little of the action. Their humours were superimposed, and served little purpose in forwarding the plot. On the other hand, Otter's humours are much more closely associated with the character of the man, and they contribute effectively in moving the action toward its conclusion. *Epicoene* was written at the height of Jonson's powers, while the other braggarts were products of apprenticeship or of the period of his "dotages."

My next Hypocritical Man is a woman, Lady Politic Would-be of *Volpone*. She is the representative of a kind of person that Jonson most thoroughly detested, the woman who inserts herself into the world of men even while she is using her woman's body for bargaining purposes. Lady Would-be, with the foolish Knight, her husband, is visiting Venice on a sort of conjugal grand tour. The Lady has become one of those striving to be made heir to Volpone, along with three men consumed by greed, Voltore, Corbaccio, and Corvino. She may not be hypocritical in all things, for she has herself introduced to the chamber of Volpone as "the beauteous lady WOVLD-BEE." This she may believe, but she has (and the reader has) abundant evidence to the contrary. Her approach is heralded by this exchange between Volpone and Mosca:

> [Volp.] 'Fore heauen, I wonder at the desperate
>   valure
> Of the bold *English*, that they dare let loose
> Their wiues, to all encounters! MOS. Sir, this
>   knight
> Had not his name for nothing, he is politique,
> And knowes, how ere his wife affect strange aires,
> Shee hath not yet the face, to be dishonest.
>   (I.v.100–105)

She does indeed "affect strange aires." She can justify her statement, "I haue, a little, studied physick": "Alas, good soule! the passion of the heart. / Seed-pearle were good now, boild with syrrope of apples, / Tincture of gold, and corrall, citron-pills, / Your elicampane roote, mirobalanes—" (III.iv.51–54). But she commands other disciplines too:

> I'am all for musique: saue, i' the fore-noones,
> An houre, or two, for painting. I would haue
> A lady, indeed, t'haue all, letters, and artes,
> Be able to discourse, to write, to paint,
> But principall (as PLATO holds) your musique
> (And, so do's wise PYTHAGORAS, I take it)

Is your true rapture; when there is concent
In face, in voyce, and clothes: and is, indeed,
Our sexes chiefest ornament.
. . . .
Which o' your Poets? PETRARCH? or TASSO?' or
DANTE?
GVERRINI? ARIOSTO? ARETINE?
CIECO *di Hadria*? I haue read them all.

(ll. 68–76, 79–81)

That her claims to learning are not justified is indicated by this remarkable passage: "For the incorporating / Of these same out-
ward things, into that part, / Which we call mentall, leaues some
certaine *faeces*, / That stop the organs, and, as PLATO sayes, / As-
sassinates our knowledge" (ll. 108–12).

In Lady Would-be Jonson personifies skillfully all his great
vices—greed, hypocrisy, and folly. But whether she has a humour
is debatable. Sir Politic characterizes as a humour her desire to come
to Venice "to quote, to learne the language." Perhaps closer to
the quality of a humour is her compulsion, as Volpone says, toward
"Another floud of wordes! A very torrent!"

The fate of such a pretender to qualities not in Jonson's mind
proper to a woman, unless possibly to Sidney's niece, Lady Mary
Wroth, is predictable. When, after learning the false news of
Volpone's death, she comes to claim the inheritance she has earned
by perjury, Mosca pronounces the final comic judgment for
Jonson: "Remember, what your ladiship offred me, / To put you
in, an heire; goe to, thinke on't. / And what you said, eene your
best madames did / For maintenance, and, why not you?"
(V.iii.40–43).

Fortunately for womankind, Jonson did not make Lady Would-
be's sisters very numerous. In fact, most of the others are assembled
in *Epicoene*. Such concentration in that play is appropriate, because, as its title implies, the whole play tends toward what Jonson
calls "amphibian"—of two natures.[11] He will later apply that char-

---

[11] For a more complete discussion of Jonson's treatment of the "amphibian"
idea, see "The Allusiveness of *Epicoene*," by Edward B. Partridge, in *ELH*,
XXII (1955), 93–107.

acterization to Buckingham, merely because he is titular head of the
King's forces by land and by sea. The ladies in *Epicoene*, who appear to be what they know themselves not to be, are five in number, listed thus in "The Persons of the Play":

MAD. HAVGHTY. ⎫
MAD. CENTAVRE. ⎬ *Ladies Collegiates.*
Mʳˢ· MAVIS. ⎭

Mʳˢ· TRVSTY. │ *The La.* HAVGHTIES *woman.*
Mʳˢ· OTTER. │ *The Captaines wife.*   { *Pretenders.*

The essential hypocrisy of the whole collegiate group is manifest
in the following speeches:

> CEN. Good sir DAVPHINE, doe not trust HAVGHTY, nor
> make any credit to her, what euer you doe besides. Sir DAV-
> PHINE, I giue you this caution, shee is a perfect courtier, and
> loues no body, but for her vses: and for her vses, shee loues all.
> Besides, her physitians giue her out to be none o' the clearest,
> whether she pay 'hem or no, heau'n knowes: and she's aboue fiftie
> too, and pargets! See her in a forenoone. Here comes MAVIS, a
> worse face then shee! you would not like this, by candle-light. If
> you'll come to my chamber one o' these mornings early, or late
> in an euening, I'll tell you more. Where's HAVGHTY, MAVIS?
> ·
> DAVP. 'Slight, they haunt me like *fayries*, and giue me iewells
> here, I cannot be rid of 'hem.
> CLE. O, you must not tell, though.
> DAVP. Masse, I forgot that: I was neuer so assaulted. One loues
> for vertue, and bribes me with this. Another loues me with caution,
> and so would possesse me. A third brings me a riddle here, and all
> are iealous: and raile each at other.
>
> (V.ii.30–41, 49–56)

These true collegiates may hardly be considered humourous
characters, unless their assuming of the amphibian posture can be
considered a humour. The ladies are not in any real sense distinguished one from another. Except for the fact that Lady Haughty,
as the President, speaks more and with more authority, their
speeches could be interchanged with no harm to character or ac-

tion. The assignment of a humour to *each* could easily make such a distinction.

On the other hand, Mistress Otter, the pretender to the college, does display humourous qualities. She believes that dire mishaps follow her dreams. She chastises her husband as a pleasure, even when he has not earned chastisement. Other humourous tendencies are suggested in this characterization of her: "LA-F. I, sir: his wife was the rich *China*-woman, that the courtiers visited so often, that gaue the rare entertainment. She commands all at home. CLE. Then, she is Captaine OTTER? LA-F. You say very well, sir; she is my kinswoman, a LA-FOOLE by the mother side, and will inuite, any great ladies, for my sake" (I.iv.27–33).

These estimable ladies of *Epicoene* are not moved primarily by greed. In *Volpone* the theme of the whole play had been the power of greed to push man toward betrayal of himself and his fellows. The "amphibian"—the *epicoene*—theme which pervades this play, however, is essentially a manifestation of hypocrisy in almost all of the characters of the Humourous Group. That such a facade cannot be long maintained is a truism. Thus, from the very nature of the vehicle *Epicoene*, many of its characters manifest extraordinary foolishness.

Madame Haughty and her colleagues come out at some indeterminate stage between reform and cutting-off. They do learn something. They learn that the "men" they have made associates of the college, Sir John Daw and Sir Amorous La Foole, are no men. They discover that they are despised by the man toward whom they simultaneously direct their longings, Dauphine. And they have disclosed to the *man* Epicoene their inmost secrets: "And haue you those excellent receits, madame, to keep your selues from bearing of children?" (IV.iii.57–58).

Dame Purecraft of *Bartholomew Fair* assumes something of the same masculine posture, the same sort of hypocritical facade, but she will be more at home among hypocrites of the Puritan type. There is, however, one more woman of this species, who should be glanced at, if for no other reason than that she functions in a tragedy. She is Sempronia of *Catiline*. Her facade is that of a well-born Roman matron, who, in return for her favors, accepts handsome presents. She can "discourse the best"; "shee's a great states-woman"; she is a "very masculine" "shee-*Critick*"; she "can compose, in verse, and make quick jests, modest or otherwise"; "she can sing, and play on instruments"; she is "a mistris of the *latine* tongue, and of the *greeke*." An associate in the Catilinian conspiracy, she expects, with the help of Caesar and Crassus, to have Catiline elected consul. The Sempronia known to Sempronia is, however, quite a different woman:

> SEM. Th'art a most happy wench, that thus canst make
> Vse of thy youth, and freshnesse, in the season:
> And hast it, to make vse of. FVL. (Which is the
>   happinesse.)
> SEM. I am, now, faine to giue to them, and keepe
> Musique, and a continuall table, to inuite 'hem;
> FVL. (Yes, and they study your kitchin, more then you)
> SEM. Eate myselfe out with vsury, and my lord, too,
> And all my officers, and friends beside,
> To procure moneyes, for the needfull charge
> I must be at, to haue 'hem: and, yet, scarce
> Can I atchieue 'hem, so. FVL. Why, that's because
> You affect yong faces onely, and smooth chinnes,
> SEMPRONIA. If you'ld loue beards, and bristles,
> (One with another, as others doe) or wrinkles—
>   (II.186–99)

The usefulness of Sempronia in the action is very limited. Fulvia, who has learned of the conspiracy from Curius, refuses to join it because her position would be of less importance than that of Sempronia. She instead reveals the conspiracy to Cicero, who then ostentatiously saves Rome. If Sempronia has a humour, it is the assiduity with which she thrusts herself into the affairs of men, on the level of the state. Her cutting-off is perhaps best expressed by Longinus: "[SEM.] What! is our counsell broke vp first? AVR. You say, / Women are greatest talkers. SEM. We ha' done; / And are now fit for action. LON. Which is passion. / There's your best actiuitie, lady. SEM. How / Knowes your wise fatnesse that?

LON. Your mothers daughter / Did teach me, madame" (III.679–84). Her final dismissal is in the words of Cicero: "A states anger / Should not take knowledge eyther of fooles, or women" (IV.814–15).

We have seen in two manifestations Jonson's Hypocritical Man—the braggart who knows himself to be a coward and the woman who practices feminine wiles while asserting masculine prerogatives. Along with their hypocrisy, most representatives of both groups manifest a degree of greed and a high level of foolishness, since their pretensions inevitably must become apparent. Unless the very hypocritical facade itself can be considered a humour, few of the cowardly men or the *epicoene* women manifest a humour comparable in single-mindedness to that of, say, Fungoso in *Every Man Out of His Humour*.

More interesting to Jonson, and to us, is a third representative of the Hypocritical Man, the Puritan. He is not for Jonson representative of *all* Puritans, but rather of that segment of them whom he scornfully calls the "precisian." This Puritan is perhaps the man who comes first to mind when one is reviewing the whole gallery of Jonson's satirical portraits. Yet, there are no more individual portraits of Puritans than of poetasters, or *epicoene* women. The power of the representations of Tribulation Wholesome of *The Alchemist* and Rabbi Busy of *Bartholomew Fair*, however, is such that the Puritan almost seems to the reader to be the primary object of Jonson's scorn. Possibly this pervasive effect is achieved not so much by individual portraits, as by generalized indictments by Wit, or by Chorus, of the hypocritical precisian. It is appropriate by way of introduction to present two such essentially choric passages. The first, from *Volpone*, is spoken by Androgyno, the *"Hermaphrodite"* and "fool," as he describes the Pythagorean progress of his soul. His questioner is Nano, the dwarf:

> But, from the moyle, into whom did'st thou passe?
> AND. Into a very strange beast, by some writers
>   cal'd an asse;
> By others, a precise, pure, illuminate brother,

> *Of those deuoure flesh, and sometimes one another:*
> *And will drop you forth a libell, or a sanctified lie,*
> *Betwixt euery spoonefull of a natiuitie-pie.*
> NAN. *Now quit thee, for heauen, of that profane nation;*
> *And gently, report thy next transmigration.*
>
> (I.ii.41–48)

A second passage, this one about the female of the species, occurs when Truewit, of *Epicoene*, tries to dissuade Morose from taking a wife. Having treated possible wives who might be "faire," "foule," "rich," "noble," "fruitfull," or "learned," he arrives at the crowning disaster: "If precise, you must feast all the silenc'd brethren, once in three daies; salute the sisters; entertaine the whole family, or wood of 'hem; and heare long-winded exercises, singings, and catechisings, which you are not giuen to, and yet must giue for: to please the zealous matron your wife, who, for the holy cause, will cosen you, ouer and aboue. You beginne to sweat, sir? but this is not halfe, i' faith" (II.ii.80–86).

The best known of Jonson's precisians is Tribulation Wholesome of *The Alchemist*. But almost the whole spectrum of qualities which Jonson abhorred is represented in Rabbi Zeal-of-the-Land Busy. And almost all that he is and says can be reproduced in Jonson's own inimitable prose. The introduction to Busy is in a set "character" by Quarlous, himself one of Jonson's Wits:

A notable hypocriticall vermine it is; I know him. One that stands vpon his face, more then his faith, at all times; Euer in seditious motion, and reprouing for vaine-glory: of a most *lunatique* conscience, and splene, and affects the violence of *Singularity* in all he do's: (He has vndone a Grocer here, in Newgate-market, that broke with him, trusted him with Currans, as errant a Zeale as he, that's by the way:) by his profession, hee will euer be i' the state of Innocence, though; and child-hood; derides all *Antiquity*; defies any other *Learning*, then *Inspiration*; and what discretion soeuer, yeeres should afford him, it is all preuented in his *Originall ignorance*; ha' not to doe with him: for hee is a fellow of a most arrogant, and inuincible dulnesse, I assure you.

(I.iii.135–48)

Busy is perhaps as hungry for wealth as the famous group in *Volpone*. His methods are attested by Dame Purecraft, to whom he is suitor, herself "an assisting *sister* of the *Deacons*, and a deuouer, instead of a distributer of the alms": "Our elder, *Zeale-of-the-land*, would haue had me, but I know him to be the capitall Knaue of the land, making himselfe rich, by being made *Feoffee* in trust to deceased *Brethren*, and coozning their *heyres*, by swearing the absolute gift of their inheritance" (V.ii.66–70). To Busy's pursuit of money is added gluttony, almost as a humourous quality. Its presence and its function in the action are made manifest in this exchange between Dame Purecraft, her daughter, Win-the-Fight, and her son-in-law, John Littlewit:

> PVR. What shall we doe? call our zealous brother *Busy* hither, for his faithfull fortification in this charge of the aduersary; child, my deare childe, you shall eate Pigge, be comforted, my sweet child.
> WIN. I, but i' the *Fayre*, mother.
> PVR. I meane i' the *Fayre*, if it can be any way made, or found lawfull; where is our brother *Busy*? Will hee not come? looke vp, child.
> IOH. Presently, mother, as soone as he has cleans'd his beard. I found him, fast by the teeth, i' the cold Turkey-pye, i' the cupbord, with a great white loafe on his left hand, and a glasse of *Malmesey* on his right.
> PVR. Slander not the *Brethren*, wicked one.
> IOH. Here hee is, now, purified, Mother.
>
> (I.vi.25–38)

The gluttony of Busy is therefore highly significant in transferring the whole, not only of the Humourous Group, but also of the Choric Group, to the Fair, in fact to the booth of Ursula the Pig-Woman.

Quarlous in the passage just quoted has probably intended as a statement of Busy's humour that he "affects a violence of *Singularity* in all he do's." Part of this singularity is certainly Busy's use of language. His rhythms and his use of epithets are remarkably like those of Captain Tucca of *Poetaster* and constitute another humourous facet of Busy.[12] This is his reaction when he smells Ursula's roast pig:

> No, but your mother, religiously wise, conceiueth it may offer it selfe, by other meanes, to the sense, as by way of steeme, which I thinke it doth, here in this place (Huh, huh) yes, it doth. And it were a sinne of obstinacy, great obstinacy, high and horrible obstinacy, to decline, or resist the good titillation of the famelick sense, which is the smell. Therefore be bold (huh, huh, huh) follow the sent. Enter the Tents of the vncleane, for once, and satisfie your wiues frailty. Let your fraile wife be satisfied: your zealous mother, and my suffering selfe, will also be satisfied.
> (III.ii.78–87)

His eloquence rises to an equally high style as he overturns the table which bears Joan Trash's gingerbread figures:

> Hinder me not, woman. I was mou'd in spirit, to bee here, this day, in the *Faire*, this wicked, and foule *Faire*; and fitter may it be called a foule, then a *Faire*: To protest against the abuses of it, the foule abuses of it, in regard of the afflicted Saints, that are troubled, very much troubled, exceedingly troubled, with the opening of the merchandize of *Babylon* again, & the peeping of *Popery* vpon the stals, here, here, in the high places. See you not *Goldylocks*, the purple strumpet, there? In her yellow gowne, and greene sleeues? the prophane pipes, the tinckling timbrells? A shop of reliques!
> (III.vi.86–96)

The cutting-off of Zeal-of-the-Land is not of Jonson's usual severity. The crimes which he committed under the cover of his hypocrisy are not noticed, perhaps because they lie outside the play. He is found by Justice Overdoo to be an enormity, a "*superlunaticall* hypocrite." After the Puppet Play, his zeal overcomes him, and he prays: "I will not feare to make my spirit, and gifts knowne! assist me zeale, fille me, fill me, that is, make me full" (V.v.44–46). He then engages Puppet Dionysius in an argument, the essence of which is this, "*your old stale argument*": "PVP.

---

[12] For an excellent discussion of Jonson's use of language to display character, see *Ben Jonson and the Language of Prose Comedy*, by Jonas A. Barish (Cambridge, Mass.: Harvard University Press, 1960).

What then, Dagonet? is a Puppet worse then these? BVS. Yes, and my maine argument against you, is, that you are an *abomination*: for the *Male*, among you, putteth on the apparell of the *Female*, and the *Female* of the *Male*" (ll. 97–100). When "*The Puppet takes vp his garment*" (marginal note) and reveals that the puppets "*haue neyther* Male *nor* Female *amongst*" them, Busy's anguish almost approaches the tragic: "I am confuted, the *Cause* hath failed me."

Busy's partner in hypocrisy, Dame Purecraft, is almost as deserving of attention as Busy himself. As has been noted earlier, she might have been listed among the preceding group, the women who affect masculine prerogatives and attainments, for she engages in masculine business and rules her daughter and son-in-law with a firm hand. But once Jonson has her speak, it will readily appear that she is most at home among Jonson's precisians:

> I must vncover my selfe vnto him, or I shall neuer enioy him, for all the *cunning mens* promises. Good Sir, heare mee, I am worth sixe thousand pound, my loue to you, is become my racke, I'll tell you all, and the truth: since you hate the hypo[c]risie of the party-coloured brotherhood. These seuen yeeres, I haue beene a wilfull holy widdow, onely to draw feasts, and gifts from my intangled suitors: I am also by office, an assisting *sister* of the *Deacons*, and a deuourer, in stead of a distributer of the alms. I am a speciall maker of marriages for our decayed *Brethren*, with our rich *widdowes*; for a third part of their wealth, when they are marryed, for the reliefe of the poore *elect*: as also our poore handsome yong Virgins, with our wealthy Batchelors, or Widdowers; to make them steale from their husbands, when I haue confirmed them in the faith, and got all put into their custodies. And if I ha' not my bargaine, they may sooner turne a scolding drab, into a silent *Minister*, then make me leaue pronouncing *reprobation*, and *damnation* vnto them.
>
> (V.ii.48–66)

Largely for the purpose of the action, Jonson gives Dame Purecraft a humour of sorts. Again Jonson's words are more effective than any paraphrase:

> WIN. Sir, my mother has had her natiuity-water cast lately by the Cunning men in *Cow-lane*, and they ha' told her her fortune,

and doe ensure her, shee shall neuer haue happy houre; vnlesse shee marry within this sen'night, and when it is, it must be a Madde-man, they say.

LIT. I, but it must be a Gentle-man Mad-man.

WIN. Yes, so the tother man of *More-fields* sayes.

WIN-W. But do's shee beleeue 'hem?

LIT. Yes, and ha's beene at *Bedlem* twice since, euery day, to enquire if any Gentleman be there, or to come there, mad!

(I.ii.46–56)

Dame Purecraft finds in Trouble-all the madman she must have. Quarlous has, for a purpose not related to her, disguised himself as Trouble-all, and it is to him that she makes the revelation quoted above. These circumstances have neatly arranged her cutting-off, for Quarlous, who had earlier condemned widow-hunting—"cur-rying a carkasse, that thou hast bound thyself to alive"—decided on his course: "Why should not I marry this sixe thousand pound, now I think on't? and a good trade too, that shee has beside, ha? . . . here I may make my selfe some sauer, yet, if shee continue mad, there the question. It is money that I want, why should I not marry the money, when 'tis offer'd mee?" (V.ii.75–77, 79–82).

Among Jonson's Hypocritical Men, Tribulation Wholesome of *The Alchemist* is perhaps most carefully delineated. The secret of Jonson's power in this portrayal lies in the juxtaposition of Ananias with Tribulation. A look at Ananias first, therefore, will be useful. He is the precisian, the zealot, but not the hypocrite. He is the foe of all learning: "all's *heathen*, but the *Hebrew*"; he is a "*Dea-con*" of the "*exil'd Brethren*," who deals "with widowes, and with orphanes goods," and makes a just account if their parents were "*sincere professors.*" To him, "bells are prophane"; starch is "an idoll"; "*Traditions*" "are *Popish*, all"; he knows "no Magistrate" and therefore to him "coyning" is lawful, for the sake of the breth-ren. But he sincerely believes that "the *sanctified cause* / should have a *sanctified course.*" These beliefs of Ananias are all good Puritan doctrine.

But these beliefs stand in Tribulation's way in securing the philosopher's stone. Ananias has a humour of sorts—explosive outbreaks: "*Christ-tide*, I pray you"—which Subtle skillfully uses as an excuse to threaten destruction of the whole work: "out-goes / The fire: and down th' *alembekes*, and the fornace." Tribulation, whose beliefs are essentially the same as those of Ananias, must suppress his assistant. His arguments are masterful:

> Good *Brother*, we must bend vnto all meanes,
> That may giue furtherance, to the *holy cause*.
> . . . .
> The children of perdition are, oft-times,
> Made instruments euen of the greatest workes.
> Beside, we should giue somewhat to mans nature,
> The place he liues in, still about the fire,
> And fume of mettalls, that intoxicate
> The braine of man, and make him prone to passion.
> Where haue you greater *Atheists*, then your Cookes?
> Or more prophane, or cholerick then your Glasse-men?
> More *Antichristian*, then your Bell-founders?
> What makes the Deuill so deuillish, I would aske you,
> *Sathan*, our common enemie, but his being
> Perpetually about the fire, and boyling
> *Brimstone*, and *arsnike*?
> . . . .
> What need we haue, to hasten on the worke,
> For the restoring of the *silenc'd Saints*,
> Which ne'er will be, but by the *Philosophers stone*.
> And, so a learned *Elder*, one of *Scotland*,
> Assur'd me; *Aurum potabile* being
> The onely med'cine, for the ciuill *Magistrate*,
> T'incline him to a feeling of the cause:
> And must be daily vs'd, in the disease.
> (III.i.11–12, 15–27, 37–44)

These arguments are most effective, since Ananias has this response: "I haue not edified more, truely, by man; / Not, since the *beautifull light*, first, shone on me: / And I am sad, my zeale hath so offended" (ll. 45–47).

So much for the hypocrisy of Tribulation. He is not a fool, but he is greedy. His greed, however, is of a peculiar kind, a dangerous kind. The question of gluttony such as that of Busy does not arise.

Tribulation does want the power that wealth will bring on behalf of the *"Saints,"* in order to restore the *"silenc'd"* ones. It will make friends of the *"Hollanders"*; it will make a friend by healing "some great man in state" who has the gout, or by restoring some "Lady, that is past the feate of body." Its powers for the Saints, in the words of Subtle, are almost unlimited: "You cannot / But raise you friends. Withall, to be of power / To pay an armie, in the field, to buy / The king of *France*, out of his realmes; or *Spaine*, / Out of his *Indies*: What can you not doe, / Against lords spirituall, or temporall / That shall oppone you?" (III.ii.45–51). Tribulations's response to this speech may be the most prophetic of Jonson's utterances: "Verily, 'tis true. / We may be temporall lords, our selues, I take it" (ll. 51–52). But it is not the province of this essay to explore by what philosopher's stone the Tribulations and Ananiases, later in the seventeenth century, did become temporal lords.

In the plan proposed for this portion of the study, Gossip ("and she-Parasite") Polish of *The Magnetic Lady, or Humours Reconciled* would have been the last of the hypocrites of the Puritan type. Thereafter, a study of a group designated as professional men would have been examined as Hypocritical Men, men who know themselves not to be altogether in accordance with the front they present. But because *The Magnetic Lady*, even though almost by common consent placed among Jonson's "dotages," contains by far his most complete collection of men of the professions or crafts, Gossip Polish may be more economically handled in the context of her own play. For this study we need Jonson's entire list of *"The Persons that act"*:

LADY *Loadstone*,	The Magnetic Lady.
M^rs. *Polish*,	Her Gossip, and she-Parasite.
M^rs. *Placentia*,	Her Neice.
Pleasance,	Her Waiting-woman.
M^rs. *Keepe*,	The Neices Nourse.
MOTHER *Chaire*,	The Midwife.
M^r. *Compasse*,	A Scholler, Mathematick.
CAPTAINE *Ironside*,	A Souldier.
PARSON *Palate*,	Prelate of the Parish.
DOCTOR *Rut*,	Physician to the house.

Tim Item,	His Apothecary.
SIR *Diaph. Silkworm,*	A Courtier.
M^r. *Practise,*	A Lawyer.
SIR *Moath Interest,*	An Vsurer, or Money-baud.
M^r. *Bias,*	A Vi-politique, or Sub-secretary.
M^r. *Needle,*	The Ladies Steward, and Taylor.

A brief look at the structure of the play is desirable in order to place the members of the professions in a common context. The *supposed* niece to Lady Loadstone, Placentia, having reached the age of fourteen, is marriageable. Certain of the professional men are suitors; certain others act as the council which debates the choice of a husband. Placentia's considerable dowry remains in the custody of Sir Moath Interest, the "money-baud." The real niece, however, is Pleasance, supposed daughter to Polish, who had deliberately exchanged the girls in their cradles.

The leading candidate for the hand of the niece is Mr. Bias, the impeccable civil servant, sponsored by Sir Moath Interest. The dowry of the niece is sixteen thousand pounds, of which Bias will receive ten, and Sir Moath will retain six. Here is the facade of Bias, as expressed by Sir Moath:

> I ha' brought you here the very man! the Jewell
> Of all the Court! close Mr. *Bias*! Sister,
> Apply him to your side! or you may weare him
> Here o' your brest! or hang him in your eare!
> He's a fit Pendant for a Ladies tip!
> A Chrisolite, a Gemme: the very Agat
> Of State, and Politie: cut from the Quar
> Of Macchiavel, a true Cornelian,
> As *Tacitus* himselfe! and to be made
> The brooch to any true State-cap in Europe!
>
> . . . .
>
> I will tell you, sister,
> I cannot cry his Carract up enough:
> He is unvaluable: All the Lords
> Have him in that esteeme, for his relations,
> Corrant's Avises, Correspondences
> With this Ambassadour, and that Agent! Hee
> Will screw you out a Secret from a Statist—
>
> (I.vii.24–33, 37–43)

The real Bias is the one delineated by Compasse, who stands in the sort of combined attitude of Wit and Chorus:

> *Pal.* What is he, Mr. *Compasse? Com.* A Vi-politique!
> Or a sub-aiding Instrument of State!
> A kind of a laborious Secretary
> To a great man! (and likely to come on)
> Full of attendance! and of such a stride
> In busines politique, or oeconomick,
> As, well, his Lord may stoope t'advise with him,
> And be prescribed by him, in affaires
> Of highest consequence, when hee is dull'd
> Or wearied with the lesse.
>
> (I.vii.1–10)

Jonson's master vices—of greed, of hypocrisy, and of foolishness—are apparent in our fine civil servant. As in so many cases, unless the very maintenance of the facade be a humour, no specific humour is very prominent in Bias. However, since Jonson himself insists that humours are present, we shall assign Bias something. But first, let Jonson speak, in the first "Chorus," through the Boy:

> The *Author*, beginning his studies of this kind, with *every man in his Humour*; and after, *every man out of his Humour*: and since, continuing in all his *Playes*, especially those of the *Comick* thred, whereof the *New-Inne* was the last, some recent humours still, or manners of men, that went along with the times, finding himselfe now neare the close, or shutting up of his Circle, hath phant'sied to himselfe, in *Idaea*, this *Magnetick Mistris*. A Lady, a brave bountifull House-keeper, and a vertuous Widow: who having a young Neice, ripe for a man and marriageable, hee makes that his Center attractive, to draw thither a diversity of Guests, all persons of different humours to make up his *Perimeter*. And this hee hath call'd *Humours reconcil'd.*
>
> (ll. 99–111)

The particular humour, however, of Bias is an elusive trait. He fears to carry a challenge from Sir Diaphanous to Captain Ironside, not only because he fears the losing of his Lord's good opinion, but also because he might injure his hand and thereby spoil his "*Kallygraphy.*" He approves a "Christian valour": "Which is a

quiet patient toleration, / Of whatsoever the malitious world /
With Injury doth unto you; and consists / In passion, more then
action, Sir *Diaphanous*" (III.vi.181–84).

The mellow Jonson, who is writing a play of "*Humours reconcil'd*," does no more by way of cutting-off Bias than some
scathing observations from Compasse. Sir Moath has advanced to
Bias four hundred pounds toward the wooing of the niece, and
though Bias has lost the rich wife, the debt is forgiven:

> Good Mr. *Compasse*, for the summes he has had
> Of me, I doe acquit him: They are his owne.
> Here, before you, I doe release him. *Com.* Good!
>   *Bia.* O Sir. *Com.* 'Slid take it: I doe witnesse it:
> Hee cannot hurle away his money better.
>   *Int.* He shall get so much Sir, by my acquaintance,
> To be my friend: And now report to his Lords
> As I deserve, no otherwise. *Com.* But well:
> And I will witnesse it, and to the value;
> Foure hundred is the price, if I mistake not,
> Of your true friend in Court. Take hands, you ha'
>   bought him,
> And bought him cheap. *Bia.* I am his worships servant.
>   *Com.* And you his slave, Sir *Moath*. Seal'd, and
>   deliver'd.
> Ha' you not studied the Court Complement?
> Here are a paire of Humours, reconcil'd now,
> That money held at distance: or their thoughts,
> Baser then money.
>
>   (IV.iii.36–52)

Another suitor to Placentia, and the favorite candidate of Lady
Loadstone, is Mr. Practise. Again it is Mr. Compasse who gives us
the portrait, almost a set character:

> Or man of Law: (for that's the true writing)
> A man so dedicate to his profession,
> And the preferments goe along with it;
> As scarce the thundring bruit of an invasion,
> Another eighty eight, threatning his Countrey
> With ruine; would no more worke upon him,

Then *Syracusa's* Sack, on *Archimede*:
So much he loves that Night-cap! the Bench-gowne!
With the broad Guard o'th' back! These shew a man
Betroth'd unto the study of our Lawes!
(I.vi.14–23)

Practise is greedy enough; the other characters believe him to be a hypocrite; and he is foolish enough to be easily deceived by Compasse. He has also a humour that is very convenient for the poet. Though favored by Lady Loadstone for the hand of Placentia (the false niece), he declares himself to love Pleasance, supposed daughter to Polish. His reasons for choosing her are of a humourous origin:

Pra. I must confesse a great beholdingnesse
Vnto her Ladiships offer, and good wishes.
But the truth is, I never had affection,
Or any liking to this Neice of hers.
Com. You fore-saw somewhat them? *Pra.* I had
    my notes,
And my Prognosticks. *Com.* You read Almanacks,
And study 'hem to some purpose, I beleeve?
Pra. I doe confesse, I doe beleeve, and pray
    too:
According to the Planets, at sometimes.
Com. And doe observe the signe in making Love?
Pra. As in Phlebotomy. *Com.* And choose your
    Mistris
By the good dayes, and leave her by the bad?
Pra. I doe, and I doe not. *Com.* A little more
Would fetch all his Astronomie from *Allestree.*
Pra. I tell you, Mr. *Compasse,* as my friend,
And under seale, I cast mine eye long since,
Vpo' the other wench, my Ladies woman,
Another manner of peice for handsomnesse,
Then is the Neice (but that is *sub sigillo,*
And as I give it you) in hope o' your aid,
And counsell in the busines.
(IV.ii.21–41)

This astrological predilection is the handle by which Compasse is able to secure the license and wed Pleasance and her fortune. Nor is Practise cut off, for in reward for his assistance in forcing Sir Moath to disgorge the dowry of Pleasance—now grown to "three-score thousand"—he receives from Compasse a handsome office at court, of which Compasse has the "reversion," "Surveyor of the Projects generall."

Of the gallery of professional portraits in *The Magnetic Lady*, only one more should be looked at in depth—that of Sir Moath Interest, the "Money-baud." He is brother to the Lady Loadstone, and the custodian of her niece's portion. In the cases of Practise and Bias, the hypocrite was introduced in a set "character," spoken by another. For Sir Moath, however, his own words suffice: he proposes to deny to his niece all but ten thousand of the sixty thousand to which her portion has grown, to "pay me for my watch, and breaking of my sleepes." In case there is "clamour" and "envie," he is prepared:

> Let 'hem exclaime, and envie: what care I?
> Their murmurs raise no blisters i' my flesh.
> My monies are my blood, my parents, kindred:
> And he that loves not those, he is unnaturall:
> I am perswaded that the love of monie
> Is not a vertue, only in a Subject,
> But might befit a Prince. And (were there need)
> I find me able to make good the Assertion
> To any reasonable mans understanding,
> And make him to confesse it.
>
> (II.vi.37–46)

He proceeds to "eightly" in showing that the love of money is a virtue. Some of his reasons are surprising: "The Prince hath need / More of one wealthy, then ten fighting men"; "your wise poore men / Have ever beene contented to observe / Rich Fooles" (ll. 66–67, 92–94).

Sir Moath's love of money is turned into a humourous trait, rather unnecessarily, in the fifth act. Doctor Rut had diagnosed Placentia's pregnancy as a "timpanie," and confidence in his professional attainments must be restored. Needle, the Lady's steward and tailor, will "faine a distemper." In his illness, he sees an "Indian Mag-pie," the spirit of an alderman's widow who had loved

Sir Moath. The spirit, the Mag-pie, buries three hundred thousand gold pieces in the garden and twice as many in the well. Sir Moath, who had overheard all this, of course falls into the well, comes out wet, with no pieces, and is in danger of arrest for five hundred thousand pounds "Fright-Baile" unless he pays Pleasance's portion in full. Sir Moath's cutting-off has been closer to the standard Jonsonian practice, since it is done largely in terms of his humour.

Two other professional men of *The Magnetic Lady* fall into the category of hypocrites, Parson Palate and Doctor Rut. Both are formally introduced by epigrammatic "characters," made by "a great Clarke / As any'is of his bulke, (*Ben: Ionson*)." Both epigrams suggest hypocrisy, professional incompetence, and the trace of a humour—in the case of Palate, love of food, and of Rut, violent and obscene language. But little is done with the humours, and apparently Jonson does not concern himself with any cutting-off in their cases.

The peculiar qualities of *The Magnetic Lady*, its diversity of portraits and its apparent revival of the technique of the humours, have turned the course of this essay from its predetermined path. Perhaps a further digression is permissible, in order to do justice to Captain Ironside, who would otherwise lie outside our rigid scheme of comic characters.

The redoubtable Captain, "*Rudhudibras*" to the more timorous characters, is a distinguished professional soldier, longtime friend to Mr. Compasse. He is introduced, against his will, by Compasse, to the feast which will accompany the momentous decision about the proper husband for Placentia. He has a strong humour, which in a contemporary cliché might be stated as being unwilling to suffer fools gladly. Being at the feast, he tells us what he sees and proposes a course of action:

> . . . i' the house,
> I heare it buzz'd, there are a brace of Doctors,
> A Foole, and a Physician: with a Courtier,
> That feeds on mulbery leaves, like a true *Silke-*
>   *Worme*:

A Lawyer, and a mighty Money-Baud,
Sir Moath! has brought his politique *Bias* with
    him:
A man of a most animadverting humor:
Who, to indeare himselfe unto his Lord,
Will tell him, you and I, or any of us,
That here are met, are all pernitious spirits,
And men of pestilent purpose, meanely affected
Vnto the State wee live in: and beget
Himselfe a thankes, with the great men o' the
    time,
By breeding Jealouses in them of us,
Shall crosse our fortunes, frustrate our endeavours,
Twice seven yeares after: And this trick be call'd
Cutting of throats, with a whispering, or a pen-
    knife.
I must cut his throat now: I'am bound in honour,
And by the Law of armes, to see it done:
I dare to doe it.
                        (II.vi.116–35)

This terrible resolution disperses the guests, but they are reas-
sembled by Parson Palate, who, as we have noted, has a predilection for food. The second meeting is also dissolved by the Captain,
who is so unable to stomach what he sees going on at the table
that his "sword of Justice" must come into play, even though it is
only a wine glass:

    Com. Were you a mad man to doe this at table?
And trouble all the Guests, to affright the Ladies,
And Gentlewomen? *Iro.* Pox upo' your women,
And your halfe man there, Court-Sir *Amber-gris*;
A perfum'd braggart: He must drinke his wine
With three parts water; and have Amber in that too.
    Com. And you must therefore breake his face
      with a Glasse,
And wash his nose in wine. *Iro.* Cannot he drinke
In Orthodoxe, but he must have his Gums,
And Panym Drugs? *Com.* You should have us'd the Glasse
Rather as ballance, then the sword of Justice;
But you have cut his face with it, he bleeds.

Come, you shall take your Sanctuary with me;
The whole house will be up in armes 'gainst you
 else,
Within this halfe hour; this way to my lodging.
                                        (III.ii.1–15)

Such a terrible display serves so to "affright the Ladies," that
Placentia's "timpanie" is induced, between acts as it were, to become "the bravest boy."

Jonson, after showing us several Bobadils and Otters, has given
us here a true soldier, even if in caricature. Jonson most handsomely
rewards the "fortitude" of Captain Ironside. The reward is no
less than Lady Loadstone herself, who elsewhere in this essay has
been given a provisional place among the Deities. She herself makes
the award:

Well, wee are all now reconcil'd to truth.
There rests yet a Gratuitie from me,
To be conferr'd upon this Gentleman;
Who (as my Nephew *Compasse* sayes) was cause,
First of th' offence, but since of all th'amends.
The Quarrell caus'd th' affright; that fright
     brought on
The travell, which made peace; the peace drew on
This new discovery, which endeth all
In reconcilement. *Com.* When the portion
Is tender'd, and receiv'd. *Int.* Well, you must
     have it,
As good at first as last [*Lad*] 'Tis well said,
     brother.
And I, if this good Captaine will accept me,
Give him my selfe, endow him with my estate,
And make him Lord of me, and all my fortunes.
                                        (V.x.126–39)

And finally, Mrs. Polish, "Gossip and she-Parasite," who led us
into *The Magnetic Lady*, deserves a note as an accomplished hypocrite. She might have appeared, as has been said, among the Puritans or the masculine women. She substituted Placentia for Pleasance in the cradle, for, as she says, the sake of the inheritance. It is

her own daughter who gives birth during the play to Mr. Needle's child. A few of her own lines will reveal her hypocrisy and her posture among her betters: "*Pol.* Shee is a noble Aunt! / And a right worshipfull Lady, and a vertuous; / I know it well! *Rut.* Well, if you know it, peace. / *Pal.* Good sister *Polish*, heare your betters speake. / *Pol.* Sir, I will speake, with my good Ladies leave, / And speake, and speake againe" (I.iv.19–24). These lines in which she is speaking of Lady Loadstone's niece are enough to reveal her ignorant Puritanism:

> *Pol.* She would dispute with the Doctors of
> Divinity
> At her owne table! and the Spitle Preachers!
> And find out the *Armenians. Rut.* The *Arminians?*
> *Pol.* I say the *Armenians. Com.* Nay, I say
> so too!
> *Pol.* So Mr. *Polish* called 'hem, the *Armenians!*
> *Com.* And *Medes*, and *Persians*, did he not?
> *Pol.* Yes, he knew 'hem,
> And so did Mistris *Steele*! she was his Pupill!
> The *Armenians*, he would say, were worse then
> Papists!
> And then the *Persians*, were our Puritanes,
> Had the fine piercing wits! *Com.* And who, the
> *Medes?*
> *Pol.* The midle men, the Luke-warme Protestants!
> *Rut.* Out, out. *Pol.* Sir, she would find them
> by their branching:
> Their branching sleeves, brancht cassocks, and
> brancht doctrine,
> Beside their Texts. *Rut.* Stint Karlin, Ile not
> heare:
> Confute her, Parson. *Pol.* I respect no Persons,
> Chaplins, or Doctors, I will speake. *Lad.* Yes,
> so't be reason,
> Let her. *Rut.* Death, she cannot speake reason.
> *Com.* Nor sense, if we be Masters of our senses!
> (I.v.10–27)

In the category of Hypocritical Men—those who present an appearance contrary to what they know themselves to be—three more Jonsonian characters of some stature remain to be examined. All are men of the law, a profession to which Jonson devotes many notable satiric passages. His general attitude toward the lawyer is expressed in Epigram XXXVII, "ON CHEV'RILL THE LAWYER": "No cause, nor client fat, will CHEV'RILL leese, / But as they come, on both sides he takes fees, / And pleaseth both. For while he melts his greace / For this: that winnes, for whom he holds his peace."

In *The Magnetic Lady* Jonson has mellowed and has, in an attitude of reconciling humours, let off Mr. Practise, his lawyer, with no more than an occasional satiric thrust. But, he was not so lenient with Picklock of *The Staple of News* and Voltore of *Volpone*. Picklock betrays all his friends and clients in the hope that by perjuring himself about a deed of trust he may claim a great inheritance. That he sees himself clearly is indicated in this passage: "Tut, I am *Vertumnus*, / On euery change, or chance, vpon occasion, / A true *Chamoelion*, I can colour for't. / I moue vpon my axell, like a turne-pike, / Fit my face to the parties, and become, / Streight, one of them" (III.i.34–39).

Peni-Boy Junior, the prodigal of *The Staple of News*, has in his protection the Lady Pecunia, whose favors he scatters promiscuously and foolishly. His most grandiose proposal is the founding of "*Canters Colledge*," with pretenders in several occupations for its "Professors." Picklock is to read "*Littletons tenures*." He is qualified, as is evident from this exchange:

> [P.IV.] But Picklocke, what wouldst thou be? Thou
>   canst *cant* too.
> PIC. In all the languages in *Westminster-Hall*,
> *Pleas, Bench*, or *Chancery. Fee-Farme, Fee-Tayle*,
> *Tennant in dower, At will*, For *Terme of life*,
> By *Copy of Court Roll, Knights seruice, Homage*,
> *Fealty, Escuage, Soccage*, or *Frank almoigne*,
> *Grand Sergeanty*, or *Burgage*.
>   (IV.iv.102–08)

After Peni-Boy Canter, the supposed beggar, has revealed himself as father to Peni-Boy Junior and has taken Pecunia into his protection, Picklock, who had been Trustee, flatly denies the trust. He represents himself as acting from the highest motives: "O, good heauen knowes / My conscience, and the silly latitude of it! / A narrow-minded man! my thoughts doe dwell / All in a *Lane*, or line indeed; No turning, / Nor scarce obliquitie in them. I still looke / Right forward to th'intent, and scope of that / Which he would go from now" (V.i.72–78). His real intentions, however, are otherwise: "If I can now commit Father, and Sonne, / And make my profits out of both. Commence / A suite with the *old man*, for his whole state, / And goe to *Law* with the Sonnes credit, vndoe / Both, both with their owne money, it were a piece / Worthy my night-cap, and the Gowne I wear, / A *Picklockes* name in *Law*" (ll. 99–105).

If Picklock has a humour, it is again probably in terms of language. He has a "Fore-head of steele, and mouth of brasse," according to Peni-Boy Canter. He is to be "Coyted Over the Barre," and as the play ends, the "Stentor" is "safe enough in a wooden collar."

The Vulture—such is Jonson's characterization of Voltore of *Volpone*. In a play almost exclusively devoted to the examination of human greed, to a searching-out of the levels of degradation to which it can take a man, Voltore is one of Jonson's major symbols. He has been noticed to some extent already in the discussion of Mosca. That parasite tells Voltore how much he is to be admired for a mass of abuses: the giving of "forked counsell"; taking "prouoking gold on either hand"; having a tongue loud and "per-plex'd."[13] What Mosca says is taken as high compliment by Voltore. Mosca's encomium emphasizes the hypocrisy of Voltore, and in its extensive dwelling on the Advocate's skill in language pos-sibly sets up his pride in that skill as a humourous quality.

The eloquence of Voltore comes to be sorely needed by Mosca and Volpone, and the Advocate can rise to the occasion. To a panel of judges, "The Avocatori," has been reported the attempt of Volpone to ravish Celia. There is danger that a hearing will not

[13] This passage in its entirety is quoted in the section above on the Broker.

only destroy the profitable enterprise of Mosca and Volpone but also will jeopardize their lives. Preparations, however, have been made: "Is the lie safely conuai'd amongst vs?" The lie is a monstrous one, conveyed with all the eloquence on which Voltore prides himself:

> This lewd woman
> (That wants no artificiall lookes, or teares,
> To helpe the visor, she has now put on)
> Hath long beene knowne a close adulteresse,
> To that lasciuious youth there; not suspected,
> I say, but knowne; and taken, in the act;
> With him; and by this man, the easie husband,
> Pardon'd: whose timelesse bounty makes him, now,
> Stand here, the most vnhappie, innocent person,
> That euer mans owne goodnesse made accus'd.
>
> (IV.v.34–43)

There is a great deal more of Voltore's oration, much of it as false as the lines quoted above. The truth lies in the response of Bonario: "BON. Most honour'd fathers, / I humbly craue, there be no credit giuen / To this mans mercenary tongue. AVOC. 2. Forbeare. / BON. His soule moues in his fee. AVOC. 3. O, sir. BON. This fellow, / For six *sols* more, would pleade against his maker" (ll. 93–97). But the "lie" prevails. A further hearing "ere night" will be held to announce "what punishment the court decrees vpon 'hem." That hearing occurs after the news of Volpone's "death" has been circulated. It opens considering a memorandum from Voltore that all he had said in the previous hearing had been false. Then he learns that Volpone is not dead. Voltore denies the memorandum. To make the denial credible, at Volpone's suggestion he becomes "possest": "God blesse the man! / (Stop your wind hard, and swell) see, see, see, see! / He vomits crooked pinnes! his eyes are set, / Like a dead hares, hung in a poulters shop! / His mouth's running away! doe you see, signior? / Now, 'tis in his belly" (V.xii.23–28).

The cutting-off of Voltore is perhaps the most severe that can come to a lawyer; he is disbarred and banished: "Thou VOL-

TORE, to take away the scandale / Thou hast giu'n all worthy men, of thy profession, / Art banish'd from their fellowship, and our state" (ll. 126–28).

Before we proceed to the Would-Be Man, a little collecting of observations about the Hypocritical Man is required. He was described originally as one who seems, in Hamlet's meaning of the word, something other than he knows himself to be. The coward presents the brave man; the ignorant woman, the learned; the usurer, the generous man. To some of his peers, and to all of his betters, in the play, there is no doubt of his hypocrisy; but it is not always possible to establish from his own mouth a knowledge of what he really is.

Greed—the desire for wealth or power—is in almost all cases the moving force behind the hypocritical appearance. The very effort to impose his false front on the world implies in the Hypocritical Man a degree of foolishness, for his attempt cannot succeed, at least in Jonson's plays.

The humours are not of paramount importance in this man, unless one makes the assumption that the effort to sustain the facade is the humour. But the truly humourous character in Jonson wants to be something or to have something for its own sake. The Hypocritical Man, on the other hand, wants money, or power, and the appearance is not an end in itself, but a means to an end. Yet to a lesser degree, the humours do play a part in the careers of almost all the Hypocritical Men. To a surprising degree, the humour consists in the use of a particular kind of language, or the use of words to an excess. Frequently the humour is of significance in getting bits of the action effected. It is also frequently associated with the cutting-off of the hypocrite.

Seldom indeed does this man escape Jonson's comic justice. Captain Tucca's cowardice is fully revealed, and he must wear a vizard "that he may looke *bi-fronted*, as he speakes." Lady Would-be's future will lie in the suburbs; Zeal-of-the-Land Busy is "confuted"; Sir Moath Interest must disgorge *all* the dowry, with accumulated interest. The hypocrisy is revealed for all to see.

THE WOULD-BE MAN

The last class into which the humourous characters naturally fall takes its name from Sir Politic Would-be of *Volpone*. It has been pointed out earlier that the humourous characters have been divided into three groups on the basis of their awareness of their own nature or natures of the people and circumstances in the midst of which they find themselves. This Would-Be Man lives in a world of make-believe, blissfully assuming himself to be something that he is not. In general he is stupid, or foolish; he can be easily led—wound up—by Wit or Broker; he has just enough knowledge of what he would be to present a superficial appearance thereof, in clothing or style of hair or speech. His conduct among his fellows is conceived exclusively in terms of presenting the appearance of what he conceives himself to be. He is the truly humourous character, for his "affects, his spirits, and his powers" all "runne one way." Only in rare instances is the Would-Be Man capable of learning. Hence, he is seldom redeemed, but his cutting-off is not so severe as that of the Hypocritical Man. Jonson may well let him off with exposure and ridicule that will render him innocuous. The reason for this comparative gentleness on the part of Jonson is easy to find. Few of these Would-Be Men are truly greedy, and few are conscious hypocrites. In those cases where greed joins the basic foolishness of the Would-Be Man, castigation is severe.

These Would-Be Men, whose only existence is in their humours, though there are among them a few who defy classification, fall generally into three groups. There are the "Poetasters," who take their designation naturally from the early comedy. The epithet "Poet-Ape" might have served, from Epigram LVI, which will serve as a good introduction to the breed:

> Poore POET-APE, that would be thought our chiefe,
> Whose workes are eene the fripperie of wit,
> From brocage is become so bold a thiefe,
> As we, the rob'd, leaue rage, and pittie it.

At first he made low shifts, would picke and gleane,
  Buy the reuersion of old playes; now growne
To'a little wealth, and credit in the *scene*,
  He takes vp all, makes each mans wit his owne.
And, told of this, he slights it. Tut, such crimes
  The sluggish gaping auditor deuoures;
He markes not whose 'twas first; and after-times
  May iudge it to be his, as well as ours.
Foole, as if halfe eyes will not know a fleece
  From locks of wooll, or shreds from the whole peece?

A second group consists of those who imagine themselves to be accomplished courtiers. The designation "Courtling" is appropriate for them, a locution used by Jonson in the titles of Epigrams LII and LXXII. The third group consists of those who are essentially fools, but think themselves to be wise men. Jonson has a character of this sort in his masque *The Fortunate Isles*—"Merefoole." In *Bartholomew Fair* Justice Overdoo is once called a "deliberate fool." But a better name than either comes from that accolade supposedly given to James I by Henry IV of France—"the wisest fool in Christendom." Poetasters, Courtlings, and Wise Fools constitute the bulk of Jonson's completely humourous characters.

Jonson has better-known Poetasters than Crispinus of *Poetaster*, but none of the others is treated at so great a length, nor shown from so many points of view. Jonson's statement in the *Conversations* is generally accepted as identifying Crispinus: "he had many quarrells with Marston beat him & took his Pistol from him, wrote his Poetaster on him the beginning of y^m were that Marston represented him jn the stage jn his youth given to Venerie" (ll. 284–87). Crispinus is not of course a literal representation of John Marston.[14] He is rather the vehicle of an indictment of a bad poet, with enough personal touches in terms of language and perhaps appearance that Marston would inevitably come into the minds of the audience. Demetrius Fannius, also of *Poetaster*, is probably conceived in such a manner as to suggest Thomas Dekker, "a

---

[14] For additional discussion of the identification of Marston and Dekker, see my article "Ben Jonson in Ben Jonson's Plays," *Studies in English*, III (1962), 1–17. Reprinted here as Chapter II.

dresser of plaies about towne." Sufficient notice of him as Poetaster will accompany the examination of Crispinus. It has been noted that for the Poetasters, the Wise Fools, and the Courtlings, the facade—that which the man *believes himself to be—is* the humour, the source from which springs every decision he reaches. Crispinus and his fellows are not hypocrites. They sincerely believe themselves to be poets. Such a belief is possible, of course, because they are utterly devoid of knowledge about poets or poetry. It is also true that they are not particularly greedy. Crispinus wants, not money, but admission to a select circle, to which he is by nature ineligible.

With those general observations as preparation, we can allow Crispinus to present, to indict, himself. He has come to the house of Albius, the citizen, to visit his cousin Cytheris. Present also are Ovid, Gallus, and Propertius, who are real courtiers, and real poets. Chloe, a "gentlewoman borne," is much impressed by the courtesy of the poet-courtiers. Crispinus is smitten by her great beauty. As a consequence he arrives, through this exchange, at a momentous decision:

> CHLO. What gentlemen are these? doe you know them?
> CRIS. I, they are *poets*, lady.
> CHLO. *Poets?* they did not talke of me since I went, did they?
> CRIS. O yes, and extold your perfections to the heauens.
> CHLO. Now in sinceritie, they be the finest kind of men, that euer I knew: *Poets?* Could not one get the Emperour to make my husband a *Poet*, thinke you?
> CRIS. No, ladie, 'tis loue, and beautie make *Poets*: and since you like *Poets* so well, your loue, and beauties shall make me a *Poet*.
> (II.ii.66–77)

Crispinus has perhaps another humour besides the overriding general one—a love for hard words. He uses some of those words in the process of implementing his decision to become a poet:

> ALBI. Will you not stay? and see the iewels, sir? I pray you stay.
> CRIS. Not for a million, sir, now; Let it suffice, I must relinquish; and so in a word, please you to expiate this complement.
> ALBI. Mum.

CRIS. Ile presently goe and enghle some broker, for a *Poets* gowne, and bespeake a garland: and then ieweller, looke to your best iewell yfaith.

(ll. 218–26)

The next step in this progress of a poet becomes evident when Crispinus encounters Horace, a true poet, on the street:

CRIS. 'Slid, yonder's HORACE! they say hee's an excellent *Poet*: MECOENAS loues him. Ile fall into his acquaintance, if I can; I thinke he be composing, as he goes i' the street! ha? 't is a good humour, and he be: Ile compose too.
. . . .
CRIS. Sweet HORACE, MINERVA, and the *Muses* stand auspicious to thy desseignes. How far'st thou, sweete man? frolicke? rich? gallant? ha?
HORA. Not greatly gallant, sir, like my fortunes; well. I'm bold to take my leaue, sir, you'ld naught else, sir, would you?
CRIS. Troth, no, but I could wish thou did'st know vs, HORACE, we are a scholer, I assure thee.
HORA. A scholer, sir? I shall bee couetous of your faire knowledge.
CRIS. Gramercie, good HORACE. Nay, we are new turn'd *Poet* too, which is more; and a *Satyrist* too, which is more then that: I write iust in thy veine, I. I am for your *odes* or your *sermons*, or any thing indeed; wee are a gentleman besides: our name is RVFVS LABERIVS CRISPINVS, we are a prettie *stoick* too.

(III.i.3–7, 13–28)

The unfortunate Horace must hear his verses, just made in tribute to the beauteous Chloe: "*Rich was thy hap, sweet, deintie cap, / There to be placed: / Where thy smooth blacke, sleeke white may smacke, / And both be graced. / White*, is there vsurpt for her brow; her forehead: and then *sleeke*, as the *paralell* to *smooth*, that went before. A kind of *Paranomasie*, or *Agnomination*: doe you conceiue, sir?" (ll. 85–91).

The next choice made by Crispinus on his way to becoming a poet is an obvious one. The wealthy and powerful Mecoenas is the patron of poets. Since Horace refuses to introduce him, Crispinus can find a way: "Nay, I'le bribe his porter, and the groomes of his chamber; make his doores open to mee that way, first: and then, I'le obserue my times. Say, he should extrude mee his house to day; shall I therefore desist, or let fall my suite, to morrow? No: I'le attend him, follow him, meet him i' the street, the high waies, run by his coach, neuer leaue him. What? Man hath nothing giuen him, in this life, without much labour" (ll. 271–78).

The next stage of Crispinus is to become a professional poet. He falls under the spell of the redoubtable Captain Tucca, accepts him for a sort of patron, and agrees with Histrio (thinly disguised by Jonson as a representative of the Lord Chamberlain's Company) to produce, in collaboration with Demetrius, a play maligning Horace.[15] Jonson shows Crispinus in all the attitudes which he detests in the would-be poet—sycophancy, plagiarism, detraction, plus very bad writing, especially barbaric diction and loose rhythms. Just before the Heavenly Banquet, Crispinus sings as his own a "ditti" "borrowed" from Horace. Though he himself has taken part as Mercury in the Heavenly Banquet, he joins Lupus in finding it a threat to the life of Augustus because Ovid and his friends had rented "a scepter, and a crowne for IOVE, and a *caduceus* for MERCVRY" (IV.iv.11–13).

It is the share of Crispinus in this folly of the informer Lupus that brings him into the presence of Caesar, and Virgil and the other true Poets. Once the folly of the conspiracy has been blown away, Gallus and Tibullus conceive the indictment, and all those present, all characters belonging to the group of Wits, concur. Severe indeed is the charge: "... CRISPINAS, Poetaster, *and* plagiary: *the other*, by the name of *DEMETRIVS FANNIVS*, playdresser, *and* plagiary ... *haue most ignorantly, foolishly, and (more like your selues) maliciously, gone about to depraue, and calumniate the person and writings of* QVINTVS HORACIVS FLACCVS, *here present*, poet, *and* priest *to the* Muses ... *taxing him, falsly, of* selfe-loue, arrogancy, impudence, rayling, filching by translation"

---

[15] That play, the shabby *Satiromastix*, does get written. It was published in 1602, with only the name of Dekker on the title-page.

(V.iii.218–20, 224–28, 231–32). The evidence is damning. Crispinus confesses this effusion to be his:

> *Rampe vp, my* genius; *be not retrograde:*
> *But boldly nominate a spade, a spade.*
> *What, shall thy lubricall and glibberie* Muse
> *Liue, as shee were defunct, like punke in stewes?*
> . . . .
> *Alas! That were no moderne consequence,*
> *To haue cothurnall buskins frighted hence.*
> *No; teach thy* incubus *to poetize;*
> *And throw abroad thy spurious snotteries,*
> *Vpon that puft-vp lumpe of barmy froth,*
> . . . .
> *Or clumsie chil-blain'd iudgement; that, with oath,*
> *Magnificates his merit; and bespawles*
> *The conscious time, with humorous fome, and brawles,*
> *As if his organons of sense would crack*
> *The sinewes of my patience. Breake his back,*
> *O* Poets *all, and some: For now we list*
> *Of strenuous venge-ance to clutch the fist.*
> (ll. 275–78, 280–84, 286–92)

The evidence against Demetrius is not quite so powerful, but it is enough:

> *Our* Muse *is in mind for th'vntrussing a* poet,
> *I slip by his name; for most men doe know it:*
> *A* critick, *that all the world bescumbers*
> *With* satyricall *humours, and* lyricall *numbers:*
> . . . .
> *And for the most part, himselfe doth aduance*
> *With much self-loue, and more arrogance.*
> . . . .
> *And (but that I would not be thought a prater)*
> *I could tell you, he were a translater.*
> *I know the authors from whence he ha's stole,*
> *And could trace him too, but that I vnderstand*
> *'hem not full and whole.*
> (ll. 302–305, 307–308, 310–313)

Jonson is now ready for the cutting-off. Horace has pills "that should purge / His braine and stomach of those timorous heates." Crispinus does vomit—and up come "terrible, windy wordes": *"Glibbery," "lubricall," "turgidous," "ventositous," "oblatrant," "prorumped," "obstupefact"*—these and many more. Horace, after this inhuman punishment, is lenient. After Crispinus has been locked up for a week in some dark place, a bit of Cato, Terence, Plautus, and Homer, among others, he suggests, should suffice for a cure. But Caesar is not so lenient; he has the final words in the play: "It is the bane, and torment of our eares, / To heare the discords of those iangling rimers, / That, with their bad and scandalous practices, / Bring all true arts, and learning in contempt. / But let not your high thoughts descend so low, / As these despised obiects; Let them fall, / With their flat groueling soules" (ll. 615–21).

In the portrait of Crispinus we have had one of Jonson's most powerful satirical attacks. It has been the portrait, not of the hypocrite, or of the greedy man, but that of the fool as pretender in the sacred role of poet. We have noted that the humour of Crispinus has been the struggle to achieve his conception of a poet, but that the use of the hard words is a sort of superimposed humour. It should be noted also that the winding-up of Crispinus, the commentary about him, and the cutting-off have all been in the hands of a Wit or of a Choric figure.

The first play presented by Herford and Simpson in their *Ben Jonson* is *A Tale of a Tub*, a work which may contain both Jonson's earliest and latest Poetasters. As editors, they take the position that the play is basically early work, revised late in Jonson's career.[16] The Poetaster of *A Tale of a Tub* who may repre-

---

[16] The conclusions of Herford and Simpson are as follows:

A Tale of a Tub, in the form in which it has come down to us, consists therefore of (1) the original play, written about 1596 or 1597, clear traces of which survive in the extant text, (2) the 1633 reissue of this discarded work, in which Jonson inserted his satire on Inigo Jones and—in all probability—recast the original prose passages in verse form, (3) the final touches of revision forced upon him by the

sent early work of Jonson is Miles Metaphor, Clerk to Justice Pre-amble. The Poetaster of the late version is the In-and-In Medlay of the late scenes only, a thinly disguised version of Inigo Jones. This study as it has progressed has revealed one thing not suspected by the writer at its inception, that in many cases the humour lies in the realm of language. Such was notably the case with Captain Tucca, with Bobadil, with Zeal-of-the-Land Busy. Such is also the case—as his name implies—with Miles Metaphor. He has no significant part in the play beyond the running of er-rands. He is foolish enough, cowardly enough, and greedy enough to betray his master's counsel. But the one quality which he mani-fests in all encounters is his love for the similitude. The following is a fair sample of Metaphor's style:

> Be't knowne unto you, by these presents, then,
> That I *Miles Metaphore*, your worships Clarke:
> Have ene beene beaten, to an Allegory,
> By multitude of hands. Had they beene but
> Some five or sixe, I' had whip'd 'hem all, like tops
> In *Lent*, and hurl'd 'hem into *Hoblers*-hole;
> Or the next ditch: I had crack'd all their costards,
> As nimbly as a Squirrell will crack nuts:
> And flourish'd like to *Hercules*, the Porter,
> Among the Pages. But, when they came on
> Like Bees about a Hive, Crowes about carrion,
> Flies about sweet meats; nay, like water-men
> About a Fare.
>
> (III.vii.38–50)

His finest flight into the world of comparisons, however, is this: "Let not the mouse of my good meaning, Lady, / Be snap'd up in the trap of your suspition, / To loose the taile there, either of her truth, / Or swallow'd by the Cat of misconstruction" (IV.iv.25–28).

Censor. As much as he could save of Vitruvius Hoop was clumsily attached to In-and-In Medlay; and it is possible that the flat and colourless epitome of the play, which now constitutes the "motion", replaced something more pungent of which Inigo may have had reason to complain. (III, 3)

Of no interest in himself as an artistic creation, Miles Metaphor does have historic significance in the work of Jonson, both as an early manifestation of the Poetaster and in the use of mannerisms of language as an important device in the individualizing of character and motivation of actions through the humours.

A second Poetaster in *A Tale of a Tub*, In-and-In Medlay, is also of considerable historical interest. He is at home in the portion of the play written about 1597 as a clown, a rustic who can speak good stage dialect:

> Masters, take heed, let's not vind too many:
> One's enough to stay the Hang-mans stomack.
> There is *Iohn Clay*, who is yvound already;
> A proper man: A Tile-man by his trade:
> A man as one would zay, moulded in clay:
> As spruce as any neighbours child among you:
> And he (you zee) is taken on conspition.
>
> (III.i.24–30)

A Tale of a Tub was first licensed for performance in 1633, with certain provisos: "*1633, May 7.* 'R. for allowinge of *The Tale of the Tubb*, Vitru Hoop's parte wholly strucke out, and the motion of the tubb, by commande from my lorde chamberlin; exceptions being taken against it by Inigo Jones, surveyor of the kings workes, as a personal injury unto him. May 7, 1633,—*2l.* 0.0' " (*Var.*iii. 232).[17] Therefore, having lost Vitruvius Hoop, Jonson converted Medlay from clown to a Poetaster who resembles Inigo Jones. The metamorphosis from cooper to joiner to architect takes place in "The *Scene* interloping" between scenes one and two of Act IV. Medlay introduces himself thus:

> Indeed, there is a woundy luck in names, Sirs,
> And a maine mysterie, an' a man knew where
> To vind it. My God-sires name, Ile tell you,
> Was *In-and-In Shittle*, and a Weaver he was,
> And it did fit his craft: for so his Shittle

[17] Joseph Quincy Adams, ed., *The Dramatic Records of Sir Henry Herbert* (New York: Benjamin Blom, [n.d.]), p. 19.

Went in, and in, still: this way, and then that
    way.
And he nam'd me, *In-and-In Medlay*: which serves
A Joyners craft, bycause that wee doe lay
Things in and in, in our worke. But, I am truly
Architectonicus professor, rather.

                      (ll. 1–10)

By way of celebrating a pair of weddings, there is to be a feast
at Tottenham Court, the home of Lady Tub. Squire Tub, her son,
in the absence of "a Cooper at *London* call'd *Vitruvius* ... Or old
Iohn Haywood," commissions Medlay to write a "Masque" re-
capitulating the momentous events of the day. There are certain
difficulties attending the agreement:

> *Med.* I have a little knowledge in designe,
> Which I can varie Sir to *Infinito*.
> *Tub. Ad Infinitum* Sir you mean. *Med.* I doe.
> I stand not on my Latine, Ile invent,
> But I must be alone then, joyn'd with no man.
> This we doe call the Stand-still of our worke.
>   *Tub.* Who are those wee, you now joyn'd to your
>   selfe?
>   *Med.* I meane my selfe still, in the plurall
>   number,
> And out of this wee raise our *Tale of a Tub*.
>   *Tub.* No, Mr. *In-and-In*, my *Tale of a Tub*.
> By your leave, I am *Tub*, the Tale's of me,
> And my adventures! I am Squire *Tub*,
> *Subjectum Fabulae. Med.* But I the Author.
>   *Tub.* The Worke-man Sir! the Artificer!
>   (V.vii.10–23)

The masque is in due time produced, as a puppet-show, a "*Motion.*" Its Prologue will be enough to show Jonson's technique—
even in a "dotage"—of indicating that a carpenter is not a poet:

> *Med.* Thus rise I first, in my light linnen
>   breeches,
> To run the meaning over in short speeches.
> Here is a *Tub*; a *Tub* of *Totten-Court*;

An ancient *Tub*, hath call'd you to this sport:
His Father was a Knight, the rich Sir *Peeter*;
Who got his wealth by a *Tub*, and by Salt-Peeter:
And left all to his Lady *Tub*; the mother
Of this bold Squire *Tub*, and to no other.
Now of this *Tub*, and's deeds, not done in ale,
Observe, and you shall see the very *Tale*.
(V.x.8–17)

Jonson's next Poetaster of whom we know is Antonio Balladino of *The Case Is Altered* (1597?). He, like Metaphor and Medlay, a very minor character, is probably Anthony Munday, "*Pageant* Poet to the City of *Millaine*." But Crites, and the redoubtable Horace, have not yet manifested themselves, and Jonson pays little attention to Balladino: "True sir, they would haue me make such plaies [nothing but humours], but as I tell hem, and they'le giue me twenty pound a play, I'le not raise my vaine" (I.ii.71–73).

Master Matthew of *Every Man in His Humour*, Jonson's third Poetaster, though he is perhaps a slight rehearsal for Crispinus, needs less attention. Though Matthew is a fool, he is not greedy, nor is he a hypocrite. His principal offense is plagiarism—"hee utters nothing, but stolne remnants." He is wound up by the Wits Knowell and Wellbred to the reciting of his thefts from Marlowe and others. Matthew comes to the attention of Justice Clement, the choric dispenser of fates, as a "poet." The Justice "challenges" him "at *extempore*." The passage continues:

> WELL.   . . . Hee is all for the pocket-*muse*, please you command a sight of it.
> CLEM. Yes, yes, search him for a tast of his veine.
> WEL. You must not denie the Queenes Iustice, Sir, vnder a writ o' rebellion.
> CLEM. What! all this verse? Bodie o'me, he carries a whole realme, a common-wealth of paper, in's hose! let's see some of his subiects!
> *Vnto the boundlesse Ocean of thy face,*
>   *Runnes this poore riuer charg'd with streames of eyes.*
> How? this is stolne!

E.KN. A *Parodie!* a *parodie!* with a kind of miraculous gift, to
make it absurder then it was.
CLEM. Is all the rest, of this batch? Bring me a torch; lay it
together, and giue fire. Clense the aire. Here was enough to haue
infected, the whole citie, if it had not beene taken in time! See,
see, how our *Poets* glorie shines! brighter, and brighter! still it in-
creases! o, now, it's at the highest: and, now, it declines as fast. You
may see. *Sic transit gloria mundi.*

(V.v.15–34)

Sir John Daw of *Epicoene* looks somewhat like the earlier
Poetasters. He truly believes himself to be a poet, and all his postures, his choices, during the course of the play are made in terms of
that misconception of himself. They are of course influenced also
by the fact that he is a fool and a coward. They are further influenced by his secondary humour, one of which the other characters
make much—he is "the only talking Sir of the towne."

But Jonson uses Daw for a very different purpose from that for
which Crispinus was conceived. The play *Poetaster* is concerned
primarily with poetry, as it is rightly used or as it is abused. Virgil
represents the ideal practitioner of the art of poetry; a Horace who
looks remarkably like Jonson is a near-perfect exponent; the
courtier poets and Ovid, the poet of love, are acceptable examples;
and Crispinus, who looks like John Marston, is the epitome of
abusers of poetry, as plagiarist, sycophant, detractor, and abuser of
language. *Poetaster* has for its theme the glorification of poetry,
rendered more effective by the contrast between the true poet and
the poetaster.

But *Epicoene* has quite a different theme, its major thrust being
not praise of the noble, but attack through many exemplars of
what is to Jonson detestable, that which is "of two natures," the
"amphibian." A touch of this *epicoene* quality extends to almost
every character in the play, even to the three members of our group
of Wits. But Jonson's Poetaster in this play, Sir John Daw, is put
to work by the poet in many more ways than were any of his predecessors. He is not guilty of plagiarism, but he does utter some ex-

tremely bad poetry, one of his efforts being an actual statement of
the very theme of the play:

> *Silence in woman, is like speech in man,*
>   *Deny't who can.*
>
> . . . .
>
>   *Nor, is't a tale,*
> *That female vice should be a vertue male,*
> *Or masculine vice, a female vertue be:*
>   *You shall it see*
>   *Prou'd with increase,*
> *I know to speake, and shee to hold her peace.*
>
> (II.iii.123–24, 126–31)

Not only, however, does Daw state the motif of *Epicoene*; he
is the primary male manifestation of it. His humour, "the only
talking Sir," is the predominant one among Jonson's male characters displaying humours. Even his cowardice is exceptional.
Though La Foole is a "braue, heroique coward," Daw is merely a
"whiniling dastard." He is admitted, as an associate, to the "Colledge," a group of women who assume masculine prerogatives.
Though there is little likelihood of his effecting an amatory con-
quest, he boasts of his prowess.

But Sir John Daw's work is not yet done. Through his participation in the farcical but magnificent scene of the mock duel,
he is highly useful to Jonson in the creation of pure spectacle. He
served the same function in the preparatory scene, the drinking
bout involving Captain Otter's Bull, Bear, and Horse.

These qualities of Daw are all put to work in the action with
remarkable skill by Jonson. His propensity for talking, together
with his cowardice, lead him to admit that he has known Epicoene,
a boy, "carnally." This revelation at the end of the play leads to
Morose's desperate avowal—"I am no man"—and to the wonderful
response of Centaur, "Bridegroome vncarnate" (V.iv.44, 49).

The cutting-off of Sir John is not, as was the case with Matthew
and Crispinus, in terms of his pretensions to poetry, but rather in
terms of the general theme of the play, plus Daw's humour of talking. It is spoken by Truewit, after it has been revealed that Epi-

coene is a boy: "You are they, that when no merit or fortune can make you hope to enioy their bodies, will yet lie with their reputations, and make their fame suffer. Away you common moths of these, and all ladies honors. Goe, trauaile to make legs and faces, and come home with some new matter to be laught at: you deserue to liue in an aire as corrupted, as that wherewith you feed rumor" (V.iv.237–43).

The last of the Poetasters is Madrigal (George Wither?) of *The Staple of News*. He is slightly greedy, for he is one of the lesser suitors to the Lady Pecunia; but he is not a hypocrite, for he really believes himself to be a poet; nor is he altogether a fool, for he can write rhythmically and at least make sense, as in this madrigal on the virtues of Pecunia:

> *As bright as is the* Sunne *her Sire,*
> *Or* Earth *her mother, in her best atyre,*
> *Or* Mint, *the Mid-wife, with her fire,*
>   *Comes forth her Grace!*
> *The splendour of the wealthiest* Mines!
> *The stamp, and strength of all imperiall lines,*
> *Both maiesty and beauty shines,*
>   *In her sweet face!*
> *Looke how a Torch, of Taper light,*
> *Or of that Torches flame, a Beacon bright:*
> . . . .
> *Or of that Beacons fire, Moone-light:*
>   *So takes she place!*
>   (IV.ii.95–104, 106–07)

He, like the Doctor, the Lawyer, the Captain, the Courtier, is guilty of canting. Peni-Boy Canter, the Chorus, makes the charge: "My Eg-chind *Laureat*, here, when he comes forth / With *Dimeters*, and *Trimeters*, *Tetrameters*, / *Pentameters*, *Hexameters*, *Catalecticks*, / His *Hyper*, and his *Brachy-Catalecticks*, / His *Pyrrhicks*, *Epitrites*, and *Choriambicks*. / What is all this, but canting?" (IV.iv.54–59). He is guilty, however, of poetic heresy, for he believes that "The perfect, and true straine of poetry, / Is rather to be giuen the quicke *Celler*, / Then the fat *Kitchin*" (IV.ii.5–7).

This assertion is refuted by Lickfinger, the Cook, who uses it as a starting point for his praise of the "Master-Cooke," who may be Shakespeare.[18]

Madrigal's humour has, of course, been his approach to all matters from his posture as poet. His cutting-off is properly given to Peni-Boy Canter, who perhaps identifies Madrigal's original by an adjective in the fifth line:

> Doe I despise a learn'd *Physician*,
> In calling him a *Quack-Saluer*? or blast
> The *euer-liuing ghirlond*, alwaies greene
> Of a good *Poet*? when I say his *wreath*
> Is piec'd and patch'd of dirty witherd flowers?
> Away, I am impatient of these vlcers,
> (That I not call you worse) There is no sore,
> Or Plague but you to infect the times. I abhorre
> Your very scent.
>
> (IV.iv.164-72)

We have looked at the Poetasters as men utterly deceived about themselves and their relationships to their associates, men who sincerely believe themselves to be what they are not and can never be, poets. The constant presentation of the imagined identity constitutes their humours, with frequently a secondary humour also apparent, such as the inevitable similitudes of Miles Metaphor. A second group, resembling the Poetasters in conception, function, and fate will be designated, after Jonson, as Courtlings. Jonson's attack on the Poetasters was essentially that they disgraced a sacred calling, of which he himself was a worthy practitioner. His grievance against the Courtling, aside from the fact that he is dangerous to the state, is that the Courtling is a detractor of the virtues of poets and scholars. A portion of this resentment appears in Epigram LII:

> TO CENSORIOVS COVRTLING.
> COVRTLING, I rather thou should'st vtterly
> Dispraise my worke, then praise it frostily:
> When I am read, thou fain'st a weake applause,

[18] See footnote 8 above.

As if thou wert my friend, but lack'dst a
   cause.
This but thy iudgement fooles: the other way
Would both thy folly, and thy spite betray.

The difference between the true courtier and Jonson's Courtling
is neatly pointed out in this brief passage from *The Staple of
News*: "A worthy *Courtier*, is the ornament / Of a *Kings Palace*,
his great *Masters* honour. / This is a moth, a rascall, a Court-rat, /
That gnawes the common-wealth with broking suits, / And eating grieuances!" (IV.iv.140–44).
   The most fully developed of these "Court-rats" is Fastidius
Briske of *Every Man Out of His Humour*, who may just possibly
be, like Crispinus, a John Marston. Here is Jonson's introduction
of Fastidius in his "character": "*A Neat, spruce, affecting Courtier,
one that weares clothes well, and in fashion; practiseth by his glasse
how to salute; speakes good remnants (notwithstanding the Base-
violl and Tabacco:) sweares tersely, and with variety; cares not
what Ladies fauour he belyes, or great Mans familiarity: a good
property to perfume the boot of a coach*" (ll. 36–41). He is not
greedy, in the sense that Volpone and Mosca and their victims
were. He is partly a hypocrite, for though he sincerely believes
himself to be admired at the court, he can easily invent favors
from great ladies, courtesies from great men. We must perhaps
call him a fool, for he does not learn anything, even in a play almost the sole action of which is to cure assorted follies, or humours.
The humour of Fastidius consists in being always busy in the activities which in his opinion make the courtier: the use of a rarified
language, much like that of Osric in *Hamlet*; courtship of ladies,
with accounts of imagined conquests; accounts, again imaginary, of
consultations with great lords; duelling; but, above all, dress—
"what bright-shining gallant's that?"
   Though in many cases we have seen Jonson using Wit or Chorus
to establish the folly of one of the humourous characters, he does
not use that technique with Fastidius Briske, except for the final assessment. The massive satirical portrait grows almost every time

Fastidius speaks. He gives his concept of the court, in language which he believes appropriate to the courtier:

> A man liues there, in that diuine rapture, that hee will thinke himselfe i' the ninth heauen for the time, and lose all sense of mortalitie whatsoeuer; when he shall behold such glorious (and almost immortall) beauties, heare such angelicall and harmonious voyces, discourse with such flowing and *ambrosian* spirits, whose wits are as suddaine as lightning, and humorous as *nectar*; Oh: it makes a man al *quintessence*, and *flame*, & lifts him vp (in a moment) to the verie christall crowne of the skie, where (houering in the strength of his imagination) he shall behold all the delights of the HESPERIDES, the *Insulae Fortunatae*, ADONIS gardens, *Tempe* or what else (confin'd within the amplest verge of *poesie*) to bee meere *vmbrae*, and imperfect figures, conferr'd with the most essentiall felicitie of your court.
>
> (IV.viii.18–32)

Fastidius is in debt for some thousands of pounds, partly to pay for the gifts that a courtier must present and partly for dress. It is not surprising once he has explained the virtues of apparel:

> Why, assure you, signior, rich apparell has strange vertues: it makes him that hath it without meanes, esteemed for an excellent wit: he that enioyes it with means, puts the world in remembrance of his means: it helps the deformities of nature, and giues lustre to her beauties; makes continuall holy-day where it shines; sets the wits of ladies at worke, that otherwise would be idle: furnisheth your two-shilling ordinarie; takes possession of your stage at your new play; and enricheth your oares, as scorning to goe with your scull.
>
> (II.vi.45–54)

The expense one must undergo in maintaining proper apparel is apparent as we hear his account of a duel with Signior Luculento, the cause being "the same that sundred AGAMEMNON, and great THETIS sonne." Only a portion of the hazards involved appear in the lines below:

> Sir, I mist my purpose in his arme, rasht his doublet sleeue, ran him close by the left cheek, and through his haire. He againe, lights me here (I had on, a gold cable hatband, then new come vp, which I wore about a murrey *French* hat I had) cuts my hatband

(and yet it was massie, gold-smithes worke) cuts my brimmes, which by good fortune (being thicke embrodered with gold-twist, and spangles) disappointed the force of the blow: Neuer-thelesse, it graz'd on my shoulder, takes me away sixe purles of an *Italian* cut-worke band I wore (cost me three pound in the ex-change, but three daies before.) . . . .

. . . .
Here (in the opinion of mutuall dammage) wee paus'd: but (ere I proceed) I must tell you, signior, that (in this last encounter) not hauing leisure to put off my siluer spurres, one of the rowels catcht hold of the ruffle of my boot, and (being *Spanish* leather, and subiect to teare) ouerthrowes me, rends me two paire of silke stockings (that I put on, being somewhat a raw morning, a peach colour and another) and strikes me some halfe inch deepe into the side of the calfe; Hee (seeing the bloud come) presently takes horse, and away. I (hauing bound vp my wound with a peece of my wrought shirt)—

. . . .
Rid after him, and (lighting at the court-gate, both together) embrac'd and marcht hand in hand vp into the presence: was not this businesse well carried?
(IV.vi.81–91, 108–18, 120–22)

The cutting-off of Fastidius is all the more severe when one considers the nature of the play in which he appears. As its title implies, restoration rather than cutting-off is the intent in *Every Man Out of His Humour*. The greedy Sordido is reclaimed; the scurrilous Buffone has his lips sealed, literally, with candle wax; the envious Macilente is no longer envious; the uxorious Deliro has moved a step forward, perhaps into the state of jealous husband. But Fastidius, in prison for a riot he did not create, remains there—to this day—for his debts. His epitaph is pronounced by Macilente:

What, doe you sigh? this it is to kisse the hand of a countesse, to haue her coach sent for you, to hang poinards in ladies garters, to weare bracelets of their haire, and for euery one of these great fauours to giue some slight iewell of fiue hundred crownes, or so, why 'tis nothing. Now, Monsieur, you see the plague that treads o' the heeles of your fopperie: well, goe your waies in, remoue your selfe to the two penny ward quickly, to saue charges.
(V.xi.44–51)

Jonson's second Courtling is Asinus Lupus of *Poetaster*. In Fastidius Briske, Jonson emphasized foppish, effeminate qualities. Briske's activities reached only the perimeter of the court, and never touched on matters which might affect the state. Lupus, on the other hand, as a Tribune has access to Caesar himself, to whom, for an expected reward, he undertakes to be informer. One feels that there is much of Polonius in him. He is greedy and is foolish, but is not a hypocrite. His humour, not a very pronounced one, is the presentation of his facade, that of a wise servant to the state. He has not a secondary humourous quality, such as the necessity for bright-shining apparel of Fastidius Briske.

As one might expect in *Poetaster*, which is essentially a discourse on poets and poetry, the informing of Lupus is directed against the poets themselves. In the early stages of the play Ovid Junior has been surprised by his father devoting his attention, not to the law, but to poetry, the composition of a tragedy in particular. Asinus Lupus undertakes, in a fine piece of self-revelation, to point out the iniquities of poets and players:

> Indeed, MARCVS OVID, these players are an idle generation, and doe much harme in a state, corrupt yong gentrie very much, I know it: I haue not beene a *Tribune* thus long, and obseru'd nothing: besides, they will rob vs, vs, that are magistrates, of our respect, bring vs vpon their stages, and make vs ridiculous to the plebeians; they will play you, or me, the wisest men they can come by still; me: only to bring vs in contempt with the vulgar, and make vs cheape.
>
> (I.ii.36–44)

Later in the play, after thus vigorously attacking the players, Lupus aligns himself with Histrio, who may be Augustine Phillips of the Lord Chamberlain's Company. The poet-courtiers have in hand a "heauenly banquet," the parts to be distributed as follows: "OVID will be IVPITER; the Princesse IVLIA, IVNO; GALLVS here APOLLO; you CYTHERIS, PALLAS; I will bee BACCHVS; and my Loue PLAVTIA, CERES: And to install you, and your husband, faire CHLOE, in honours, equall with ours; you shall be a Goddesse, and your husband a God" (IV.ii.42–47).

Histrio has informed Lupus of the request of the courtiers to rent properties. Lupus scents danger to the state, and presumably a nice reward for himself: "*Caduceus?* and *petasus?* Let me see your letter. This is a coniuration; a conspiracy, this. Quickly, on with my buskins: I'le act a *tragoedie*, i' faith. Will nothing but our gods serue these *poets* to prophane? dispatch. Plaier, I thanke thee. The Emperour shall take knowledge of thy good seruice. Who's there now? Looke, knaue. A *crowne*, and a *scepter?* this is good: rebellion, now?" (IV.iv.14–20).

Augustus, at first shocked by such an abuse of sacred poetry, is soon mollified by the true poets; and the whole affair is brushed aside in a sentence spoken by Mecoenas and directed at Lupus: "Princes that will but heare, or giue accesse / To such officious spies, can ne're be safe: / They take in poyson, with an open eare, / And, free from danger, become slaues to fear (IV.vii.57–60).

But Lupus is not yet finished as informer-courtier. He has probably unlawfully searched "HORACE his studie, in MECOENAS his house," and found an "*embleme*"—the picture of a vulture and a wolf preying on an ass. This "*distich*" accompanies the emblem: "*Thus, oft, the base and rauenous multitude / Suruiue, to share the spoiles of fortitude*" (V.iii.79–80).

Lupus forces admittance to the sacred reading by Virgil of his own *Aeneid* to announce the treason he has discovered. He interprets the eagle as Caesar, the wolf as himself, Lupus, and the ass as himself, Asinus. Once Horace has explained his emblem, the cutting-off of Asinus Lupus is required, and one feels that he stands for many a real or fancied enemy of Jonson. Caesar's charge is in physical terms: "Let him be whipt. LICTORS, goe take him hence, / And LVPVS, for your fierce credulitie, / One fit him with a paire of larger eares" (ll. 128–30). One Deity has spoken. It remains for the second, the poet Virgil, to speak Jonson's mind about the informer, whether he be a Courtling or merely a "politique *Picklocke* of the *scene*":

CAESAR hath done like CAESAR. Faire, and iust
Is his award, against these brainelesse creatures.

> 'Tis not the wholesome sharpe moralitie,
> Or modest anger of a *satyricke* spirit,
> That hurts, or wounds the bodie of a state;
> But the sinister application
> Of the malicious, ignorant, and base
> Interpreter: who will distort, and straine
> The generall scope and purpose of an authour,
> To his particular, and priuate spleene.
>
>   (ll. 135-44)

The next Courtling to be considered is Fitton of *The Staple of News*. He is a member of a sort of Chorus of Jeerers, his ostensible task in the play being to gather the news of the court for the Staple. In reality, he contributes nothing to the action. He is merely on display, but he represents a slightly different version of the courtier than the foppish Briske or the informer Lupus. Fitton will undertake, for a consideration, to get a suit, or a "project," forwarded in the court. The whole Fitton, language, function, and effectiveness, is in this passage spoken by the Chorus, Peni-Boy Canter:

> With all your *fly-blowne proiects*,
> And lookes-out of the *politicks*, your *shut-faces*,
> And reseru'd *Questions*, and *Answers* that you game
>   with, As
> Is't a *Cleare business*? will it *mannage well*?
> *My name* must not be vs'd else. Here, *'twill dash*.
> Your *businesse has receiu'd a taint*, giue off,
> I may not *prostitute my selfe*. Tut, tut,
> *That little dust I can blow off*, at pleasure.
> *Here's no such mountaine, yet, i' the whole worke*,
> But a light purse may leuell. I will *tyde*
> This *affayre* for you; giue it *freight*, and *passage*.
>   (IV.iv.63-73)

Our supply of Courtlings is almost exhausted. There are in *The New Inn* several persons of the proper class and vocation. But since their actions are as romantic as a Ben Jonson can achieve, and since they are as a whole proposed to us for admiration, not for censure, they may be omitted from a discussion of humourous characters, with one slight exception. Lovel, in a court-of-love posture, discourses for one hour on the nature of valor. His arguments must be noted in connection with the examination of our last Courtling, Sir Diaphanous Silkworm of *The Magnetic Lady*. Bias, also a courtier, of the same play, was discussed earlier in a digression. Sir Diaphanous is a slighter version of Fastidius Briske. He is, like so many of the characters of *The Magnetic Lady*, first presented to us in a sort of "character" of a courtier. The speaker is Compasse: "Sir *Diaphanous Silke-worme*? / A Courtier extraordinary; who by diet / Of meates, and drinkes; his temperate exercise; / Choise musick; frequent bathes; his horary shifts / Of Shirts and Wast-coats; meanes to immortalize / Mortality it selfe; and makes the essence / Of his whole happinesse the trim of Court" (I.vi.3–9). The very presence of Sir Diaphanous at dinner is so offensive to the redoubtable Captain Ironside that he must "brake his face with a Glasse, and wash his nose in wine." The offenses of Sir Diaphanous are indeed great, according to the Captain: "Pox upo' your women, / And your halfe man there, Court-Sir *Amber-gris*: / A perfum'd braggart: He must drinke his wine / With three parts water; and have Amber in that too" (III.ii.3–6). This insult to Sir Diaphanous is intolerable. He and the choric commentator, Compasse, discuss it:

> *Silk.* There's nothing vexes me, but that he
>   has staind
> My new white sattin Doublet; and bespatter'd
> My spick and span silke Stockings, o' the day
> They were drawne on: And here's a spot i' my hose
>   too.
>   *Com.* Shrewd maimes! your Clothes are wounded
>   desperately,
> And that (I thinke) troubles a Courtier more,
> An exact Courtier, then a gash in his flesh.
>   *Silk.* My flesh? I sweare had he giv'n me
>   twice so much,
> I never should ha' reckon'd it. But my clothes
> To be defac'd, and stigmatiz'd so foulely!
> I take it as a contumely done me
> Above the wisdome of our Lawes to right.
>   (III.iv.7–18)

This confrontation at dinner has been useful to Jonson in several ways: it has established the humour of Sir Diaphanous; it has created such a furor that the "Timpanie" of Placentia has been reduced—into a fine baby boy; it has set up the arrangements for a duel, arrangements which provide Jonson with material for further characterization of Bias, Sir Diaphanous, and the wily Compasse; and it has provided Jonson with some skillful satire on Jonson. In *The New Inn* Jonson had Lovel, a man of unquestionable bravery, discourse for an hour about valor, in a court-of-love situation, after talking for an earlier hour about love. Lovel pronounces that there is no valor except that for the public good; and that conflict for reputation, or because of passion, or to redress an injury, is beneath the brave man. In *The Magnetic Lady* Captain Ironside knows only *Fortitude*, which he calls valor for the public. Sir Diaphanous accuses him of having read Jonson's *The New Inn*. Sir Diaphanous, in his shirt for fear of having his doublet torn by a sword, avoids conflict with a seven-step discourse on valor, point seven of which is a "Christian valour," which could not deface the "divine image in a man."

The items in Sir Diaphanous' discussion have been for the most part a reworking of the discourse of Lovel in *The Magnetic Lady*. He arrives, if one places the two discourses side by side, at the amazing position that the very same conduct that is valor in the brave man is sheer cowardice in the coward. One is left to guess whether the exposition of Sir Diaphanous represents a later and wider view of the subject of valor, or is a realistic Jonson of 1632 poking fun at an apparently romantic Jonson of 1629.

Like the Poetaster who truly believes himself to be a poet, or the Courtling who thinks himself to be a true courtier because he has a new suit, the Wise Fool truly believes himself to be what he is not. He expects admiration for the soundness of his judgments and the timeliness of his decisions. Needless to say, the line of demarcation between him and his two neighbors among the Would-Be Men cannot be closely drawn. But presenting him in an essay like this is extremely difficult, for it is only out of the mass of his own utterances that his portrait emerges.

One does not *like* many of Jonson's characters: not the Choric figures, for their very massiveness is forbidding; not the Wits, except for Brainworm, for it is all too apparent that they know themselves to be witty; not the Brokers, unless possibly the rascally Face; not the Deities, for perfection does not much appeal to mortal man. The Mistaken Man we can like a little, for he shares some of our frailties, as does Justice Overdoo; Poetaster and Courtling have qualities that almost automatically repel us—sycophancy, greed, extreme vanity.

But one creation of Jonson's we can like—Bartholomew Cokes of *Bartholomew Fair*. For him the world is full of wonders and full of friends. Misfortunes cannot trouble him, nor criticism dampen his spirits. He wants to see his marriage license because he never saw one. Although he is in the presence of his bride-to-be, Grace Welborne, the sight of John Littlewit's wife elicits this: "a pret[t]y little soule, this same Mistris Littlewit! would I might marry her." Bartholomew must go to the Fair, his Fair, and his going is useful to Jonson in getting everybody else to the Fair. But the consequences will be alarming. They are predicted by Bartholomew's testy Governor, Humphrey Waspe: "If he goe to the *Fayre*, he will buy of euery thing, to a Baby there; and household-stuffe for that too. If a legge or an arme on him did not grow on, hee would lose it i' the presse. Pray heauen I bring him off with one stone! And then he is such a Rauener after fruite! you will not beleeue what a coyle I had, t'other day, to compound a businesse between a *Katerne*-peare-woman, and him, about snatching! 'tis intolerable, Gentlemen" (I.v.113–20).

Waspe's dire predictions do all come to pass. As refreshments for his forthcoming wedding celebration, Bartholomew buys all Joan Trash's rotten gingerbread; and for favors for the guests at those festivities, he buys all Leatherhead's baubles, drums, soldiers, and hobby horses, but he leaves them with the sellers. He loses one purse in his rapt attention to Justice Overdoo's oration against tobacco; the second he loses while listening to Nightingale's ballad warning the audience against cutpurses; he loses hat, cloak, sword in trying to steal pears from the Costermonger's overturned stall.

But at the Puppet Play, Bartholomew is at the very peak of his happiness. The tiny players lying in their basket fascinate him: "which is your *Burbage* now ... your best *Actor*. Your *Field*?" There is even a sort of wisdom in his observations about them: "Well, they are a ciuill company, I like 'hem for that; they offer not to fleere, nor geere, nor breake iests, as the great *Players* doe: And then, there goes not so much charge to the feasting of 'hem, or making 'hem drunke, as to the other, by reason of their little-nesse. Doe they vse to play perfect? Are they neuer fluster'd?" (V.iii.96–101).

As the puppet play takes its bawdy—many critics say obscene—way with Marlowe's revered poem, *Hero and Leander*, Cokes almost becomes one of the actors: he interprets hard passages for the audience, and he applauds well-directed blows or epithets. We feel only disappointment when we cannot accept his invitation in the last line of the play—"yes, and bring the *Actors* along, wee'll ha' the rest o' the *Play* at home."

Bartholomew is really of very little use to Jonson, except as spectacle: he helps to assemble all the visitors at the Fair; he neatly manages the cutting-off of Humphrey Waspe—"you ha' beene i' the Stocks, I heare." He perhaps assists in bringing Justice Overdoo out of the disguise of Arthur of Bradley, so that there will be no further search for enormities. There is in him not a touch of avarice, of hypocrisy. He is, literally, a humour personified, and we are only thankful that he never learns that he is not wise, and that he did not become husband to the formidable Grace Welborne.

Though we can share in Bartholomew's joy in the wonders of the Fair, we can take little pleasure in the sinister prodigies that surround Sir Politic Would-be of *Volpone*. A few excerpts from his first conversation with Peregrine, one of Jonson's Wits, will establish Sir Politic's massive folly:

> POL. My name is POLITIQVE WOVLD-BEE. PER. O,
>   that speaks him.
> A Knight, Sir? POL. A poore knight, sir. PER.
>   Your lady

Lies here, in *Venice*, for intelligence
Of tyres, and fashions, and behauiour,
Among the curtizans? the fine lady WOVLD-BEE?
   POL. Yes, sir, the spider, and the bee, oft
   times,
Suck from one flowre. PER. Good sir POLITIQVE!
I cry you mercie; I haue heard much of you:
'Tis true, sir, of your rauen. POL. On your
   knowledge?
   PER. Yes, and your lyons whelping, in the
   Tower.
   POL. Another whelpe! PER. Another, sir.
   POL. Now, heauen!
What prodigies be these? The fires at *Berwike*!
And the new starre! these things concurring,
   strange!
And full of omen! Saw you those meteors?
   PER. I did, sir. POL. Fearefull! Pray you
   sir, confirme me,
Were there three porcpisces seene, aboue the bridge,
As they giue out? PER. Sixe, and a sturgeon, sir.

. . . .
There was a whale discouer'd, in the riuer,
As high as *Woolwich*, that had waited there
(Few know how manie mon'ths) for the subuersion
Of the *Stode*-Fleet. POL. Is't possible? Beleeue
   it,
'Twas either sent from *Spaine*, or the *Arch-dukes*!
SPINOLA'S whale, vpon my life, my credit!
Will they not leaue these proiects?

. . . .
       [PER.] He that should write
But such a fellow, should be thought to faine
Extremely, if not maliciously.
               (II.i.25–41, 46–52, 58–60)

Sir Politic understands what constitutes wisdom in a statesman—
"to know the houre when you must eat your melons, and your
figges." He is perhaps a little greedy, for he expects to become
wealthy by serving the state of Venice with red herrings from
Rotterdam. He will secure the safety of the state by allowing only

known patriots to possess tinder boxes. He will prevent importation of the plague by foreign ships by interposing onions cut in half, "which doth naturally attract th'infection." It is wisdom for a man who deals with matters of state to keep a diary:

> A rat had gnawne my spurre-lethers; notwithstanding,
> I put on new, and did goe forth: but, first,
> I threw three beanes ouer the threshold. *Item,*
> I went, and bought two tooth-pickes, whereof one
> I burst, immediatly, in a discourse
> With a *dutch* merchant, 'bout *ragion del stato.*
> From him I went, and payd a *moccinigo,*
> For peecing my silke stockings; by the way,
> I cheapen'd sprats: and at S$^{t.}$ MARKES, I vrin'd.
>   (IV.i.136–44)

The cutting-off of Sir Politic is like all his other affairs, entirely outside the action of *Volpone.* Peregrine, in disguise as a merchant, tells Sir Politic that the Peregrine to whom Sir Politic had boasted of his wisdom had betrayed him to the Senate, reporting that he had "a plot to sell the state of *Venice*, to the *Turke.*" Three "Mercatori," prepared by Peregrine, appear to make an arrest. But the wise Sir Politic has prepared himself for such an emergency: "Mary, it is, sir, of a tortoyse-shell, / Fitted, for these extremities: 'pray you sir, helpe me. / Here, I' haue a place, sir, to put backe my leggs, / (Please you to lay it on, sir) with this cap, / And my blacke gloues, I'le lye, sir, like a tortoyse, / Till they are gone" (V.iv.54–59). As an additional precaution, he has his wife's women burn all his papers. Sir Politic will "to sea," "Creeping, with house, on backe: and thinke it well, / To shrinke my poore head, in my politique shell" (ll. 88–89).

One other Wise Fool is studied at length by Jonson, Fabian Fitzdottrell of *The Devil Is an Asse.* He is made the focus of all lines of action in the play, for he combines, massively, two of the great vices, folly and greed. His punishment is in terms of his vices, for at the end of the play he is his wife's ward, all the property being in her name, and he believes himself to be a cuckold, which he is not. (For a more complete discussion of Fitz-dottrell, see the article in Chapter IV, "The Cloaks of *The Devil is an Asse*.")

There are also a few minor manifestations of the breed of Wise Fool. Master Stephen of *Every Man in His Humour* knows precisely how to become a gentleman: ". . . an'a man haue not skill in the hawking, and hunting-languages now a dayes, I'll not giue a rush for him. They are more studied then the *Greeke*, or the *Latine*. He is for no gallants companie without 'hem" (I.i.41–44). Madam Moria of *Cynthia's Revels* is almost an allegorical representation of folly. Cupid's assessment of her is sound: "One that is not now to be perswaded of her wit, shee will thinke her selfe wise against all the iudgements that come. A lady made all of voice, and aire, talkes any thing of any thing" (II.iv.12–15). Jonson's next member of this unfortunate brotherhood is Albius of *Poetaster*. He can quickly manifest himself in his own words: "Hee that would haue fine ghests, let him haue a fine wife; he that would haue a fine wife, let him come to me" (II.ii.211–13). He is not, however, important enough for Jonson to assign him any fate in the play—even cuckoldry.

The last of this group of minor Wise Fools is Sir Amorous La Foole of *Epicoene*. The credentials of Sir Amorous for membership in the fraternity are impeccable: "They all come out of our house, the LA-FOOLES o' the north, the LA-FOOLES of the west, the LA-FOOLES of the east, and south—we are as ancient a family, as any is in *Europe*—but I my selfe am descended lineally of the *french* LA-FOOLES—and, wee doe beare for our coate *Yellow*, or *Or*, checker'd *Azure*, and *Gules*, and some three or foure colours more, which is a very noted coate, and has, some-times, beene solemnely worne by diuers nobilitie of our house" (I.iv.37–45). He has no greed, but is hypocritical, for he would be thought a man. He has a slight humour, of which Jonson makes good use, the making of feasts. His punishment is severe, for the full extent of his *epicoene* quality is displayed.

RECAPITULATION

The essential thesis of this study can be stated very simply in terms of three. There are three basic groups of characters—the Choric, the Broker, the Humourous. The first, the Choric, speaks much of Jonson's thought and executes his decrees. Those of the second group, the Brokers, not in themselves objects of Jonson's attack, are merely manipulators seeking to prey on those of the Humourous Group; and as such are immensely useful to Jonson in arranging a full display of vices. It is in the third group, the Humourous, that the vices are to be castigated.

With this third group a second set of three manifests itself, for the members of the group fall into three broad categories, largely in terms of knowledge of self. One member of the Humourous Group merely labors under some misapprehension about his personal circumstances or the intentions of his associates. He has been labeled the Mistaken Man. A second member of the Humourous Group knows what he *is*, but devotes his efforts to sustaining an image of that which he knows himself *not to be*. Him we have called the Hypocritical Man. A third member believes himself to be that which he is not, and by that misapprehension all his actions are governed. He is the Would-Be Man, after Sir Politic of *Volpone*.

The third set of three is more universalized, in that it comprehends what to Jonson are the basic vices: greed, hypocrisy, and what we have earlier called "foolness." Though one or the other may appear to a small degree in a member of the Choric Group, or to a much greater extent in one of the Brokers, the extended study of them, and the cure or punishment of them, is effected almost altogether with reference to members of the Humourous Group.

We can, at this point, observe still another set of three. The basic vices—greed, hypocrisy, and folly—are displayed, and castigated, immediately, in certain of the *personae* of the play, but

Jonson makes it abundantly clear, principally through his formal Choruses, that they are also in the audience. And, if they are in the audience, obviously they are also in mankind at large, where they may be cured, as in this play, or should be castigated, as in that.

But, in this assemblage of sets of three, what of the humours— as in "Comedy of Humours"? Morose's humour is an almost pathological aversion to noise. It differs in degree, but not in kind, from a trait which possesses most of us when we have passed the age of consent. But this quality, in its excess, does lead Morose into conduct which is inordinately vindictive, and into other conduct which is the height of folly. But it is this secondary conduct, rather than the mere presence of the humourous trait, which is the object of Jonson's concern. The humour is a technique useful in shaping characterization and in furnishing probability for action; it is a means, not an end.

Morose was listed earlier among that portion of the Humourous Group which we have called the Mistaken Man. His compeers in that group are generally men of substance, of standing in the community, of professional competence. Such a man is Kitely of *Every Man in His Humour*. Perhaps his competence is momentarily lessened by the fact that he fears he may be, or may become, a cuckold. As a humour, this fear is useful to Jonson in getting on with the action. But in Kitely there is no greed, no hypocrisy, no innate foolishness. His humour has served its purpose, we cure it, and Kitely is his own man again, as are most of his compeers among the Mistaken men.

In the second Humourous Group, the Hypocritical Man, the humour is again not the principal object of attack. The hypocrisy itself is the primary target for Jonson. But such a man is by his very nature self-serving and usually greedy. He is in a sense two men— the one he knows himself to be and the one of the facade that he presents. He is a fool to the extent that he believes the facade may prevail indefinitely. He remains, therefore, basically the same, whether presented as soldier, Puritan, liberated woman, courtier, or lawyer.

We may say, if we wish, that Captain Tucca's humour is the presentation of the facade of "tall man," a commander in Caesar's wars. But it must be remembered that a humour is a "peculiar quality" that "doth draw all his affects, his spirits, and his powers . . . to runne one way." What makes the actions of a Tucca all run one way is *greed*—for money, for influence, for recognition. So universal a quality is hardly what Jonson had in mind as a humour. Perhaps we should look further.

In addition to greed, a quality that many of these Hypocritical men have in common is facility in the use of language. This is the chief vehicle by which the facade is maintained and the necessary persuasion is accomplished. Captain Tucca's sonorous epithets, Bobadil's heroic oaths, Captain Otter's Latinisms, Busy's rhetorical flourishes, Metaphor's similitudes, Lady Politic Would-be's interminable discourse—these are all methods of differentiation among characters, all devices useful to Jonson in forwarding what is essentially the poet's action. While these skills in, or perhaps misuses of, language have satirical and spectacular value, they are not the primary object of Jonson's didactic efforts. Again they are a means, not an end.

The thrust of this paper has been toward the isolation of types of characters, in terms of personal qualities and functions in a play. No effort has thus far been made to observe the effect on a particular play of the presence, or absence, or predominance, or abundance, of representatives of the various groups. The final observations in the essay will be based on a glance at the use of the members of the various categories in some of Jonson's masterpieces, and in some of his failures.

The presence of a play in a current anthology is not perhaps an absolute mark of excellence, but for present purposes it is a satisfactory criterion. The most frequently offered plays are *Volpone* and *The Alchemist*, while *Every Man in His Humour* and *Epicoene* are much less popular representatives of Jonson's work. But *Bartholomew Fair* is superior to either of the latter, and is perhaps even on a par with *Volpone* and *The Alchemist*. In these three plays, then, we might examine the presence or absence, the number, and the variety of our comic personages.

If the three plays nominated above are Jonson's best—which are his worst? Anthologists cannot help us. In fact, the Herford and Simpson work and an elusive Everyman edition in two volumes, are perhaps the only modern printings where the entire list of plays may be found. The only alternative, aside from subjective likes and dislikes, is an examination of the reception of Jonson's plays by Jonson's audience. That criterion, of course, does not necessarily coincide with Jonson's own opinion of his work.

Cynthia's Revels did not secure to Jonson the favor of the Queen, though it is obviously a bid for her attention. Perhaps the play was not well received by its audience either, for Jonson has his "Epilogue" say this:

> Let's see; to lay the blame
> Vpon the Childrens action, that were lame.
> To craue your fauour, with a begging knee,
> Were to distrust the writers facultie.
> To promise better at the next we bring,
> Prorogues disgrace, commends not any thing.
> Stifly to stand on this, and proudly approue
> The play, might taxe the maker of *selfe-Loue.*
> I'le onely speake, what I haue heard him say;
> *By (—) 'tis good, and if you lik't, you may.*
>   (ll. 11–20)

Poetaster suffered a similar fate, though perhaps for different reasons. In the "apologeticall Dialogue," *"which was only once spoken vpon the stage,"* Jonson gives us his reason for the play's unpopularity: "...they say you tax'd / The Law, and Lawyers; Captaines; and the Players / By their particular names" (ll. 81–83). Jonson of course denies the allegation, but the very accusation drives him to a momentous decision:

> And, since the *Comick* Mvse
> Hath prou'd so ominous to me, I will trie
> If *Tragoedie* haue a more kind aspect.
> Her fauours in my next I will pursue,

Where, if I proue the pleasure but of one,
So he iudicious be; He shall b' alone
A Theatre vnto me.

(ll. 222–28)

The two plays just mentioned were very early work. A third that did not receive public acclaim is *The New Inn*, a very late play (1629). One suspects Jonson's hand in the editorializing on the title page of the Quarto of 1631:

> As it was neuer acted, but most
> negligently play'd, by some,
> the Kings Seruants.
> And more squeamishly beheld, and censu-
> red by others, the Kings Subiects.[19]

To argue that the use and the ordering of the basic comic characters are causes of excellence, or the lack thereof, in Jonson's plays would be inadvisable. But it can be argued that as the personality of Jonson, as reflected in his characters, becomes less obtrusive, the plays become, if not greater works of art, at least more acceptable by the popular and the courtly audience. As the didacticism becomes less overt, it becomes more powerful.

The table presented on the following page shows the distribution in the six plays designated roughly as most, and as least, successful of the various types of characters examined in the course of this study. Minor characters are not represented, and in some cases another classification might fit a character equally well.

It has been pointed out earlier that Jonson fancied himself as soldier, scholar, critic, and poet. These specific attainments are displayed, or noted, in Crites of *Cynthia's Revels* and Horace of *Poetaster*, who have earlier been given the designation of Chorus. Their massive presence, in the elucidation of follies and the management of the fates of their companions on the stage, is not highly entertaining to an audience. When Jonson entrusts some of their commentary and manipulation of fates to the Wits, the action is livelier, the commentary more pithy. But when the presence of a

[19] Reproduced in *Ben Jonson*, VI, 395.

DISTRIBUTION OF THE BASIC COMIC CHARACTERS IN SIX OF JONSON'S PLAYS

	The Choric Group			The Broker Group		The Humourous Group		
	Chorus	Wit	Deity	Broker	Plyant Woman	Mistaken Man	Hypocritical Man	Would-Be Man
Volpone (1606)		[Mosca]		Volpone Mosca	Celia		Voltore Corbaccio Corvino Lady Would-be	Sir Politic
The Alchemist (1610)	Lovewit(?)	[Face]		Face Subtle Dol	Dame Plyant	Kastril	Tribulation Ananias	Surly Mammon Dapper Drugger
Bartholomew Fair (1614)		Win-wife Quarlous		The ten Fair-Folk	Mistress Littlewit Mistress Overdoo	Justice Overdoo	Busy Dame Purecraft	Littlewit Cokes
Cynthia's Revels (1600)	Crites	[Cupid] [Mercury]	Cynthia Cupid Mercury					The eight "Deformities" Male and Female
Poetaster (1601)	Horace	Ovid Tibullus Gallus	Caesar Virgil (?)				Tucca	Crispinus Albius Chloe Lupus Demetrius
The New Inn (1629)	Host(?)	Beaufort Latimer Lovel Prudence		Fly			Sir Glorious	

MOST SUCCESSFUL *(Volpone, The Alchemist, Bartholomew Fair)*

LEAST SUCCESSFUL *(Cynthia's Revels, Poetaster, The New Inn)*

Deity is required to sanction the imposition of fates, one fears that the real purpose of the Deity may be to place the final accolade on a Crites, or a Horace, or a Jonson. One is driven to the conclusion that the massive presence of members of the Choric Group reduces the dramatic effectiveness of Jonson's work.

A glance at the table above is enough to show a small part, at least, of the rise of Jonson's dramatic powers. The heart of that rise lies in the decrease in importance of the Choric Group, the employment of a Broker Group, and the increase in number and diversity of the members of the Humourous Group.

In the mature plays Jonson no longer needs the Wits as winders-up. Such a Broker as Mosca can supply enough winding-up, and the self-revelation of a Busy is far more powerful satiric commentary than even a Wellbred or a Truewit can provide. A Deity is re-quired to lend authority to the punishments meted out by a Horace, but a mature Jonson can make the punishments not only fit, but grow out of, the crimes.

The unfortunate objects of attention by members of the Choric Group or Broker Group assume a much greater role in the mature plays. Occasionally one of them can learn something, as does Justice Overdoo, and so escape punishment. Not so fortunate is the Hypo-critical Man, for his exposure and cutting-off are almost always effected. With Jonson's maturing also comes a wider range of hypocrites—cowardly man-of-war, liberated woman, Puritan, pro-fessional man.

Occasionally a member of Jonson's third group of Humourous victims can escape punishment, provided there is no greed in him. Bartholomew Cokes is an example of such a man. But if he profanes the sacred calling of the poet, his fate can be unhappy indeed. Hardly less severe is his fate if he, in the posture of a courtier, serves, not the state, but himself.

Jonson reaches his highest achievement when he ceases to make the humours themselves an object of attack and uses them instead as a means of differentiation among representatives of much more basic vices. When, in addition to this lesson, he has also learned to omit the massive person Jonson from his *dramatis personae*, and let the poet Jonson construct magnificent satirical actions, he attains perhaps the height of excellence in comedy of the realistic sort. That he falls short of the attainment of Shakespeare is partly due to the fact that while Shakespeare was looking at the noble and the idealistic in man, Jonson was too often looking at the ignoble and the base.

II.

BEN JONSON
IN BEN JONSON'S PLAYS

Ben Jonson was never able to leave himself altogether out of his plays, though, after the early comedies, he speaks largely in the prefatory matter, or with the voices of many of his *dramatis personae.* Beginning with *Every Man in His Humour,* however, there is in the early comedies a single character of majestic proportions, who is the principal dispenser of rewards and punishments, and the chief repository of right opinion. He is scholar, soldier, poet, critic, censor of morals and manners. One has only to leaf through the pages of *Timber,* or *Conversations with Drummond,* or of the introductory matter to the plays, to see that Jonson strongly felt himself to be indeed scholar, soldier, poet, critic, censor of morals and manners.

It is my purpose in this paper to examine the careers of these characters who reflect the personality of Jonson himself in the plays *Every Man in His Humour, Every Man out of His Humour, Cynthia's Revels* and *Poetaster.*[1] I wish to show how each does

---

[1] Since *Every Man in His Humour* is not the earliest of Jonson's known plays, perhaps *A Tale of a Tub* and *The Case Is Altered* should be mentioned. *A Tale of a Tub* may have existed in some form at a very early date, but in all likelihood the one thing in which Ben speaks directly for himself is the attack on Inigo Jones (Herford and Simpson, III, 77–92, *passim*). This is clearly an interpolation, probably of a later date in his career. Similarly, in *The Case Is Altered,* the attack on Anthony Munday as Antonio Balladino (Herford and Simpson, III, 106–107), and the attack on pseudo-critics dragged in by Valentine (Herford and Simpson, III, 136–37), are probably interpolations made some little time after original composition. Perhaps anticipatory of the later exploits of Doctor Clement and his successors, however, is the Olympian ratification of fates by Maximilian, for a total of nine characters:

> Max. Well, I will now sweare the case is alterd. Lady fare you

manifest the qualities on which Jonson prided himself; how each is useful to Jonson in the management of the action; and how each has major choric function as the chief custodian of right opinion, though he may not be a convenient vehicle for the expression of the truly comic.

That these characters have some kinship with Ben himself is suggested by his remark to Drummond that "he had many quarrells with Marston beat him and took his Pistol from him, wrote his Poetaster on him."[2] That the idea of having himself as a character in one of his own plays is not unacceptable to him is suggested by his further word to Drummond that "he heth a Pastorall jntitled the May Lord, his own name is Alkin Ethra." Whether or not the *May Lord* and *The Sad Shepherd* are the same, it is worth noting that in the latter play there is a character "Alkin," the "Sage."[3]

Jonson's own Captain Tucca, borrowed for *Satiromastix* by Dekker, in the following passage makes a useful identification:

> No you staru'd rascal, thou't bite off mine eares then, you must haue three or foure suites of names, when like a lowsie Pediculous vermin th'ast but one suit to thy backe: you must be call'd *Asper*, and *Criticus*, and *Horace*, thy tytle's longer a reading then the Stile a the big Turkes: *Asper, Criticus, Quintus, Horatius, Flaccus*.[4]

---

well, I will subdue my affections. Maddam (as for you) you are a profest virgin, and I will be silent. My honorable Lord *Ferneze*, it shall become you at this time not be frugall, but bounteous, and open handed, your fortune hath been so to you. Lord *Chamount*, you are now no stranger, you must be welcome, you haue a faire, amiable and splendi[dio]us Lady: but signior *Paulo*, signior *Camillo*, I know you valiant; be louing. Lady I must be better knowne to you. Signiors for you, I passe you not: though I let you passe; for in truth I passe not of you. Louers to your nuptials, Lordings to your dances. March faire al, for a faire March, is worth a kings ransome.

(Herford and Simpson, III, 189, 190, 55–67)

[2] C. H. Herford and Percy Simpson, editors, *Ben Jonson* (Oxford: Clarendon Press, 1925), I, 140. This edition will be the source of all passages taken from *Every Man in His Humour*. The text quoted will be that of the Quarto of 1601.

[3] *Ibid.*, VII, 7.

[4] *The Dramatic Works of Thomas Dekker*, ed. Fredson Bowers (Cambridge: Cambridge University Press, 1953), I, 325.

Dekker himself, in his *To the World,* prefixed to *Satiromastix,* in a most thorny piece of prose, denies the presence of Jonson in *Every Man in His Humour:*

> *I meete one, and he runnes full Butt at me with his Satires hornes, for that in vntrussing* Horace, *I did onely whip his fortunes, and condition of life, where the more noble* Reprehension *had bin of his* mindes Deformitie, *whose greatnes* if his Criticall Lynx *had with as narrow eyes, obseru'd in himselfe, as it did little spots vpon others: without all disputation,* Horace *would not haue left* Horace *out of* Euery man in's Hvmour.[5]

Dekker is correct, of course, in assuming that Jonson did not make "His mindes Deformitie" an object of his attack in *Every Man in His Humour.* It is my contention, however, that there is in the play a character of the Asper-Criticus-Horace type, a dispenser of justice and a custodian of right opinion, Doctor Clement. It is the careers of Clement, Asper, of *Every Man out of His Humour,* Criticus, of *Cynthia's Revels,* and Horace, of *Poetaster,* that I wish to trace.[6]

---

[5] *Ibid.,* 309.

[6] It is not my intention to say that Clement, Asper, Criticus, Horace are intended literally to represent Jonson himself, except perhaps in the case of Horace. The opinions of students of Jonson's work are not markedly at variance with my own. R. A. Small, in *The Stage-Quarrel Between Ben Jonson and the So-Called Poetasters* (Breslau: Verlag von H. & H. Marcus, 1899), 27-28, says, "In Every Man out of his Humour, Cynthia's Revels, and the Poetaster, Jonson has left us a three-fold presentation of himself under the names of Asper, Crites (called Criticus in the quarto edition of Cynthia's Revels and in Dekker's Satiromastix), and Horace. There is no question that all three were meant for him." Herford and Simpson (I, 347) say that Asper and Crites "speak Jonson's mind if they do not reflect his person"; that Horace is "less like Jonson than Asper and Crites" (I, 422); they say also, however, that Jonson did not represent himself in *Every Man in His Humour.* E. K. Chambers, in *Elizabethan Stage* (Oxford, 1923), III, 364, 365, doubts that Jonson would have praised himself as highly as he praises Criticus and states that Horace is Jonson himself. Ralph W. Berringer, in "Jonson's *Cynthia's Revels* and the War of the Theaters" (*PQ,* XII, 1-22) says "that, in *Satiromastix,* a good part of Dekker's satire is devoted to pointing out and mocking this early habit of Jonson's of setting up a character annoyingly like himself as a quasi-hero.... The emphasis... is upon the identity of Horace, the idealized self-portrait of Jonson, and Criticus" (11). Many other statements could be cited, but their tenor would be essentially that of those I have quoted.

The first major appearance, therefore, of what I shall call the Horace-character as spokesman for, and with many of the characteristics of, Ben himself occurs in the first quarto of *Every Man in His Humour*. The Doctor Clement of the quarto is altogether a more distinguished man than Justice Clement of the folio of 1616. He is introduced by this exchange:

> *Lo. iu.* Doctor *Clement*, what's he? I haue heard much speech of him.
> *Pros.* Why, doest thou not know him? he is the *Gonfaloniere* of the state here, an excellent rare ciuilian, and a great scholler, but the onely mad merry olde fellow in Europe: I shewed him you the other day.
> *Lo. iu.* Oh I remember him now; Good faith, and he hath a very strange presence me thinkes, it shewes as if he stoode out of the ranke from other men. I haue heard many of his iests in Padua: they say he will commit a man for taking the wall of his horse.
> *Pros.* I or wearing his cloake of one shoulder, or anything indeede, if it come in the way of his humor.
>
> (III.ii.45–57)

Two elements of some interest in this description do not appear in the corresponding passage in the folio, the titles of "Doctor" and "Gonfaloniere."

On almost all occasions when he is addressed in the play, Clement is "Master Doctor." One is reminded of the "Doctor" who points out the lessons of *Everyman*; of Faustus, with his almost boundless knowledge; of the doctors in *Friar Bacon and Friar Bungay*; of the Doctors Bellario and "Balthazar" of *The Merchant of Venice*.

Not only, however, is the Doctor a learned man, a scholar, but he is also "the *Gonfaloniere* of the state here." This is indeed an exalted title, with connotations at once religious, civil, and military: "The head of the Signoria in the Florentine republic"; "the champion of the Church in its quarrels with the Emperor."[7]

In addition to the qualities noted, Doctor Clement is a poet in his own right, offering to enter into competition with Matheo in

---

[7] Alfred Hoore, *An Italian Dictionary* (Cambridge: Cambridge University Press, 1925).

verses "in honor of the Gods," or, failing that "height of stile," "a steppe or two lower then." He is a critic also, for he concurs in Lorenzo junior's impassioned defense of poetry, "Blessed aeternall, and most true deuine." But, while agreeing that "Nothing can more adorne humanitie," he also notes that

> election is now gouernd altogether by the influence of humor, which insteed of those holy flames that should direct and light the soule to eternitie, hurles foorth nothing but smooke and congested vapours, that stifle her vp, & bereaue her of al sight & motion.
>
> (V.iii.344–48)

Finally Doctor Clement, though a most severe judge of mistaken humour in poet or gull, has his own humour: he dons his armor to greet a "soldier"; he competes with a "poet" in the making of verses "extempore"; and in honor of the wit of Musco, he clothes that rascal in his own robes for the evening's mirth. He is not, however, like most of his associates in the play a humours character. His "affects, his spirits, and his powers" do not all "runne one way." His humour is little more than a whim of secondary importance in the full life of the man pictured in the passage quoted.

Doctor Clement's usefulness to the playwright in *Every Man in His Humour* is enormous in the conduct of the plot; his pronouncements terminate, with reward, or punishment, or reconciliation, all lines of action. His value is equally great in the choric function, the stating of right opinion, the establishing of significance in the light of normal human conduct. Though the follies of a Stephano, a Bobadillo or a Matheo manifest themselves abundantly, Jonson deliberately uses Doctor Clement at the end of the play to summarize and evaluate these follies. The lack of foundation of the jealous humours of Cob and Tib, of Thorello and Biancha, is made manifest only through the skillful questioning of Doctor Clement. It is through his careful analysis that Matheo's plagiarism is exposed; that the senior Lorenzo's contempt for poetry is overcome; that Lorenzo junior's eulogies are tempered.

A far more important task than the establishing of right opinion is the utterance of *the truly comic, the flash of insight which sets in perspective many elements of character, of circumstance, of wit and ignorance in conflict.* This high privilege is accorded to several of the characters in *Every Man in His Humour,* particularly Lorenzo junior, Guilliano and Musco. Yet, again, the summary statements are reserved for Doctor Clement. Having donned his armor to receive the "soldier" Bobadillo, when he learns of Bobadillo's cowardice, he hits the true comic note with "here take my armour quickly, twill make him swoone I feare." Or, when he orders the burning of Matheo's stolen "Conceit," he can achieve the choric comment without either invective or moralizing: "Conceite, fetch me a couple of torches, sirha, I may see the conceite: quickly! its very darke!"

In *Every Man out of His Humour* there is a far more complex manifestation of these characteristics of Jonson himself, reaching full definition only in the union of Asper and Macilente. The formal introduction of Asper, the Presenter, though well known, should perhaps be repeated:

> *He is of an ingenuous and free spirit, eager and constant in reproofe, without feare controuling the worlds abuses; One, whome no seruile hope of Gaine, or frostie apprehension of Daunger, can make to be a* Parasite, *either to* Time, Place, *or* Opinion.
>
> (A3^r.2–5)[8]

This is a man of whom it might be said, as of Doctor Clement, "it shews as if he stoode out of the ranke from other men."

It is this Asper who knows what the humours are:

> As when some one peculiar qualitie
> Doth so possesse a man, that it doth draw
> All his affects, his spirits, and his powers
> In their confluctions all to runne one way,
> This may be truly said to be a Humor.
>
> (B2^v.114–18)

[8] The text used for *Every Man out of His Humour* is that of the Quarto of 1600 as reproduced in The Malone Society Reprints, (R. P. Wilson and W. W. Greg, eds. *Every Man out of His Humour,* Oxford University Press, 1920). This and the passages immediately following are from the preliminary matter.

It is he who has written the play with two sorts of spectators in mind. The first are those of the "Apish, or Phantasticke straine," whom he would "giue them pils to purge." The other is the

> attentive auditors,
> Such as will joine their profit with their pleasure,
> And come to feed their vnderstanding parts.
> (B4ʳ.215–17)

Then, says Asper:

> Ile melt my braine into invention,
> Coine new conceits, and hang my richest words
> As polisht jewels in their bounteous eares.
> (B4ʳ.220–22)

By way of implementing this promise Asper will "goe To turn Actor, and a Humorist." The actor he becomes is Macilente, soldier, scholar, traveller, who "has oile and Fire in his pen." While Macilente does not have formally assigned to him the official judicial position of a Doctor Clement, it is he who metes out judgments and punishments, as his successors Criticus and Horace will do.

Macilente then is Asper—with a humour—envy. It is, however, an envy not altogether blame-worthy, for it is directed only toward those things which are truly desirable and are possessed unworthily by the objects of envy. He is, however, as Doctor Clement was not, a full-fledged humours character, for his envy "doth draw All his affects, his spirits, and his powers In their confluctions, all to runne one way." The movement of *Every Man out of His Humour* is essentially the purgation of the humour of Macilente by the process of removing the meat it feeds on. Through his manipulations are purged successively the humours of Sir Puntarvolo, Saviolina, Shift and Sogliardo, Buffone, Fungoso, Deliro and Fallace. Whether Fastidius Briske is cured is doubtful, but he is certainly punished. With the dismissal of Fastidius, Macilente feels a change:

> Now is my soule at peace,
> I am as emptie of all Envie now,
> As they of Merit to be envied at,

My Humour (like a flame) no longer lasts
Than it hath stuffe to feed it, and their vertue,
Being now rak't vp in embers of their Follie,
Affords no ampler Subject to my Spirit;
I am so farre from malicing their states,
That I begin to pittie 'hem.

(R2^r.4333–4341)

His envy purged, Macilente is once more Asper:

Wel, Gentlemē, I should haue gone in, and return'd
to you as I was *Asper* at the first: but (by reason the Shift would
haue been somewhat long, and we are loth to draw your Patience
any farder) wee'le intreat you to imagine it.

(R4^r.4463–4467) [9]

In *Every Man out of His Humour* the more serious choric functions have, to some extent, been performed *a priori* by Asper in
introductory matter. But in the play itself, while some invective is
entrusted to Carlo Buffone, and some technical explanations to
Mitis and Cordatus as "Grex," it is to Macilente that the definition
and evaluation of the humour—the folly—is given. His language is
that of satire, and frequently it becomes direct invective. Sogliardo
is the "Mushrompe" gentleman, a "dustie Turfe," a "clod"; Sordido
is "a pretious filthy damned rogue / That fats himselfe with expectation / Of rotten weather, and vnseason'd howers"; Fungoso
is a "painted Iay with such a deale of outside"; to Deliro he can
wish "Now Horne vpon Horne pursue thee, thou blind egregious
Dotard."

Macilente can poison Sir Puntarvolo's dog; he can hold the con-
stable at bay while Sir Puntarvolo seals up Buffone's beard with
wax; he can mock Fastidius Briske imprisoned for the "riot" which
he himself fashioned; he can say to Fallace in the presence of her
disillusioned husband Deliro "gi' him not the head, though you
gi' him the horns."

---

[9] This passage is from the "*Catastrophe*," of the first playing, which "many
seem'd not to relish," since Elizabeth is represented as present in person, and
taking part in the cure of Macilente's envy. The substituted ending has a
similar passage beginning "and now with *Asper's* tongue (Though not his
shape)."

But it is only after he has been purged of his envy and has again become Asper that he can speak in a vein approaching the comic: after having begged the audience for a *"Plaudite,"* he says "why, you may (in time) make lean *Macilente* as fat as *Sir John Fallstaffe."*

The Criticus of *Cynthia's Revels* has most of the essential qualities of Doctor Clement and of Asper-Macilente. Though not a soldier, "For his valour, tis such, that he dares as little to offer an Iniury as receiue one." He is a "scholler," in the opinion of Amorphous "a triuiall fellow, too meane, too coarse for you to conuerse with." He "smels all Lamp-oyle," and he wears "a piece of *Serge,* or *Perpetuana*." As poet, in the opinion of Anaides "he does nothing but stab." Arete several times calls attention to his "invention"; the masque, which provides the resolution of all problems, and which has the approval of Cynthia herself, is his. As did Doctor Clement and Asper, he stands out above the rank of common men:

> A creature of a more perfect and diuine temper; One, in whom the *Humors* & *Elements* are peaceably met, without aemulation of Precedencie: he is neither to fantastickly *Melancholy*; too slowly *Phlegmatick,* too lightly *Sanguine,* or too rashly *Cholerick,* but in al, so composd and order'd; as it is cleare, Nature was about some full worke, she did more then make a man when she made him.
>
> (II.iii.D^{4v}–E$_1$^{r}) [10]

The words are those of Mercury himself. The purgation of the humour of envy which we saw in Asper-Macilente remains effective: in fact the balance of his nature is such that no humour can obtain a foothold.

The function of Criticus in *Cynthia's Revels* is in one sense less than that of Asper-Macilente. For Macilente almost without conscious intent achieves such an effect that he and the other characters are purged of their follies and returned to themselves. It is through him almost singlehanded, that the playwright's goals are

---

[10] All quotations are from the first quarto: *The Fountain of Self-Love. Or Cynthia's Revels.* Written by Ben: Jonson, For Walter Burre, 1601.

achieved. On the other hand, the ultimate achievement of Criticus is greater, for he achieves not a purgation, but a complete reversal of character in the courtiers in *Cynthia's Revels*. He has, also, the distinction of being the worthy instrument of Mercury, of Cynthia and of Arete, and of being the accepted suitor of Arete.

Though Jonson says in his Prologue that *Cynthia's Revels* has "*Words aboue Action: Matter, aboue wordes,*" there is an action of sorts. It is the announced assault by Cupid on the court of Cynthia, on the occasion of her revels; this action of Cupid is thwarted by Mercury, first by fostering the qualities of the Fountain of Self-Love, and then by his sponsorship of, and his conduct in, the masque at the end of the play. Criticus is the author of this masque. The suggestion that it be written comes from Cynthia, through Arete; it is Arete who insists that the performers be Hedon, Anaides, Amorphus, Asotus, the "male Deformities," and their female counterparts, Philautia, Phantaste, Moria, and Gelaia. It is to Mercury principally that Criticus prays that, as formerly in Mercury's service, his invention may thrive. The happy "invention," however, of having each of the victims of self-love play his opposite (*e. g.* Anaides, "*the* impudent" plays "good audactie") is his own; it is also his invention that Cupid plays his opposite, "Anteros," while Mercury plays only in his identity as a page.

Doctor Clement was a dispenser of justice by function of his office; Asper-Macilente dispensed not justice, but rather mercy, purgation, and he did it in an entirely unofficial capacity, and he was himself a subject of his own purgation. Criticus is also a dispenser of justice, but not by virtue of his own authority. The power is delegated by Cynthia to Arete, by Arete to Criticus. The cure of the "deformities" was effected by the mere fact that as a consequence of the masque Cynthia took note of them. The punishment, the singing of the Palinode while visiting the "*weeping crosse,*" and the visit to the "Well of Knowledge, *Helicon,*" is devised and imposed by Criticus.

Criticus shares the choric function along the way with Mercury, with Cupid, and with Arete, but it is chiefly to him that the formal indictment of folly is given. At the end of Act I, in a set speech of forty-four lines, Criticus though having particular reference to Asotus and Amorphus, in what is almost a choral ode, generalizes on the follies of the courtiers:

> O vanity,
> How are thy painted beauties doated on,
> By light, and emptie Ideots?
> . . . .
> "While fooles are pittied, they wax fat, and prowde.
> (C4ʳ–C4ᵛ.Dlʳ)

Again in the third scene of Act III, in a set piece, Criticus shrugs off the detractions of "poore pittious Gallants":

> So they be ill men,
> If they spake worse, twere better: for of such
> To be disprais'd, is the most perfect praise.
> . . . .
> Their Enuy's like an Arrow, shot vpright,
> That in the fall endangers their owne heads
> (Flᵛ.F2ʳ)

In the following scene (III.iv), with Arete, he further anathematizes the courtiers, men and women: Hedon, the "proud, and spangled Sir," "scarce can eate for registring himself"; Anaides, "some subtill *Proteus*, . . . One that dares / Doe deeds worthy the Hurdle, or the Wheele, / To be thought some body"; the ladies, "A sixth times worse Confusion then the Rest," "such *Cob-web* stuffe, / As would enforce the commonst sense abhorre / Th'*Arachnean* workers."

Examples might be multiplied, but the foregoing passages are sufficient to show that it is to Criticus that Jonson gives much of the function essential in all plays, of setting abnormal conduct against the normal, of pointing out the distinction between wise conduct and foolish. His task is made easy in this play because the follies are set up, not primarily as humours, but as allegory, and are set in contrast to the absolute perfections of Arete and Cynthia.

Cynthia's Revels has more of the truly comic than has *Every*

Man out of His Humour, but to Criticus himself is given little but satirical invective. Early in the play (I.iv) this exchange has something beyond the merely satirical:

> *Amo.* *Lucian* is absurde, he knew nothing: I will beleeue my owne Trauels, before all the *Lucians* of *Europe*; he doth feed you with fictions, and leasings.
> *Crit.* Indeed (I thinke) next a Traueller he do's prettily well.
> (I.iv.Cl^v)

And in those scenes of the Folio, which do not appear in the Quarto (V.i–v), (Criticus) takes part in the courtiers' games, assuming a role appropriate to that proposed by Mercury:

> Well, I haue a plot vpon these prizers, for which I must presently find out CRITES, and with his assistance, pursue it to a high straine of laughter, or MERCVRIE hath lost of his mettall.
> (IV.v.148–51) [11]

Envy was an evil that must be purged from Asper-Macilente; Criticus had none himself, and envy is not possible among the victims of the Fountain of Self Love. Envy, however, does play an important part in *Poetaster*, but it lies in the detractors of Horace, not in Horace. In fact he rebukes Caesar himself for imputing it to him:

> And for my Soule, it is as free, as *Caesars:*
> For, what I knowe is due, I'le giue to all.
> "He that detracts, or enuies vertuous Merit,
> "Is still the couetous, and the ignorant spirit.
> (V.i.K2^r) [12]

Horace has the other qualities that we have seen in his predecessors. While not specifically a soldier, his reputation is such as to change Captain Tucca's threats to fair greetings when Horace passes over the stage: "my good *Poet*; my *Prophet*; my Noble *Horace*." Even his "vntrusser" Crispinus concedes his valor:

---

[11] Herford and Simpson, *op. cit.*, IV, 130.
[12] All quotations are from the first quarto: *Poetaster or the Arraignment:* Composed, by Ben. Ionson. for M. L., 1602.

PYRG. I, but Master; take heed how you giue this out, *Horace* is a Man of the Sword.

CRISP. 'Tis true, introth: they say, hee's valiant.

(IV.vii.I2^r)

Horace is also a man of letters, as were his predecessors. Doctor Clement was an amateur of poetry; Asper-Macilente a satirist; Criticus is the author of the masque, a man of "invention." Horace, however, is one among many honored poets, second only to Virgil himself, honored of Mecoenas and Caesar. The appurtenances of the earlier scholars are not so observable in Horace, the smell of lamp oil, the leanness, the serge. He is, however, considered by Caesar worthy to analyze the spirit and learning of Virgil. Criticus of *Cynthia's Revels* is rather wistfully in search of friends at court and is frankly seeking for Cynthia's favor. Horace, on the other hand, is the object of the envy of Demetrius largely because of his associations:

> *Virg.* Demaund, what cause they had to maligne *Horace.*
>
> *Demet.* In troth, no great cause, not I; I must confesse: but that he kept better companie (for the most part) then I: and that better men lou'd him, then lou'd me: and that his writings thriu'd better then mine, and were better lik't & grac't: Nothing else.
>
> (V.iii.M2^v)

In fact Horace, sure of his friends, takes almost equal pride in the nature and number of his enemies:

> Enuie me still; so long as *Virgill* loues me.
>
> . . . .
>
> I would not wish but such as you should spight them.
>
> (V.iii.M2^v.M2^r)

Like his predecessors, too, is Horace in the authority he wields. Doctor Clement exercised it by virtue of his position; Asper-Macilente assumed moral, though not civic, authority; that of Horace is delegated by Caesar and Virgil. His authority extends, however, only to the Poestasters. Other judgments, against Captain Tucca, against Asinus Lupus, the earlier banishment of Ovid, are reserved to Caesar himself.

This analysis of the successive characterizations of the Horace-character shows a sort of evolution of two sorts: (1) through the humours, to a position of lofty balance, above the lesser men who are subject to them; (2) from a position of civic authority, through one of power as satirist and scholar, to one of intellectual authority as critic, prophet, poet.

Analogous to the evolution in personal traits are the shifts in functions of the Horace-character. We have already noted that the disposition of the fates of almost all the characters lay in the hands of Doctor Clement; that Macilente insofar as he invented the machinery of purgation of the humours, carried a similar responsibility. We have noted also that Criticus was not the instigator, nor the principal mover in the action of *Cynthia's Revels*, but was rather the agent through whom Mercury, Cynthia and Arete fended off the attack of Cupid. In *Poetaster* also he is an agent, but only for that portion of the action which involves the Poetasters themselves.

Though Jonson says that he wrote *Poetaster* on Marston, the play is far more than a personal attack on a personal enemy. It is, in fact, almost an apology for poetry, using like Sidney's *Apology*, the idea of right use and abuse. Many levels of analysis appear, from the blatant and self-seeking abuse of Tucca, Ovid Senior and Asinus Lupus to the near divine judgment of Virgil.

At the lowest level of those who, as "poets" abuse poetry, is Crispinus. While Caesar, Virgil, Mecoenas, Tibullus and Gallus all have epithets for Crispinus, the essential comment on this "Hydra of discourse" is reserved for Horace, in the pills which purge Crispinus of the "terrible, windy words." Demetrius, the "dresser of plays," is perhaps a trifle higher in the scale of "poets" than Crispinus, and the essential comment is again that of Horace:

> Rather, such speckled creatures, as thy selfe,
> Should be aschew'd and shund: such, as will bite
> And gnaw their absent Friends, not cure their Fame;
> Catch at the loosest Laughters, and affect
> To be thought Iesters; such, as can deuise
> Things neuer seene, or heard, t'impayre mens Names.
>   (V.iii.Ml^r)

Next in order is the group of courtier-poets, Gallus, Tibullus, Propertius, Ovid. All these have mistresses, but only Propertius and Ovid find the final purpose of poetry in service to their mistresses. Upon the death of Cynthia, Horace is the disapproving reporter of the news that Propertius has immured himself in the tomb with her. Ovid is banished by Caesar—"for thy violent wronge, / In soothing the declin'd Affections / Of my base daughter." Gallus, Tibullus and Ovid are scathingly rebuked by Caesar for their part in the "Heavenly Banquet," even though both Horace and Mecoenas intercede for them. Horace's comment on the "Heavenly Banquet" places it, however, in the proper perspective:

> innocent Mirth,
> And harmelesse pleasures, bred, of noble wit.
> > (IV.vii.I2^r)

Caesar himself reconsiders, and pardons Gallus and Tibullus, applauded by Mecoenas and Horace.

Though all these court-poets are to some extent proteges of Mecoenas, it is with Horace that Mecoenas, as patron, is most associated. There is in the quarto no considered statement of the nature of Horace's poetry. Yet to Horace himself is given the statement which measures his work:

> Enuie me still; so long as *Virgill* loues me,
> *Gallus*, *Tibullus*, and the best-best *Caesar*,
> My deare *Mecoenas*; while these, with many more
> (Whose names I wisely slip) shall think me worthy
> Their honour'd, and ador'd Society,
> And read, and loue, prooue, and applaud my *Poemes*;
> I would not wish but such as you should spight them.
> > (V.iii.M2^v–M3^r)

Seated at Caesar's right hand, "*Romes* Honour," Virgil, is clearly at the highest level of the poets in *Poetaster*. Before his arrival to occupy the seat of honor, there is a sort of critical seminar among Caesar, Mecoenas, Tibullus, Gallus and Horace. Horace as "the poorest, / And likeliest to enuye, or to detract," is invited to speak first. Horace, after rebuking Caesar for imputing envy to a "know-

ing spirit," is given the two principal speeches in commendation of
Virgil. The second of these, in response to Caesar's question "what
thinks, Materiall *Horace*, of his learning," is cleverly designed, not
only as right opinion of Virgil, but indirectly of Horace:

> His Learning labours not the Schoole-like *Glosse*,
> That most consists in *Ecchoing Wordes*, and *Termes*,
>
> . . . .
> But a direct, and *Analyticke* Summe
> Of all the worth and first effectes of *Artes*,
> And for his *Poesie*, 'tis so ramm'd with Life,
> That it shall gather strength of Life, with being;
> And liue heareafter, more admir'd, then now.
>   (V.i.K₂ᵛ)

The character and function of Horace deny him, in *Poetaster*,
participation in most of the lighter scenes. He hits the comic note
occasionally in his first encounter with Crispinus:

> *Crisp.* Troth no; but I could wish thou didst
> know vs, Horace; we are a *Scholer*, I assure thee.
>   *Hor.* A *Scholer* Sir? I shall be couetous of your
> faire knowledge.
>   (III.i.D₂ᵛ)

He can strike it with Asinus Lupus toward the end of the play:

> *Lupus.* An *Asse*? Good still!: That's I, too.
> I am the *Asse*. You meane me by the *Asse*.
>   *Mecoenas.* 'Pray thee, leaue braying then.
>   *Hor.* If you will needs take it, I cannot with
> Modestie giue it from you.
>   (V.iii.Ll ᵛ)

But his is not a part of this magnificent fooling associated with
the heavenly banquet:

> *Crisp.* O yes, and extoll your perfections to
> the heauens.
>   *Chl.* Now in sincerity, they be the finest kind
> of men, that euer I knew; *Poets*? Could not one
> get the Emperor to make my husband a *Poet*,
> thinke you?

> *Crisp.* No Ladie, 'tis Loue, and Beauty make
> *Poets*: & since you like *Poets* so well, your Loue,
> and Beauties shall make me a *Poet*.
>
> (II.ii.C4ʳ)

Nor does Horace have a part in this exchange:

> *Chlöe. Mercury?* that's a *Poet?* is't?
> *Gall.* No, Ladie; but somewhat enclyning that
> way: hee is a Herald at Armes.
> *Chlöe.* A Herald at Armes? good: and *Mer-*
> *cury?* pretty: he ha's to doe with *Venus*, too?
> *Tibull.* A little, with her face, Ladie; or so.
>
> (IIII.iii.G4ʳ)

In these four towering figures, Doctor Clement, Asper-Macilente, Criticus and Horace, all conceived to some extent in the image of Ben himself, we have seen a highly profitable apprenticeship for the poet. We have seen him happily seize on the humours as dramatic material in Doctor Clement and others in *Every Man in His Humour*; we have seen him make their purgation in Macilente and his victims almost the entire content of *Every Man out of His Humour*; we have Criticus by definition placed far above any humour in *Cynthia's Revels*, and the humours themselves of the other characters pushed so far as to become almost allegorical qualities. In *Poetaster* we have seen in such people as Captain Tucca, Chloe, and possibly even Horace himself a return to the happier humours climate of *Every Man in His Humour*, but only in conjunction with more weighty material and action.

Through the career of this Horace-character, Jonson has learned a lesson of equal importance with reference to the action. Doctor Clement, as a repository for civil authority, could adjudge all matters for all characters. Macilente, without visible authority, could make himself judge, in matters of manners and morals, for all his victims. Criticus could, through his powers as poet, exercise delegated authority, again in matters of manners and morals. Horace, also with delegated authority, could pronounce judgments only in those realms in which he was qualified as poet and critic. Jonson has learned that neither a Clement nor a Horace can carry the entire action of a comedy.

As the careers of these men show the development of Jonson in the choice of his materials and the organization of his actions, so too they have demonstrated a maturing in what I have called the choric aspects of his art. From gentle, and essentially comic ridicule in *Every Man in His Humour*, Jonson passed to the heavily satiric invective of *Every Man out of His Humour*. In *Cynthia's Revels*, Criticus retained the satire and the invective, but was capable of lighter touches on occasion. In *Poetaster*, there is much more of the truly comic, and its use is much more widely distributed among the characters; invective is much less prominent, and the satire of Horace is directed largely at the unhappy poetasters.

After *Poetaster*, Doctor Clement, Asper, Criticus and Horace are gone, but their functions remain, in the hands of lesser men. Humours will continue to be punished, as that of Morose in *Epicoene*, but by the skillfully concerted action of all characters, rather than by the diligent intent of one. Or they will be purged as was that of Justice Overdoo, by the mere observation of the consequences of his own folly. Critical judgments on the nature and function of poetry will continue, but in passages addressed "To the Readers," as in *Sejanus*, or in the "Prologue," as in *Epicoene*. There will continue to be custodians of right opinion, but they will be lesser men, such as Arruntius and Lepidus of *Sejanus*, or Peni-boy Canter of *The Staple of News*. The custody of the action will not be entrusted to a Macilente, but it will be managed by Jonson himself, in such magnificent interweavings of action and motive as *Epicoene* and *The Alchemist*.

Of these towering figures who wield so much authority in act and idea, Horace is the last. They were certainly unwieldy as a major device for conducting the action; their chief weapon was direct invective or massive satire; their responsibilities were too weighty for them to indulge in much comment of a truly comic sort. Their arrogance created detractors, not without cause, for Ben himself. Perhaps it was these considerations which led Jonson to the momentous, if short-lived, decision announced in the "apolo-geticall Dialogue" ("only once spoken upon the stage") which is appended in the folio to *Poetaster*:

> And, since the *Comick* Muse
> Hath prou'd so ominous to me, I will trie
> If Tragoedie haue a more kind aspect.
>   (Herford and Simpson, IV.324.222–24)

III.

SOME ANTECEDENTS
OF THE PUPPET PLAY
IN BARTHOLOMEW FAIR

I

The literary antecedents of the Puppet Play in Jonson's *Bartholomew Fair* have been generally listed as two: The Marlowe / Chapman *Hero and Leander*, and the Edwards play, *Damon and Pythias*.[1] It is my wish to add a third item to this list, the *Lenten Stuffe* of Thomas Nashe, for it is here that Jonson might have found in juxtaposition the stories of Hero and Leander and King Dionysius, who is associated with Damon and Pythias in Jonson's play. The question of this juxtaposition is of importance since what Jonson has produced in the Puppet Play is a new action carried on jointly by the four characters Hero, Leander, Damon, and Pythias, rather than a recapitulation of the action found in either of the sources.

That he is indebted to Marlowe, Jonson very quickly makes clear, by two exact quotations from *Hero and Leander*: "Guilty of true loue's blood" and "the other, Sestos hight" (V.iii.112–113).[2] Other details used by the playwright are the Thames for the Hellespont; Puddle Wharf for Abidus; the Bankside for Sestos; the intervention of Cupid, in the person of Jonas the drawer; and not a candle's end, but a whole candle, for the light in the tower—proposed, but not used. Needless to say, Jonson does not borrow

---

[1] C. H. Herford, Percy and Evelyn Simpson, *Ben Jonson* (11 vols.; Oxford: The Clarendon Press, 1925), X, 209. This edition will be the source of all passages from *Bartholomew Fair*, and the quotations will be noted in the body of the paper by act, scene, and line.

[2] Phyllis B. Bartlett (ed.), *The Poems of George Chapman* (London: Oxford University Press, 1941), 112.

any of Marlowe's poetry, or his romantic approach to the meeting of the lovers.

Jonson's use of *Damon and Pythias*, by Richard Edwards, is of the same casual sort. The two friends are associated with Dionysius (The Younger), Tyrant of Syracuse. They quarrel—not as in Jonson's play, over the favors of Hero—but over the question of which shall die for the other. Dionysius becomes their friend, but not a keeper of a school, and not a ghost. And Pythias is to the executioner a "pretty boy," as to Lanthorne Leatherhead he is "pretty Pythias."

The relationship between the Puppet Play and Nashe's *Lenten Stuffe* first becomes apparent when Nashe, who is glorifying the Red Herring, casually uses the herring to expound the myth of Dionysius and Jupiter.[3] Nashe's Dionysius was "a good wisefellow, for he was afterwards a schoolemaster and had played the coatchman to *Plato*, and spit in Aristippus the Philosopher's face." According to Nashe he went to Corinth, "of a tyrant to become a frowning pedant and schoolmaister." Nashe has confused two entirely different men of the name Dionysius, one who was, according to Diogenes Laertius, the teacher of Plato, and the tyrant whose name is associated with the names of Damon and Pythias.[4] Jonson's Dionysius was a schoolmaster in a Scrivener's gown, and a ghost besides.

Nashe's playful account of how the subjects of Dionysius believed the red herring to be Jupiter in one of his many forms, and of how Dionysius disabused them of the belief—"flead him, and thrust him downe his pudding house at a gobbe"—leads him by his own strange logic, into an account of "howe the Herring first came to be a fish."

Nashe gives credit for part of his account of this metamorphosis to "diuine Musaeus" and to a "diuiner muse than him, Kit Marlowe." In Nashe's rollicking version of the tale, Leander dwelt at

[3] R. B. McKerrow (ed.), *The Works of Thomas Nashe* (6 vols.; London: Sidgwick and Jackson, Ltd., 1910), III, 194–201.

[4] Diogenes Laertius, *Lives of Ancient Philosophers*, trans. R. D. Hicks (2 vols.; London: William Heinemann, 1925), I, 279.

Abidos, and "his mistris or Delia" at Sestos. They were assisted in their loves by Cupid, and by a nurse—a "mother Mampudding." Nashe's story envisions a seven-day contention between the Wind and the Hellespont. Leander braved it, his body was washed up at the foot of Hero's tower, and she, when she could not reach his body, resigned herself to the "boystrous woolpacks of ridged tides."

The Gods in assembly—according to Nashe—grieving at what had transpired, determined a suitable destiny for Hero: she became that "flanting Fabian," "Cadwallader Herring." Leander, who in destiny as in life must be separated from her, became the Ling, and must inhabit the "vnquiet cold coast of Iseland."

My suggestion that Jonson was influenced in writing his Puppet Play by Nashe's *Lenten Stuffe* rests on three fairly minute relationships. The first is that his treatment of Dionysius, as has been already suggested, is closer to that of Nashe than to any other source he might have used, such as Edwards or Diogenes Laertius. The second is the association of Jonson's Hero with herring—"She is come over into Fish-street to eat some fresh herring." The third is the injection rather forcibly into his dialogue of the word "Fabian." Hero—as the herring—was "of all fishes the flanting Fabian." In Jonson's play Pythias and Damon "under their clokes they have of Bacon a gammon." But Hero, "*will not be taken, after sacke, and fresh herring, with your* Dunmow-*bacon.*" The dialogue continues:

PVP.P. *You lye, it's* Westfabian.
LAN. *Wesphalian* you should say.
                                              (V.iv.322,323)

Such a passage is certainly an effort to make something of the word "Fabian"—though of course it is not necessarily Nashe's "Fabian." The likelihood, however, that *Lenten Stuffe* was in Jonson's mind at the time of writing *Bartholomew Fair* is increased by two other circumstances: in it Nashe pays Jonson a graceful, if undeserved, tribute on *The Case Is Altered*; and *Lenten Stuffe* was written during Nashe's "exile" after the unfortunate incidents associated with the lost *Isle of Dogs* with which Jonson was also associated.

II

For clarity in the references I shall make later, perhaps a little account of the conduct of the Puppet Play should be given. In his *History of the English Puppet Theater*, George Speaight suggests that Jonson's small actors were finger puppets; that the puppets exchanged their gibes and blows as they appeared above the top of a small stand.[5] Leatherhead, now "Lanthorne," in his own person describes the manner in which, at first sight, near Puddle Wharf, after Hero has been rowed across the Thames by Puppet Cole, the waterman, Hero and Leander were smitten with mutual love; and he tells how Cupid, disguised as Jonas the drawer, in a private room at the Swan, forwarded their union. In his own person also he tells of the arrival of Damon and Pythias at the tavern to break up their arrangements. Lanthorne, when he intervenes, is beaten—not badly—by the Puppets Damon and Pythias. Leander, though urged by Lanthorne, interferes only to the extent of calling Damon a "*Goat-bearded slaue.*" This exchange has been conducted in language highly offensive to the ears of modern critics, but its only consequence is that Hero is labelled "whore," and soundly beaten about the "hanches." It is only after these events are concluded that the puppet, Ghost of Dionysius, enters the dialogue, to demolish the Puritan Busy in the argument about the respectability of players.

When commentators on *Bartholomew Fair* arrive at the Puppet Play, many tend to pass it over in embarrassed silence, pausing merely to castigate its bad taste; a few give a hasty statement of its function in the play.[6] I wish to offer, not the argument, but

[5] George Speaight, *The History of the English Puppet Theatre* (New York: John de Graff, 1955), 57–60.

[6] C. G. Thayer, *Ben Jonson* (Norman, Oklahoma: University of Oklahoma Press, 1963), speaks of "excruciatingly obscene forms" in it, and notes that

merely the speculation, that its internal significance may be a little greater than most critics have allowed. I suggest that, along with the three literary antecedents mentioned above, contemporary events of 1613–1614 contributed much to the shaping and flavor of this contrivance—that Jonson may be saying that recent matters at the court are even less palatable than the obvious iniquities of the Fair. The matters of court to which I refer are of course those surrounding the Essex divorce.

The course I am about to take is a tortuous one, and it will lead at most to fragile and inconclusive evidence concerning the point I propose, that the Puppet Play contains references to contemporary events. Along the way it will be advisable to touch on certain specific points: that Jonson normally makes the fullest use of his material in terms of action, of characterization, of comic comment, or perhaps of overt didacticism, and that he does not apparently make such use of the *text* of those parts of the Puppet Play which concern Hero and Leander and Damon and Pythias; that Jonson was in a position to have some knowledge of the goings-on associated with the great nullity action; that he did during the years 1613–1615 glance in his plays at contemporary matters; that he does in fact, in the text of *Bartholomew Fair* itself, alert his audience to expect something contemporary; and that the attitude of contemporary Londoners toward participants in the nullity proceedings was not necessarily that taken by modern historians.

The booth in which the Puppet Play takes place is the *locus* for all the comic resolutions in the play, but not one line of it, except the addendum between Zeal-of-the-Land Busy and the Ghost of Dionysius, contributes in any way directly to the punishment or

---

it "reduces a classical theme to ludicrous absurdity" (152, 153). To Herford and Simpson it is a "hideous burlesque of *Hero and Leander*" (I, 145). To J. J. Enck in *Jonson and the Comic Truth* (Madison, Wisconsin: The University of Wisconsin Press, 1957) it "rounds out the play in exhibiting what the Smithfield men and women are not" and "becomes the critic of the men who misunderstand the Fair" (199). To Eugene M. Waith (ed.), *Bartholomew Fair* (New Haven, Connecticut: Yale University Press, 1963), it is an "appalling vulgarization of the stories of Hero and Leander and Damon and Pythias" (17).

reform of any character.[7] Humphrey Waspe loses his authority over Bartholomew in the booth, but before the Puppet Play formally begins, and largely as a consequence of Humphrey's presence in the stocks. Justice Overdoo reveals himself immediately after the confutation of Busy, but his realization that he is only "*Adam*, Flesh and blood" comes through the revelations of Quarlous, and as a consequence of activities before the Puppet Play. The list could be lengthened to include the comic fates of Dame Purecraft, of the Littlewits, John and Win, of Mistress Overdoo—indeed all the visitors to the Fair except Bartholomew—all of which are resolved in the booth, but not resolved in any sense by the dialogue among puppets Hero, Leander, Damon, Pythias, and their mentor, Lanthorne Leatherhead. Only Bartholomew Cokes is visibly concerned with the dialogue, and he is at the end precisely the same Bartholomew whom we met in the first act. Not only are the lines of the Puppet Play not concerned in the action, but it is almost equally apparent that they serve none of Jonson's other usual purposes: they are surely not intended for attack, or praise, by way of parody, on *Hero and Leander*; nor is there any overt didacticism, unless it should be construed as a moral lesson that Mistress Hero is beaten, and that Puppet Jonas takes up the "brawle" with the "word"—"Whore-masters all."

Though the visitors to the Fair are all given appropriate comic punishments or cures, the denizens, the professionals, of the Fair all escape the justice of the comic poet, even the cutpurse Edgworth whose exploits become known to all. Ursula and Leatherhead, Joan Trash and Whit the bawd are subjected to no consequence, no moral judgment. It seems not inappropriate to assume that they are the world—life which is as it is—the locale of man's journey—, as of Bunyan's Pilgrim's, and that only the visitors to that Fair are to be judged, as they manifest, each in his own way, their follies or illusions. Ursula, according to Busy, has "the

---

[7] For an excellent article dealing with these resolutions see "Bartholomew Fair and Its Puppets," by Jonas A. Barish, *MLQ*, XX (March, 1959), 3–17.

marks upon her of the three enemies of man, the world, as being in the *Faire*, the Devill, as being in the fire; and the Flesh, as being her selfe." If one entertains this idea, then—since the Puppet Play and its booth are part of the Fair—the question arises as to what segment of the world the Puppet Play represents. And it is not far to another assumption—that it may be the Court of James. Certainly that court was as superficial—as far removed from reality —as the puppets. And certainly it could produce for the Londoner, the Englishman, consequences as revolutionary as those meted out to the travellers in Jonson's comic world. Whether or not such an assumption be of any validity, it is certain that the most notorious concerns of that Court in 1613 were the matters of the Essex divorce, and that they were in some degree known to most Englishmen, and were, on the whole, disapproved of by them. This is Gardiner's assessment of the situation:

> For four months the trial had formed the general topic of conversation wherever men met together in public or in private. The effrontery of the Countess, the shameless meddling of the King and of the courtiers, the truckling subserviency of Neile and his supporters, were discussed with a remarkable unanimity of abhorrence in every corner of the land. The sober stood aghast at James' disregard for the decencies of life, whilst the lighthearted laughed at the easy credulity with which he took for granted all the tales of a profligate woman.[8]

And probably they were not unknown to Ben Jonson. "Before the end of June, 1613, at latest, Jonson had returned home [from his unhappy experience abroad as tutor to Sir Walter Raleigh's son] and parted with his pupil."[9] The principals in the affair were these: on the one side, Robert Devereaux, Third Earl of Essex; the Earl of Southampton; and William, Lord Knollys, great uncle to

[8] Samuel R. Gardiner, *The History of England* (10 vols.; London: Longmans, Green, and Company, 1885), II, 174.

[9] Herford and Simpson, I, 69. The passage continues: "On June 29 he was in London, and witnessed the swift destruction of the Globe by fire, during the performance of *Henry VIII*. He appears to have resumed at once his ordinary activities. *Bartholomew Fair*, played in October, 1614, must have occupied much of his time during the preceding months of that year."

young Essex;[10] on the other side, Lady Essex, the former Frances Howard; her father, the Earl of Suffolk; her great-uncle, the Earl of Northampton; the favorite, Robert Carr, Lord Rochester, later Earl of Somerset; and among, but not altogether of these, the ill-fated Sir Thomas Overbury. That Jonson had some contact with most of these principals is made evident in his poems, and in the *Conversations with Drummond*. One of the Epigrams (LXVII) is addressed to the Earl of Suffolk, probably soon after Suffolk was instrumental in Jonson's release from imprisonment in connection with *Eastward Ho*. His association with Northampton is recorded by Drummond:

> Northampton was his mortall enimie for brawling on a St Georges day one of his attenders, he was called before ye councill for his Sejanus and accused both of popperie and treason by him.[11]

For the marriage, in 1606, of the young Earl of Essex and his Lady, Frances, Jonson had written one of his early masques, *Hymenaei*. Jonson did not write the official masque for the marriage of Frances to Robert Carr,[12] but he did write, for "the day after the Marriage," *A Challenge at Tilt*, and soon thereafter *The Irish Masque*. On the day of the marriage he sent to Somerset a congratulatory poem that may be read either as laudatory, or satirical. It begins:

> They are not those, are present with theyre face,
>   And clothes, and guifts, that only do thee grace
> At these thy Nuptials; but, whose heart, and thought
>   Do wayte vpon thee; and theyre Loue not bought.[13]

His relationship with Sir Thomas Overbury[14] is all in one line in

---

[10] These two as friends of Essex, met with the Earls of Northampton and Suffolk sometime in May to consider the course to be pursued with reference to the divorce proceedings (Gardiner, II, 169). Southampton's championship of the young Earl's cause is also expressed in a letter to Sir Ralph Winwood on August 6 (Nichols, *Progresses of James*, II, 672).

[11] Herford and Simpson, I, 141.

[12] The masque for the wedding was written by Thomas Campion; see Chambers, *Elizabethan Stage*, III, 245.

[13] Herford and Simpson, VIII, 384; XVIII, 1–5.

[14] Sir Thomas Overbury, confidential secretary and principal adviser to Rochester, was bitterly opposed to the marriage. The disapproval was probably expressed openly in his "Wife," which Jonson knew. But he was in

the *Conversations*: "Overbury was first his friend, then turn'd his mortall enimie." The occasion of this enmity is probably also noted in the *Conversations*:

> The Countess of Rūtland was nothing inferior to her Father S. P. Sidney in Poesie. Sir Th: Overburie was in love with her, and caused Ben to read his wyffe to her, which he with ane excellent grace did & praised the Aūthor. that the Morne Therafter he discorded with Overbūrie, who woūld have him to intend a sūte yt was unlawfull. the lines my Lady Keepd in remembrance he comes to near, who comes to be denied.[15]

Finally, that Jonson did indeed comment on the conduct of some of the principals in the nullity action is made clear by this item in the conversations:

> he heth a Pastorall jntitled the May Lord, his own name is Alkin Ethra the Countess of Bedfoords Mogibell overberry, the old Countesse of Suffolk ane jnchanteress other names are given to somersets Lady, Pembrook the Countess of Rutland, Lady Wroth.

In the years 1613–1616 Jonson was interested in contemporary affairs at least to the extent of noting them in his plays, and commenting on them in retrospect in the *Conversations*. There are easily recognizable references in *Bartholomew Fair* to the actors Taylor and Ostler, as well as references by name to Burbage and Field, and almost certain reference to Inigo Jones as Lanthorne Leatherhead. And something of the sort was at least contemplated, according to this record in the *Conversations* with reference to *The Devil is an Asse*:

> a play of his upon which he was accused the Divell is ane ass, according to Comedia Vetus, in England the divell was brought in either wt one Vice or other, the Play done the divel caried away the Vice, he brings in ye divel so overcome wt ye wickednes of this age that he thought himself ane ass. παρεργως is discoursed of the Dūke of Drown land, the King desyred him to conceal it.[16]

---

prison, so that his interference in the proceedings might be stopped, and he was dead of poison, through the instrumentality of Frances, before the nullity was granted.

[15] Herford and Simpson, I, 138, 213–219.

[16] *Ibid.*, I, 143, 144.

The curious reference is unexplainable, but is thus accounted for by Herford and Simpson:

> Nothing is known of this affair on independent evidence. But it may be inferred that some part of the satire, in the play as originally performed, struck home, that Jonson at the king's request softened or effaced the personal point, real or apparent, and that this revised version is represented by the printed text.[17]

The "Induction" to *Bartholomew Fair* has for its final element of agreement between the poet and the audience a warning not to conceal any "State decipherer" who might

> search out, who was meant by the *Gingerbread-woman*, who by the *Hobby-horse-man*, who by the *Costard-monger*, nay, who by their *Wares*. Or that will pretend to affirm (on his owne *inspired ignorance*) what *Mirror of Magistrates* is meant by the *Iustice*, what great *Lady by the Pigge-woman*, what *conceal'd States-man*, by the *Seller* of *Mouse-trappes*, and so of the rest.
>
> ("Induction," 139–45)

Yet as Act V opens at the booth of the puppets, Leatherhead appears to alert the audience to something contemporary:

> But the Gunpowder-plot, there was a get-penney! I haue presented that to an eighteene, or twenty pence audience, nine times in an afternoon. Your home-borne proiects proue euer the best, they are so easie, and familiar, they put too much learning i' their things now o'dayes: and that I feare will be the spoile o' this.
>
> (V.i.11–17)

In Scene iii, Bartholomew reads the play bill, which names "The ancient moderne history of *Hero* and *Leander*." Finally, in the Epilogue, the poet may be suggesting some connivance on the part of the King himself:

> *Your* Maiesty *hath seene the* Play, *and you*
> *can best allow it from your eare, and view.*
> *You know the scope of* Writers, *and what store*
> *of leaue is given them, if they take not more,*
> *And turne it into* licence: *you can tell*
> *if we have us'd that* leaue *you gave us, well.*
>
> ("Epilogue," 1–6)

[17] *Ibid.*, II, 152.

The next point I wish to make on my way toward what I have already termed as fragile evidence of contemporary allusion is that events did not look to the Londoners of 1613–1614 quite as they look today. That point will I think become clear if we permit John Chamberlain to tell most of the story of the goings-on relevant to the divorce. Chamberlain was not of the court—had no part in its intrigues and struggles for power. But he was able to learn enough of events to keep Sir Dudley Carleton and Sir Ralph Winwood and other diplomats abroad informed of significant activity. He was, like Mr. Ambler of *The Staple of News*, a frequenter of "the middle Ile" of Saint Paul's Cathedral. What he knew Jonson might know—or Jonson's audience—but it is unlikely that much more was known to them.

A brief account of the affairs of Essex and his lady up to 1613 is necessary, however, before we let Chamberlain tell his story. The marriage of the young people took place in 1606, when the young Earl was in his thirteenth year and Frances Howard was a year or two younger. The marriage may have been instigated or forwarded by James, in the hope of healing the factional wounds left over from the days of Elizabeth.[18] The young couple were immediately separated, and the young Earl spent the next three years in travel, while the bride remained in England, no doubt much of the time in Court, under the tutelage of her mother, the "ịnchanteress" of the lost *May Lord*. She was noticed favorably by the young Prince Henry, but after his death her affections became concentrated on the rising favorite, Robert Carr.

The next stage of the story is told effectively by Arthur Wilson, the historian of the reign of James:

Her *Husband* having been now three or four years beyond the *Seas* (sick with absence from her whom his desires longed after) came over again, and found that *Beauty*, which he had left *innocent*, so *farded* and *sophisticated* with some Court *Drug* which had wrought upon her, that he became the greatest *Stranger* at home. His patience made way for him a while, and he bore up

[18] *Cf.* my article, "*Troilus and Cressida* and Elizabethan Court Factions," *Studies in English*, V (1964), 43–66.

with a *gentle gale against the stream* of this *Womans* affections, which ran altogether (unknown) into another *chanel*. Nor was her *reputation* yet become so *robust* (being of a tender growth) to *strike* his ears with *reproaches*, and therefore he imputed her sly *entertainments* to a *Maiden bashfulness*. . . . He went to the Earl of Suffolk . . . to reduce his Daughter to the obedience of Wife. . . . Her Husband she looked upon as a private person, and to be carried by him into the *Country* out of her *element* . . . were to close . . . with an insufferable torment. . . . Chartley was an hundred miles from her *happines* and a little time thus lost is her *eternity*. When she came thither . . . she shut herself up in her Chamber . . . .[19]

With those preliminaries, we are ready to let Chamberlain take up the account:

> The Countesse of Essex was going downe to her Lord into Staffordshire and some of her carriage was sent away, but she hath since chaunged her purpose and is come to this towne.
>
> (August 11, 1612)[20]

> There was a divorce to be sued this terme twixt the earle of Essex and his Lady, and he was content (whether true or fained) to confesse insufficiencie in himself, but there happened an accident of late that hath altered the case; his Lady sought out and had many conferences with a wise woman, who (according to the course of such creatures) drew much monie from her and at last cousened her of a jewell of great value, for which beeing prosecuted and clapt in prison, she accuses the Lady of divers straunge questions and propositions, and in conclusion that she dealt with her to make away her Lord, (as ayming at another marke) upon which scandall and slaunder the Lord Chamberlain and other her frends thincke yt not fit to proceede in the divorce.
>
> (April 29, 1613)

> The divorce twixt the earle of Essex and his Lady is on foote, and hath ben argued twise or thrise at Lambeth before certain commissioners, but *a huis clos*. The greatest difficultie is that though he be willing to confesse his insufficiencie towards her, yet he would

[19] Arthur Wilson, *The History of Great Britain, being the Life and Reign of King James I* (London, 1653), 56–58.
[20] Norman Egbert McClure (ed.), *The Letters of John Chamberlain* (2 vols.; Philadelphia, Pennsylvania: The American Philosophical Society, 1939), I, 377 ff.

have libertie to marrie with any other, as beeing *maleficiatus* only *ad illam.* Yet some lawiers are of opinion that yf she will take her oath that he is impotent towards her, yt will serve the turne, wher-of yt is thought she will make no bones, as presuming that she is provided of a second, which I shold never have suspected, but that I know he was with her three howres together within these two days, which makes me somewhat to stagger and to thinke that great folkes to compass theyre owne ends have neither respect to frends nor followers.

(June 10, 1613)

The divorce now in question twixt the earle of Essex and his Lady is thought shalbe decided one way or other the first day of July. The opinions are divers of the successe, and the case is of so daungerous consequence that no doubt the commissioners will proceed with great warines and maturity, for yf such a gap be once let open, yt will not be so easilie stopt but that infinite incon-veniences will follow. In the meane time the Lady hath ben visited and searcht by some auncient Ladies and midwifes expert in those matters, who both by inspection and otherwise find her upon theyre oath a pure virgin: which some Doctors thincke a straunge as-severation, and make yt more difficult then to be discerned. The world speakes liberally that my Lord of Rochester and she be in love one with another, which breedes a double question, whether that consideration be like to hinder or set yt forward.

(June 23, 1613)

The Lord of Essex and his Ladies divorce goes not on so fast as was looked for. She for her part hath performed all that was required, and indured the triall; he is gon out of towne with pro-testation that he will stand to and abide whatsoever the commis-sioners shall award and injoyne, but that will not serve the turne for he must be present at some proceedings, and assignation is geven him to appeare by a certain day. Some thinke the matter wilbe protracted, to see yf yt will fall of itself yf yt be not too earnestly pursued, for yt is held a very difficult case, and can hardly be ended with satisfaction.

(July 8, 1613)

Before the Kings parting from Windsor he sent for the commis-sioners employed in the divorce of the earle of Essex and his Lady, and beeing desirous to see yt at and end, and to know theyre opinions, he found that the bishops of Ely, Coventrie and Lichfeild, the two chauncellors of the Duchie and Exchecquer, with Sir Daniell Dunne, were directly for yt, and to pronounce yt a nullitie, but the archbishop of Caunterburie the bishop of London, Sir John Bennet and Doctor Edwards Chauncellor of London were as directly against it, wherupon the King hath added two bishops more, Winchester and Rochester, and two deanes, Westminster and Paules, who together with the rest must labour in yt twixt this and Michaelmas and then geve theyre resolution, which *computatis computandis* and considering the Kings inclination is like to be for the dissolution. At my last beeing with the bishop of Ely (not long before my comming out of towne,) I found which way he bent, for he made no daintie to tell me his opinion, which I could wish were otherwise yf there be no more reason in yt then I see or conceave.

(August 1, 1613)

But that which most men listen after is what will fall out twixt the earle of Essex and Master Henry Howard,[21] who is challenged and called to account by the earle for certain disgraceful speaches of him: Perhaps I am overbold with you in this plain manner of dealing, but if you knew what indecent words and deeds have passed in the course of this suit, you would excuse yt, and thincke me modest, for what wold you say yf you shold heare a churchman in open audience demaund of him and desire to be resolved: whether he had affection, erection, application, penetration, ejaculation with a great deal of amplification upon every one of these points.

(September 9, 1613)

His Grace of Caunterburie hath lost some grace of late about the great busines, though I hope not the grace of God nor men. The marriage twixt the earle of Essex and the Lady Frauncis Howard is dissolved and pronounced a nullitie by the bishop of Winchester, who with the bishop of Rochester were only super-numerarie to the first commissioners, and so cast the balance by weight of number beeing seven to five: the morning that the matter was to be decided, the King sent expresse comaundment, that in opening they shold not argue nor use any reasons, but only geve theyre assent or dissent, and in the sentence there is no cause exprest but in these termes *propter latens et incurabile impedimentum.*

(October 14, 1613)

21 Brother of Frances.

The Vicount Rochester is lately made Lord Treasurer of Scotland. There is no certaintie of his mariage; but either yt is don, or is thought wilbe shortly, though without shew or publication till they thincke goode.

(October 27, 1613)

Upon Thursday last the Vicount Rochester was created baron of Branspeth in Westmerland and earle of Somerset. The action was don with much solemnitie. . . . The mariage was thought shold be celebrated at Audley-end the next weeke, and great preparation there was to receve the King, but I heare that the Queene beeing won and having promised to be present, yt is put of till Christmas and then to be performed at White-hall.

(November 11, 1613)

The mariage was upon Sunday without any such braverie as was looked for, only some of his followers bestowed cost on themselves, the rest exceeded not either in number or expense. She was maried in her haire and led to chappell by her bridemen a Duke of Saxonie (that is here) and the earle of Northampton her great uncle. The dean of Westminster preached and bestowed a great deale of commendation on the younge couple, on the Countesse of Salisburie, and the mother-vine (as he termed her) the Countesse of Suffolk. The Deane of the chappell coupled them, which fell out somwhat straungely that the same man, shold marrie the same person, in the same place, upon the selfsame day (after sixe or seven years I know not whether) the former partie yet living: all the difference was that the Kinge gave her the last time, and now her father.

(December 30, 1613)

Having constructed this extensive foundation, I am ready to point out touches which lead me to offer the suggestion that the affairs of Robert Carr, Frances *née* Howard, and the young Earl of Essex were called into the mind of the audience by certain lines of the Puppet Play. The puppets Hero and Leander have noted each other's charms, and with the aid of Cupid, disguised as Jonas the drawer, have entered into a compact: *"I'le for euer be thy goose, so thou'lt be my gander."* Puppets Damon and Pythias, those truest of friends, endure a true "triall of friendship" while seeking Hero. They come to blows about which has enjoyed her favors, each vehemently denying it, though the stronger asseveration of Damon seems to prevail: *"Thou hast lien with her thy selfe, I'll proue it in this place."* When Lanthorne intervenes, their blows are turned on him, and they are reconciled, to continue their mission to Hero.

They invade Hero's room, the Conney, at the Swan, announced by Lanthorne:

> *Now, heere come the friends againe* Pythias *and* Damon, *and under their cloaks they haue of bacon, a gammon.*

Their mission, according to Lanthorne, is ill-conceived:

> *Yes, but shee will not be taken*
> *after sacke, and fresh herring, with your* Dunmow-*bacon.*

It is toward the Dunmow bacon that I wish to look first.

That Jonson chose to use the reference is evidence enough that its significance would not be lost on a Jacobean audience. Its significance—a full year of domestic tranquility—is conveyed marvelously by this passage from Bishop Fuller's *Worthies*:

> *He may fetch a flitch of bacon from Dunmow.* This proverb dependeth on a custom practised in the priory of Dunmow, which was founded, saith Speed, by Juga, a noble lady, anno 1104, for Black Nuns. But it seems afterwards the property therof was altered into a male monastery; the mortified men wherein were mirthful sometimes, as hereby may appear.
>
> Any person, from any part of England, coming hither, and humbly kneeling on two stones at the church door (Which are yet to be seen) before the prior or convent, might demand, at his own pleasure, a gammon or flitch of bacon, upon the solemn taking of the ensuing oath:
>
> > You shall swear by the custom of our confession,
> > That you never made any nuptial trangression,
> > Since you were married man and wife,
> > By household brawls, or contentious strife;
> > Or otherwise, in bed or at board,
> > Offended each other in deed or word:
> > Or since the parish clerk said Amen,
> > Wished yourselfes unmarried again;
> > Or, in a twelve-month and a day,

Repented not in thought any way;
But continued true and in desire,
As when you join'd hands in holy quire.
If to these conditions, without all fear,
Of your accord you will freely swear;
A gammon of bacon you shall receive,
And bear it hence with love and good leave.
For this is our custom at Dunmow well known,
Though the sport be ours, the bacon's your own.[22]

Chaucer's reference to the bacon in the Wife of Bath's "Prologue" is well known:

But sith I hadde hem hoolly in myn hond,
And sith they hadde me yeven al hir lond,
What sholde I taken keep hem for to plese,
But it were for my profit and myn ese?
I sette hem so a-werke, by my fey,
That many a nyght they songen 'weilawey!'
The bacon was nat fet for hem, I trowe,
That som men han in Essex at Dunmowe.[23]

The two elements of the Wife's lines that I wish to emphasize are, first, the element of a wife's pleasing a husband, and second, that the association of the County of Essex with Dunmow is part of the reference. It is my suggestion that in the audience attending *Bartholomew Fair* there would be one, or a dozen, who would associate Dunmow with Essex; that it would not be a great stretch of the imagination from that association to one with the Earl of Essex; and from that, in turn, to his three years of marital difficulty. It was primarily for the purpose of pointing out this possibility that I quoted earlier in the paper from Arthur Wilson:

His patience made way for him a while.... He went to the Earl of Suffolk ... to reduce his daughter to the obedience of a Wife ... to be carried by him to Country out of her element.... Chartley was an hundred miles from her happines.

[22] John Freeman (ed.), *The Worthies of England* by Thomas Fuller (New York: Barnes and Noble), 166, 167. Fuller continues his account, giving the names of the three men who have claimed and received the bacon.
[23] F. N. Robinson (ed.), *The Works of Geoffrey Chaucer* (Boston: Houghton Mifflin Company, 1961), 78.

If the associations I have suggested were made in an audience, Hero would immediately become the lovely Frances, and Leander the all-powerful favorite, Robert Carr, Lord Rochester, Earl of Somerset.

Either Damon or Pythias would in the same manner become associated with the Earl of Essex. Pythias, for two or three reasons, seems the more likely of the two. One of the reasons lies in the line from the puppets quoted above: "Thou has lien with her thy self." A second suggestion of this identity may lie in the fact that when the puppets are introduced by Lanthorne to Bartholomew Cokes, "this with the beard" is Damon, while "this" is "pretty Pithias." Since there is a point made here of the beardlessness of Pythias, it seems worthwhile to note that Essex is, in 1613, described as "sans barbe."[24]

Immediately following the line which refers to Dunmow bacon there is this curious exchange, which has been noticed earlier in a different context:

> PVP.P.   *You lye, it's* Westfabian.
> LAN.   *Westphalian* you should say.
>
> (V.iv.322.323)

That the bacon might be Westphalian is a perfectly straight-forward reference. The province of Westphalia in Germany has been noted for centuries for its hams and bacon. One can of course assume that Jonson intended only a mistake in language. But such a trifle would be most un-Jonsonian. It is much more likely that Jonson intended the "Westfabian" to convey something to his audience—probably only the "fabian" half of the word. The occurrences of it are few. It is the name of a minor character in *Twelfth Night*, where it seems to have no special significance. In Chapman's *An Humorous Day's Mirth* (I.7.23) it appears as "flattering Fabi-

---

[24] Walter Bouchier Devereaux, *Lives and Letters of the Devereaux, Earls of Essex* (2 vols.; London: John Murray, 1853), II, 251. The writer of the letter which so describes Essex was the ambassador of the archduke, and the letter is part of the efforts to prevent the duel mentioned above between Essex and Howard. This is the relevant passage: "Le Conte d'Essex, est de moyenne stature: un peu maigre: cheveulx noirs: sans barbe: la face un peu gastee de petites verroles: age, de vingt trois ans. . . ."

an," used by a tyrannical wife toward an errant but amorous husband. In Thomas Nashe's *Lenten Stuffe* there is the "flanting Fabian"—used of Hero herself after she has been changed by the sympathetic Gods to a herring. The last of these is the only seventeenth-century occurrence noted in *NED*, except for the dictionaries, where among its synonyms are "a swash buckler, a swaggerer, a cutter, a quarreler, a roister." It appears therefore that we may gloss the exchange in such a way as to have Puppet Pythias deny vehemently the use of the Dunmow techniques, and claim for himself the more active conduct later exercised when Mistress Hero cries "O my Hanches."

One more speculation, and my fragile edifice is complete. This has to do with the intervention of Cupid in the affairs of Hero and Leander. He assumes the posture of a drawer and the name of Jonas. Bartholomew Cokes is at a loss with reference to him— "I must have a name for Cupid too."[25] I suggest—under correction from Gardiner and other historians—that under Cupid-Jonas the audience might have seen veiled reference to the council of statesmen, deans, and bishops which comprised the nullity commission. The head of that commission was George Abbott, Archbishop of Canterbury. Lanthorne explains the workings of the love-match thus: "*Cupid distinguish'd like Jonas the Drawer, From under his apron where his lechery lurks put love in her sack.*"

The copious quotations from the letters of John Chamberlain which I used earlier were included partly for their impact at this point—the suggestion that in the public mind the Bishops themselves did indeed conceal a little lechery under their aprons. The first such reference was that of June 23—"The Lady hath been visited and searcht by some auncient Ladies and midwifes expert in those matters, who both by inspection and otherwise find her upon theyre oath a pure virgin."[26] But the shock of the good Cham-

---

[25] This remark refers to the fact that Hero is his "fiddle." Leander is his "fiddlestick," Damon his "drum," Pythias his "pipe," the Ghost of Dionysius his "hobby horse," and old Cole is "Dauphin my boy." No such association is forthcoming for Cupid-Jonas.

[26] This incident is also reported by Sir Anthony Weldon. His version, however, is that Frances sent a substitute to the investigation.

berlain, and perhaps many another is evident in the letter of September ninth:

> For what wold you say yf you shold heare a churchman in open audience demaund of him and desire to be resolved: whether he had affection. . . .[27]

The onus of this passage is on simply a "churchman"—therefore presumably upon all the churchmen of the commission, among whom was not only the Archbishop, George Abbott, but also Chamberlain's lifelong friend Launcelot Andrews, Bishop of Ely.

Whether the apron of Cupid-Jonas would carry Episcopal connotations to the audience I am not prepared to say, but it is worthy of note that bishops did habitually use such aprons. I quote from the *Catholic Encyclopedia*: "Gremiale is simply an apron of silk or linen which is spread over a bishop's lap when he is seated or using the holy oils."

It is also barely possible that the name Jonas would bring to the minds of some members of the audience the name of the Archbishop Abbott—for in 1613 there was published the second edition of his *Exposition upon the Prophet Jonah*. The first edition of 1600 had stirred a goodly amount of controversy in ecclesiastical and courtly circles. It seems not unlikely that the use of the name in conjunction with the other slight pointers I have indicated might set an audience, on "the one and thirtieth day of October 1614," to deploring, or perhaps chuckling about, the goings-on that preceded the ill-fated marriage of December 26, 1613.

---

[27] See excerpts above for the letter of that date.

IV.
THE CLOAKS OF
THE DEVIL IS AN ASSE

Among the titles of Ben Jonson's plays, that of *The Devil is an Asse* is something of an anomaly. Jonson's titles fall naturally into classes: the names of persons, as *Sejanus, Volpone*; designations of individuals, which may be extended metaphorically to many members of the cast, as *The Alchemist*; qualified substantives, as *Every Man in His Humour, Every Man out of His Humour* and *The Staple of News*; only two, *The Case is Altered* and *The Devil is an Asse* are asseverations. The promise of *The Case is Altered* is fulfilled, for at the end of the play almost every one finds himself in changed circumstances, and Jonson notes the changes by repetition of the words of the title.

When, however, one is confronted by the bold assertion of the title *The Devil is an Asse*, he expects a movement that will substantiate the charge. And such a contention about Satan would have been a most difficult one to establish before a Jacobean audience which, according to Jonson, in his Prologue, has for its "*deare delight*, the Diuell of Edmunton," and which may well have heard of the "one devell too many amongst them," at a performance of Marlowe's *Doctor Faustus*.[1] Jonson's proof of the immediate and literal statement is quickly evident. Old Iniquity, by his own statement of his qualifications, by the antiquated meter in which he states them, and by the judgment of the Great Devil, qualifies as an ass. Pug's utter incompetence to conduct on Earth the affairs of Hell is quickly demonstrated by his utter inferiority

[1] E. K. Chambers, *The Elizabethan Stage* (4 Vols.; Oxford: At the Clarendon Press, 1923), III, 424.

in vice to the denizens of London. And, in view of his sending such an emissary, the judgment of the Great Devil himself is brought gravely into question. In fact, "a Boy o' thirteene yeere old made him an *Asse* / But t'other day" (V.v.50).[2]

It is to be suspected, however, that Jonson's comic apparatus was conceived for a more subtle statement than this. I submit that he offers a second reading of the title, a reversal, as it were, of the order—an "Asse" is the "Devil." He appears to be saying that folly itself, at its extreme, when accompanied by greed, is evil of a large order. In fact, when compared with the enormities of Fitz-dottrell, the professional efforts of Satan and Pug become almost innocuous. And this folly is manifested over and over in the play by the acceptance of the cloak for the man, of the dressing for the woman, of appearance for reality.

Jonson's comic process also is somewhat unique in *The Devil is an Asse*. In his typical play he has a large assemblage of characters suffering from humour, or illusion, or folly, or possibly vice. And in such a play there is usually one character whose vision is clear, and who carries the burden of revealing or curing or punishing the weaknesses of other characters. Such useful instruments are Doctor Clement of *Every Man in His Humour*, Horace of *Poetaster*, Dauphine of *Epicoene*, Arruntius of *Sejanus*, Peni-boy Canter of *The Staple of News*. Such a man has primarily a choral function.

This comic process is reversed in *The Devil is an Asse*. The focus of almost all attention, all enterprise, is Fitz-dottrell; there is no single voice of reason and right opinion, though Manly and Wittipol approach having such voices. But to almost every character is given, at some stage of the play, a word of scorn for the monstrous follies of Fitz-dottrell—an opportunity to participate in the choric comment.[3]

[2] C. H. Herford and Percy and Evelyn Simpson, *Ben Jonson* (11 Vols.; Oxford: At the Clarendon Press, 1925–1952), VI, 259.

[3] That Fitz-dottrell represents the essential evil of *The Devil is an Asse* is noted by Freda L. Townsend in *Apologie for Bartholomew Fair* (New York: The Modern Language Association, 1947): "Fitz-dottrell is the inviting center," 80. Herford and Simpson (*op. cit.*) do not consider this prob-

The foregoing observations are preliminary to a glance at some of the processes, metaphorical, logical, comic, by which Jonson establishes the rash statement of his title. The heart of his method is the proliferation of a single image, that of the "cloak." The archetypal cloak is of course that which Fitz-dottrell receives from Wittipol as payment for a fifteen minute conversation with Mistress Fitz-dottrell—the cloak which he himself most aptly calls "the price of folly." The imagery of clothing is first advanced in the opening scene, in which the Great Devil and Pug and Old Iniquity are discussing Pug's qualifications as an emissary to Earth from the Commonwealth of Hell. The nature of the Earthly vices, which are far beyond the competence of Pug, is established in terms of dress:

> They haue their *Vices*, there, most like to *Vertues*;
> You cannot know 'hem, apart, by any difference:
> They weare the same clothes, eate (o') the same meate,
> Sleepe i' the selfe-same beds, ride i' those coaches,
> Or very like, foure horses in a coach,
> As the best men and women. Tissue gownes,
> Garters and roses, fourescore pound a paire,
> Embroydred stockings, cut-work smocks, and shirts,
> More certaine marks of lechery, now, and pride,
> Then ere they were of true nobility!
>   (I.i.121–30)

The workings of this cloak image, and the numerous assumptions of the "asse" by Fitz-dottrell, are the key to the ironic effects of the play.

The word "asse" occurs many times—as an epithet—in the course of the play. It is almost always applied to Fitz-dottrell: by Wittipol, (speaking for Mistress Fitz-dottrell),

---

lem. Folly is not listed as one of the objects of Jonson's comic satire in her *The Satiric and the Didactic in Ben Jonson's Comedy* (Chapel Hill: The University of North Carolina Press, 1947) by Helena Watts Baum. J. J. Enck in his *Jonson and the Comic Truth* (Madison: University of Wisconsin Press, 1957) finds the play to be disappointing, principally because of weakness in the sentimental plot. More recently, C. G. Thayer in *Ben Jonson* (Norman: University of Oklahoma Press, 1963) finds Fitz-dottrell, in his fit of madness, to be an embodiment of the devil (171).

But such a moon-ling, as no wit of man
Or roses can redeeme from being an Asse;
(I.vi.158, 159)

by Pug, speaking to Mistress Fitz-dottrell,

Why, wee will make a *Cokes* of this *Wise Master*,
We will, my Mistresse, an absolute fine *Cokes*,
And mock, to ayre, all the deepe diligences
Of such a solemne, and effectuall Asse;
(II.ii.104–107)

by Wittipol,

WIT. Goe, you are an *Asse*. FIT. I am resolu'd on't, Sir.
WIT. I thinke you are .... Away you brokers blocke;
(II.vii.13–15)

twice by Fitz-dottrell himself, "I am not altogether, an *Asse*, good Gentlemen" (III.iii.116); and, "*A Cuckold*, and an *Asse*, and my wiues Ward" (IV.vii.78); and by Manly, as final assessment in the play, "But you'll still be an *Asse*, in spight of prouidence" (V.viii.154). Even though the title of "Asse" is awarded to no other person in the play, except of course to Satan himself, Sir Poule Either-side and the ladies Either-side and Taile-bush display the quality in abundance. And one suspects on the basis of the Prologue, that the same quality is to be found abundantly in the audience itself.

After giving his title, Jonson taxes the audience for "*allowing us no place.*" "*This tract,*" he says, "*will ne'er admit our* vice, *because of yours.*" And perhaps as an admonitory word to them against taking appearance for reality, he closes thus: "*And when sixe times you ha' seen't, / If this* Play *doe not like, the Diuell is in't.*" Though Pug's mission is ostensibly "to" Earth, the conference in the first scene between Satan, Pug, and Iniquity is held "Heere about *London*," where "it is fear'd they haue a stud o' their owne / Will put downe ours" (I.i.108–109).

The reality of the Devil, then, to Jonson, is folly, "Asse"-hood, and the primary manifestation of the nature of folly lies in Fitz-dottrell. The demonstration of his folly is through the cloak, real or metaphorical, i.e., the taking of appearance for reality. This is one of Jonson's continuing themes, stated most concisely, perhaps, in *Volpone*:

> Hood an asse, with reuerend purple,
> So you can hide his two ambitious eares,
> And, he shall passe for a cathedrall Doctor.
>   (I.ii.111–13)

Much of *Bartholomew Fair* is devoted also to the theme of purposeless folly, and there are numerous connecting links between that play and *The Devil is an Asse*. The folly of John Littlewit, the "foole-John," is never relieved. Like Fitz-dottrell, he is much taken with his wife's dressing; in fact, he admires her prodigiously in the "Spanish dress," with the "fine high shooes," the "Cioppinos" of Wittipol as the Spanish Lady in *The Devil is an Asse*. But Bartholomew Cokes is many times an "asse," as attested by Waspe, by Win-wife, by Quarlous. He is a "serious," a "resolute," a "phantasticall" fool. The sport of gulling him is, according to Edgworth, "call'd *Dorring the Dottrell*." Both Cokes and Fitz-dottrell lack souls. In *Bartholomew Fair* the point is made by Edgworth, speaking of Cokes:

> Talke of him to haue soule? 'heart, if hee haue any more then a thing giuen him in stead of salt, onely to keepe him from stinking, I'le be hang'd afore my time.
>   (IV.ii.54–56)

And of Fitz-dottrell, Wittipol says,

>   you are the wife,
> To so much blasted flesh, as scarce hath soule,
> In stead of salt, to keepe it sweete.
>   (I.vi.88–90)

The sustained image through which the folly of Cokes is manifested is, as in *The Devil is an Asse*, that of clothing, not assumed, but lost:

I ha' lost my selfe, and my cloake and my hat; and my fine sword, and my sister, and *Numps*, and Mistris *Grace*, (a Gentlewoman that I should ha' marryed) and a cutworke handkercher, shee ga' mee, and two purses to day. And my bargaine o' Hobby-horses and Ginger-bread, which grieues me worst of all.

(IV.ii.81–86)

The last speech in *Bartholomew Fair* is also given to Cokes—"and bring the *Actors* along, wee'll ha' the rest o' the *Play* at home."

One wonders whether Jonson did not indeed "bring the *Actors* along," and "ha' the rest of the *Play*" with Fitz-dottrell and company. Fitz-(son of) Dottrell, at the extremity of his folly, is a "Cokes"; the given name of Fitz-dottrell, Fabian, may be a by-product of the puppet show in *Bartholomew Fair*.[4] But it is only in *The Devil is an Asse* that this particular manifestation of human weakness becomes the object of such concentrated indignation on Jonson's part.

The movement of the play is three-fold, with Fitz-dottrell as the object, or victim, of all the lines of action. There is the en-terprise of the Kingdom of Hell, in which Pug is to serve Fitz-dottrell, in order to prove his value to his master; there is the enterprise of the tribe of brokers, led by Meercraft, to cozen Fitz-dottrell of his property; and there is the assault of Wittipol on the virtue of Fitz-dottrell's beauteous wife. In each line of action, or at the point of contact of two, the fresh follies, the fresh "cloaks" build up until the final one, the assumption by Fitz-dottrell of possession by the Devil himself. The irony of this passage is magnificent, since it is the only one of the cloaks which Fitz-dottrell is really conscious of wearing.

The first of Fitz-dottrell's follies in the realm of clothing oc-curs during his initial encounter with Pug. Pug *is* a Devil, clothed in the body of a cutpurse, the garments of gentleman-usher, and the shoes of a prostitute. Yet the wise Fitz-dottrell, refusing, be-

---

[4] In *Bartholomew Fair* a self-conscious mistake is made by Puppet Pythias, with reference to the Dunmow bacon, in calling it Westfabian in error for Westphalian. The word Fabian, according to NED, occurs in the literature of the period only in the *Lenten Stuffe* of Thomas Nashe.

cause he can find no cloven feet, to believe that he is a Devil, hires him because his name is Devil. Pug himself is deceived by his own appearance, thinking he can use his borrowed body for "venery," thinking that because he is clothed in the body of a man he, a Devil, can hold his own among the vices of man.

As soon as the enterprise of Satan and Pug has imposed the false servant on Fitz-dottrell, his confidence in his own wisdom and fortune is such that Wittipol and Manly can easily persuade him to don, in return for fifteen minutes of his wife's conversation, a magnificent cloak—one acquired from Ingine, who is of what Satan calls "our tribe of brokers." His pride in the cloak, and in his own wisdom is almost unbounded; he accepts with complacency his wife's suggestion that he may be laughed at, unconsciously predicting his course throughout the play: "Let 'hem laugh, wife, Let me haue such another cloake to morrow" (I.vi.40–41).

Having donned the cloaks provided by Satan and Wittipol, Fitz-dottrell is ripe for the more elaborate enterprise of the master-broker, Meercraft, and his lesser colleagues, Ingine, Traines, and Everill. They lead him into an elaborate sequence of follies, of acceptances of appearance, which will explain and establish the proposition of the title.

The first of this sequence is the assumption of nobility, as the "Duke of Drown'd-Land." The amazing Meercraft, proposing his project of the draining of the marshes, suggests the figure of eighteen million pounds as the possible revenue. Fitz-dottrell's cupidity, which has already led him to conjurers, has led him to take a devil for a servant, and has led him very near the prostitution of his wife, is enough to make him embrace the project, even if the added incentive of the title of Duke were absent. But, the title having been suggested, Fitz-dottrell *becomes* the Duke, and must comport himself accordingly. A minor manifestation of his asse-hood, of his wearing of the spurious cloaks, is the "Lord's face" which he must assume upon arising, a face which must not recognize even his nearest acquaintance.

While the "Lord's face" has been in preparation, the cloak motif has been at work in another segment of the play. Lady Fitzdottrell in her clothing is "Very brave," is, according to Pug, in "all this Rigging and fine Tackle," a "neat handsome vessells," "of good sayle" (II.ii.111,112). The care is not hers, but her husband's—

> hee is sensuall that way.
> In euery dressing, he do's study her.
>
> (I.iv.17.18)

Pug is naturally led to the conclusion that "No woman drest with so much care, and study, / Doth dresse her self in vaine" (II.v.22.23). Therefore, seeking to advance the cause of Hell, with a little dividend in the way of "venery" for himself, he petitions her that he may be "Stil'd o' your pleasures." This mistaking of appearance for reality secures no advancement of the cause of Hell, nor any pleasures for Pug, but only a beating from his master.

Fitz-dottrell has all confidence that he can "doe well enough" as a Duke, but his wife is "such an untoward thing" that she must be remodeled—"Is there an *Academy* for women?" There is indeed an academy, produced full-blown from the mind of Meercraft upon Ingine's whisper about the "*Spanish* gowne." Fitz-dottrell, who has taken a "sensuall" pleasure in the fine dressing of his wife, takes an even greater one in this dressing for his "Dutchesse." The trappings are elaborate: Wittipol, rather than Dicke Robinson, the player, for the Spanish woman; the broker's Spanish gown; the ring, which must be sealed for, as a present to assure admittance to the academy; Jonson's own alchemical jargon for the Spanish Lady's advice about Spanish focuses and manners; the home of Lady Taile-bush, the lady projectress, as the seat of the academy. Like the first cloak, which he bought from Wittipol with fifteen minutes of his wife's conversation, and its metaphorical successors, this cloak, this appearance, becomes reality for Fitz-dottrell.

The reality is indeed so great that when Everill demands Meercraft's time, and to account for the demand, the "*Master* of the

Dependances" springs from the fertile brain of that broker, Fitz-dottrell is eager to assume an additional cloak, that of the first client of the "office" of "*Dependances*," in order that he may pursue his quarrel with Wittipol in a manner becoming a duke, even to the making of a conveyance of his lands to a "*Feoffee.*"

His enchantment with the Spanish lady—Wittipol in Meercraft and Ingine's gown—is so great that he sends his wife into another room with the Spanish lady, who is to "melt, cast and forme her as you shalle thinke good" (IV.iv.254). The result of this meeting is actually the enlistment of Wittipol and Manly as friends and protectors of Mistress Fitz-dottrell. But the meeting will in due time provide a fresh "cloak" for Fitz-dottrell, that of cuckold, a misapprehension that will remain with him even at the end of the play.

But the work of the "cloak" of the dependancy is not over. A "*Feoffee*" must be found, and though Meercraft and Everill are assiduous candidates, Fitz-dottrell's infatuation will let him consider only the Spanish lady, and at "her" earnest request, a substitute in the person of Manly. The revelation that the Spanish lady is Wittipol gives us a fresh title for Fitz-dottrell, "Duke of Shore-ditch," and some new "cloaks," "a *Cuckold*, and an *Asse* and my wiues ward."

Though he has conceded it, the asse-hood of Fitz-dottrell is not yet fully developed, for a final "cloak" must be donned, one which brings the movement back to its starting point. At the suggestion of Meercraft he must pretend that he is possessed of a devil, as the result of witchcraft on the part of his wife and Wittipol and Manly, in order that the enfeoffment of Manly may be set aside. The trappings are provided by Meercraft and Everill, the bellows, the false belly, the mouse, while the offer of the true Devil, Pug, to give professional help is spurned. Sir Poule Either-side is brought to witness the possession, and he has qualities which make him a most willing and competent witness. In fact, he interprets all the manifestations and utterances of Fitz-dottrell in the light of Puritan language and beliefs. Urged by Meercraft, the unfortunate victim of possession speaks "languages," which are to Sir Poule a manifest proof of the presence of a Devil. The principal such speech is a passage of Greek, which in translation is this:

> Ah! Thrice, four, five, twelve times, or rather ten thousand times unhappy fate.[5]

The passage is from the *Plutus* of Aristophanes, and it is spoken by the Informer, who is shortly to lose his "witness," as Fitz-dottrell loses Sir Poule. The Informer must also give up his very handsome coat for the ragged, dirty coat of the "Just Man."

This final manifestation of the cloak motif, possession by a devil, is comparable in manner and function to the notable scenes which give the resolutions in earlier plays, such as the courts of Justice Clement, of Cynthia, of Augustus, of the Avocatori of Venice, and the Puppet show of *Bartholomew Fair*. In those, authority, legal, or moral, or comic, resolves all lines of action in terms of the cure of illusion or folly, or punishment where cure is not possible.

The manifestations of evil—of Devil-hood—in *The Devil is an Asse* have been on three levels: The professional, in Pug; those of Earth, in the broker group; and the extreme, the incurable, in Fitz-dottrell. Pug, presumably because of his utter ineffectiveness, receives what is for him a reward, the escape from Earth to the comparative paradise of Hell. The entire broker group, the brilliant Meercraft, the unspeakable Everill, Ingine and Traines, the cozen-er Guilthead, the ladies of fashion, compared with whom "there is no Hell" (V.ii.14)—all those who "had worse counsels in't"— even to the Puritan justice, Sir Poule Either-side, are by Manly, who at the end of the play is Jonson's comic spokesman, permitted to go virtually unpunished. They are merely exhorted to "repent 'hem, and be not detected" (V.viii.168). Vices they have, in vary-

---

[5] Oates and O'Neill (eds.), *The Complete Greek Drama* (2 Vols.; New York: Random House, 1938), II, 1097. The Greek which Fitz-dottrell speaks is this:

Οἴμοι κακοδαίμων, / Καὶ τρισκακοδαίμων, καὶ τετράκις, καὶ πεντάκις, / Καὶ δωδεκάκις, καὶ μυριάκις.

ing degrees, but not the ultimate vice, folly unredeemed, folly put at the service of greed.

But for Fitz-dottrell there is no redemption. When he learned of the departure of Pug from the body of the cutpurse, he abandoned almost all the cloaks—"my land is drown'd indeed" (V.viii.159). He keeps, however, one cloak, the false belief that he is a cuckold. His essential quality, that which is no cloak and which is in essence the Devil, he also keeps: in the words of Manly, "you'll still be an *Asse*" (V.viii.154).

V.
BEN JONSON AND SHAKESPEARE
1623-1626

Momentous events occurred in England in 1623, among them the trip to Spain, incognito, of Prince Charles and George Villiers, Duke of Buckingham, for the purpose of wooing the Infanta. Of hardly less import was the publication by Heminge and Condell of the First Folio of Shakespeare. A third event of a different kind and of less momentous consequence was the burning of Ben Jonson's library. We need not linger with the journey to Spain except to note that there was almost universal rejoicing when Charles returned safe—unwed—escaped as it were from the snares of Phillip and the Pope.

As a part of these rejoicings, Ben Jonson prepared a masque, *Neptunes Triumph*. It was never performed because of an insoluble question of protocol involving Spanish and French ambassadors. Portions of it were salvaged and used on Twelfth Night, 1625, in another masque, *The Fortunate Isles*, again celebrating the escape of Prince Charles, and glancing at the forthcoming union of Charles with Henrietta Maria of France.

Other portions were used in *The Staple of Newes*, acted by "His Maiesties Servants" early in 1626. It is largely these portions that I wish to juxtapose with the burning of Jonson's library and the publication of the First Folio. My starting point should perhaps be the association of Jonson with that volume. It is Jonson's initials that, without much enthusiasm, assure the reader that the Droeshout portrait was "for gentle Shakespeare cut."[1] And, probably

---

[1] The source for all quotations from the work of Shakespeare will be, for language, *The Norton Facsimile* (New York, 1968). The numbers of acts,

the best known of all Jonson's writings is his tribute in the front
matter of that volume, "To the memory of my beloved, The
AVTHOR, MR. WILLIAM SHAKESPEARE."

It seems not improbable, also, that Jonson lent touches to the two
prose items in the introductory matter to the Folio. Both appear
over the names of Heminge and Condell. In the dedicatory address
to the Earls of Pembroke and Montgomery, a glance at Jonson is
almost certainly implied in the phrase, "he [Shakespeare] not having the fate common with some [Jonson?], to be exequitor to his
owne writings." In this same address there appears one image which
may be unique with Jonson, that of the "gummes," in association
with sacrifices. He uses it thus in the dedication to Lady Mary
Wroth which precedes *The Alchemist*:

> In the age of sacrifices, the truth of religion was not in the
> greatnesse, & fat of the offrings, but in the deuotion, and zeale of
> the sacrificers: Else, what could a handfull of gummes haue done
> in the sight of a hecatombe?
>
> (V.289.1–5)[2]

The corresponding image in the First Folio is this:

> Country hands reach foorth milke, creame, fruites, or what they
> haue: and many Nations (we haue heard) that had not gummes &
> incense, obtained their requests with a leauened Cake. It was no
> fault to approch their Gods, by what meanes they could: And
> the most, though meanest, of things are made more precious, when
> they are dedicated to Temples.

Certainly much of the material of the address to the readers is
Jonsonian—the ranking of readers from foolish to wise, the cer-
tainty that the reader will "censure," the evolution of that censure,
"your six-pen 'orth, your shillings worth."[3]

---

scenes, and lines will be supplied from *Shakespeare, The Complete Works*,
ed. G. B. Harrison (New York, 1952).

[2] All passages quoted from the work of Jonson will be as they appear in
Ben Jonson, ed. by Herford and Simpson (11 vols.; Oxford, 1925–1952).

[3] This possibility that "To the great Variety of Readers" was partly Jonson's
was suggested by Steevens (Boswell's *Shakespeare* of 1820, II, 663–75), who
cited parallel passages from introductory matter to *Catiline, The New Inne*,

What does a man read who has just lost his books to the wrath of Vulcan? One possible reason for Vulcan's action, says Jonson in "Execration upon Vulcan," was that he found in Jonson's study some "pieces" of "base allay"—"parcels of a play." It is highly probable that those parcels belonged to *The Staple of Newes*, since we have no play from Jonson's hand after *The Devil is an Asse* (1615), and since the first to appear after the fire was *The Staple of Newes*. There is in that play, I believe, much echoing of Shakespeare, and very probably a specific tribute to him. Since Jonson did lose his library, and presumably his beloved Greek and Latin mentors, perhaps he was reduced to reading the work of his compeers, and the First Folio would easily come to hand. At any rate, one is reminded more of Shakespeare's plays in *The Staple of Newes* than in any other play by Jonson.

The Staple of Newes itself is a better play than scholars have conceded, though it is of course not among his greatest. But, it should certainly not be placed, with Dryden, among the "Dotages." [4] Its structure is like that of *The Devil is an Asse*, in which all lines of action converge on the greedy fool, Fitz-dottrell. The action converges in *The Staple of Newes* on the Lady Pecunia—almost an allegorical representation of wealth. The makers of news at the Staple, Cymbal and his fellows, seek to have her sojourn with them: the usurer, the "money-bawd," Peniboy Senior, strives to employ Pecunia and her servants, Mortgage, Statute, Band, Wax, and Broker, to bring him "ten in the hundred," and Peniboy Junior, to whom she is temporarily entrusted, employs her with something of the prodigality of a Timon of Athens. Peniboy Canter, in the attitude of a chorus, comments on events as they

---

The Magnetic Lady, Bartholomew Fayre, and *Discoveries*. Herford and Simpson (*Ben Jonson*, XI, 140–44) though tempted by the idea, on the whole reject it.

[4] In his *Jonson and the Comic Truth* (Madison, 1957), J. J. Enck so ranks it (250). C. G. Thayer, in his *Ben Jonson* (Norman, 1963), considers that to place *The Staple of Newes* among the "dotages" is a "gross misreading" (177). Herford and Simpson consider Jonson's "decadence" to have been suggested in *The Devil is an Asse*, but not in *The Staple of Newes*, though "disastrously clear" thereafter.

proceed, and resolves all problems at the end, with appropriate comment and punishment or reward. In a secondary choric role is Lickfinger, the cook. He is associated in a small capacity with all lines of action, but much of what he says, or of what is said of him, is extraneous to the central theme, the wooing, and the right use, of the Lady Pecunia.

In setting forth the speculation that in *The Staple of Newes* Jonson is much preoccupied with Shakespeare, that he is in some measure indebted to him, and that he incorporates in the play a massive tribute to him, I shall work along three paths. First, I shall suggest that Jonson is sufficiently indebted to *Timon of Athens* for incident, structure, and thought, that *Timon of Athens* should properly be listed among the sources of *The Staple of Newes.* I shall then collect occasional lines or phrases that may be echoes from Shakespeare's other plays. Finally, I shall follow the ubiquitous Lickfinger through various conversations to what I believe to be the tribute to Shakespeare—the passage describing "the *Master Cooke.*"

Perhaps sometime before the year 1623 Jonson set out to write a comedy about the right use of wealth. The most logical framework on which to hang such a commentary is the career of a prodigal in association with some symbol for wealth itself. These must in turn be supported by subsidiary figures such as the Miser, Peniboy Senior, the cheater, Cymbal, with his whole operation of the staple of news, and, finally, a sort of chorus, Peniboy Canter.

When Ben Jonson chose to use sources, he employed them freely, arrogantly. The list of major sources for *The Staple of Newes* is unusually long for a comedy by Jonson: *Plutus* and *The Wasps* of Aristophanes; Lucian's *Timon*; *The Deipnosophistae* of Athenaeus; *The London Prodigal*, which has been attributed to both Shakespeare and Jonson; Chaucer's *Hous of Fame*; Book five of Rabelais; and, of Jonson's own work, *The Case Is Altered, Cynthia's Revels*, and the masques *News from the New World, Neptunes Triumph* and *The Fortunate Isles.*[5] Before this essay is finished, it will appear

[5] For this information I am indebted to Herford and Simpson and to De Winter, ed., *The Staple of Newes* (New York, 1905).

that a dozen or more plays of Shakespeare's should be listed, perhaps as possible sources, perhaps as targets.

Of these many plays, however, only *Timon of Athens* appears
to have had an effect on both the structure and ideas of *The
Staple of Newes*. It is my opinion that the kinship between the two
plays is closer than editors have noted.

Jonson's prodigal, Peniboy Junior, is, I believe, partially conceived in terms of Shakespeare's prodigal, Timon.[6] There may
have been some reciprocity between the two authors—Shakespeare
for *Timon of Athens* borrowing from Jonson—and Jonson in turn
borrowing from *Timon of Athens*. Oscar J. Campbell has pointed
out that in *Timon of Athens* Shakespeare was undertaking a satirical play in the manner of Jonson's *Sejanus*.[7] The list of the eight
"principall Tragedians" which follows the text in the Jonson
Folio of 1616 has the name of Shakespeare in the fifth position.
Shakespeare's familiarity with "To the Readers" of the Quarto
may perhaps be assumed, particularly his knowledge of Jonson's
prescription for a tragic poem: "Truth of Argument, dignity of
Persons, grauity and height of Elocution, fulnesse and frequencie
of Sentence." *Timon of Athens* has much of "Elocution," and, I
believe, a self-conscious effort at "frequencie of Sentence." But
in a much more important aspect the two tragedies are alike: both
are essentially tragedies, not of an *individual*, but of a *state*. Rome,
worthy of a Sejanus, in spewing him out, places itself in subjection
to a worse man, Macro. In *Timon of Athens*, the city, guilty of
gross ingratitude on the level of the individual and of the state, and
of usury, avoids total destruction only by servile submission to
Alcibiades. In each play the author has mounted a massive satirical
attack on national corruption, the principal spokesman for Jonson
being Arruntius, for Shakespeare Timon himself, with help from
Apemantus. It is tempting to imagine that Shakespeare may have
played the part of Arruntius.

---

[6] Jonson has, of course, his own prodigal in Asotus of *Cynthia's Revels*.
Asotus is, however, a fool, as Peniboy Junior is not, and is incapable of seeing
his folly, while Peniboy Junior comes to see his clearly.

[7] Oscar J. Campbell, *Shakespeare's Satire* (New York, 1963), 168–97.

The relationships pointed out above suggest a little more likelihood that Jonson sought touches for his Prodigal in Timon, but even without them, kindred elements in the two plays indicate almost certain borrowing.

The openings of *Timon of Athens* and *The Staple of Newes* are remarkably similar: In *Timon of Athens* Poet, Painter, Jeweller and Merchant are assembled to prey on the Prodigal. In *The Staple of Newes* Fashioner, Linener, Haberdasher, Shoemaker and Spurrier are assembled for a similar purpose. In *Timon of Athens*, Apemantus warns against their rapacity. Peniboy Canter performs the same function in *The Staple of Newes*. Still in the first scene, Timon provides a dowry of three talents for a faithful servant, and pays a great debt to free Ventidius from prison. In what would for Shakespeare be still the first scene, Peniboy Junior buys for fifty pounds a place as clerk in the Staple for his follower, Tom the Barber.

Even more striking than the parallel opening scenes is the use of feasts as background for both commentary and action. In *Timon of Athens*, however, two feasts are required to accomplish what is done in *The Staple of Newes* in a single meeting in the Apollo room. It should be noted also that after the feasts, Peniboy Junior and Timon take different courses: Peniboy Junior to self-knowledge and restoration, Timon to utter misanthropy and self-destruction.

The first major accomplishment of each feast is the establishing of the mindless prodigality of Timon and Peniboy Junior. Timon makes much of refusing payment of Ventidius' debt, even though Ventidius is now rich through the death of his father. Ostentatiously also, he gives a jewel to the "1 Lord," a "trifle" to the "2 Lord," and a bay courser to the "3 Lord." Part of the representation of Peniboy Junior's folly is achieved allegorically—by his urging Pecunia to distribute her kisses promiscuously, even to Captain Shunfield, "Though he be a slugge," and to the "Poet-Sucker" Madrigal. The grand design of founding "Canters Colledge," with professorships for all the jeerers and for Lickfinger completes for Jonson the portrait of prodigality.

The list of guests at each feast has essentially the same composition: a prodigal host; his rapacious "friends"; and a single guest welcome only to the host, whose attitude throughout the feast is that of a bitter commentator on the folly and rapacity he is observing. The efforts of Apemantus in *Timon of Athens* are largely ineffective, but Peniboy Canter without mercy holds the guests up to ridicule, not only as canters like himself, but also as shabby pretenders to their professions.

In each feast also the loss by the Prodigal of his wealth is either predicted or achieved. In *Timon of Athens*, at the first feast, the steward Flavius seeks to inform Timon that he cannot pay for the rich gifts he is making, but is rebuffed. In *The Staple of Newes*, Peniboy Canter, moved beyond endurance by the folly of Canters' College, reveals himself as father to Peniboy Junior. He takes into his own protection Pecunia and her train and leaves his son only his "*Cloak*, To Travell in to Beggers Bush."

The final function of the feasting in both plays is the presentation of a sort of choric judgment on the flatterers. In *Timon of Athens* this effect is achieved by a second feast, that of the covered dishes of warm water, which Timon throws in the faces of his "guests." His accompanying invective is bitter:

> *Make the Meate be beloued, more then the Man that giues it. Let no Assembly of Twenty, be without a score of Villaines. If there sit twelue Women at the Table, let a dozen of them bee as they are. The rest of your Fees, O Gods, the Senators of Athens, together with the common legge of People, what is amisse in them, you Gods, make suteable for destruction. For these my present Freinds, as they are to mee nothing, so in nothing blesse them, and to nothing are they welcome.*
>
> (III. vi. 85–95)

The corresponding invective in *The Staple of Newes* is given to the Canter and is individualized in terms of professions: Fitton is "a moth, a rascall, a Court-rat, / That gnawes the commonwealth"; Shunfield is a "Scarre-crow / Cannot endure to heare of hazards"; the Doctor, Almanach, is a "dog-Leach" who can "erect a scheme / For my great *Madams* monkey"; Madrigal's "wreath / Is piec'd and patch'd of dirty witherd flowers."

While the opening scene and the feasting are the most obvious points in the indebtedness of Jonson, there are other items of re- semblance that are hardly less striking. One very brief passage in Act II of *Timon of Athens* may have suggested to Jonson his "Jeerers," a sort of choric group in *The Staple of Newes*, perform- ing functions not unlike those assigned to the anti-masques of the later masques. Caphis, Varro and Isidore, emissaries for three usu- rers, are proposing an assault upon Apemantus and the Foole:

> Caph. Stay, stay, here comes the Foole with Apemantus, let's ha' some sport with 'em.
>
> (II.ii.47, 48)

Further on in the exchange of jeering is this passage:

> Cap. Where's the Foole now?
> Ape. He last ask'd the question. Poor Rogues, and Vsurers men, Bauds betwene Gold and want.
>
> (II.ii.59–61)

It should be particularly noted that this passage is probably the origin of Jonson's striking epithet, "money-baud." It appears sev- eral times in *The Staple of Newes*, and later in *The Magnetic Lady*. It should also be observed that in each play, the concept money- bawd is produced by a figure primarily choric—Apemantus in the one case, Peniboy Canter in the other. Jonson's jeerers are Cymbal, Master of the Staple, Fitton, the courtier, Almanach, the "Doctor in Physick," Shunfield, the "Sea-captaine," and Madrigal, the "Poetaster." Their "game" is a concerted attack by way of insult on a helpless victim, or, in his absence, on one another. Here is a fair sample of their work in *The Staple of Newes*:

> CYM. You are a rogue. P. SE. I thinke I am Sir, truly.
> CYM. A Rascall, and a *money-bawd*. P.SE. My sur names:
> CYM. A wretched Rascall! P.SE. You will ouerflow—
> And spill all. CYM. Caterpiller, moath,
> Horse-leach, and dung-worme—
>
> (III.iv.81–85)

One other element of *Timon of Athens* may have been translated by Jonson into action, the material of these lines:

> Cracke the Lawyers voyce,
> That he may neuer more false Title pleade,
> Nor sound his Quillets shrilly.
>
> (IV.iii.153–55)

Much of the fifth act of *The Staple of Newes* is devoted to the effort of Picklocke, the man of law, who with "Fore-head of steele, and mouth of brasse" undertakes to deny the deed of trust by which he held the estate of Peniboy Canter while it—as Pecunia—sojourned with Peniboy Junior.

There is also close kinship in certain of the ideas in the two plays. On several occasions in *The Staple of Newes* there appears as part of Jonson's comdemnation of usury, the concept embodied in the last of these lines:

> CLA. No, but we heare of a *Colony* of cookes
> To be set a shore o' the coast of *America*,
> For the conuersion of the *Caniballs*,
> And making them good, eating *Christians*.
>
> (III.ii.155–58)

The theme of cannibalism is frequent in *Timon of Athens*:

> You must eate men (Timon to the Banditti)
> What a number of men eats Timon (Apemantus)
> Breakfast of enemies (Timon to Alcibiades).

A second pervasive theme in both plays is the nature and power of wealth, symbolized in *Timon of Athens* early in the play by Fortune and toward the end by "Yellow, glittering, precious Gold." In *The Staple of Newes*, the symbol throughout is, of course, the Lady Pecunia. Both Pecunia and Fortune of *Timon of Athens* have "ivory hands." There is a marked similarity among these passages, the first two from *Timon of Athens* and the other two from *The Staple of Newes*:

> O thou sweete King-killer, and deare diuorce
> Twixt naturall Sunne and fire: thou bright defiler

of *Himens* purest bed, thou valiant Mars,
Thou euer, yong, fresh, loued, and delicate wooer,
Whose blush doth thawe the consecrated Snow
That lyes on Dians lap.
Thou visible God,
That souldrest close Impossibilities,
And mak'st them kisse; that speak'st with euerie Tongue
To euerie purpose.

> (*Timon of Athens*, IV.iii.382–90)

Thus much of this will make
Blacke, white; fowle, faire; wrong, right;
Base, Noble; Old, young; Coward, valient.
Ha you Gods! why this? what this, you Gods? why this
Will lugge your Priests and Seruants from your sides:
Plucke stout mens pillowes from below their heads.
This yellow Slaue,
Will knit and breake Religions, blesse th'accurst,
Make the hoare Leprosie ador'd, place Theeues,
And giue them Title, knee, and approbation
With Senators on the Bench: This is it
That makes the wappen'd Widdow wed againe.

> (*Timon of Athens*, IV.iii.28–38)

All this *Nether-world*
Is yours, you command it, and doe sway it,
The honour of it, and the honesty,
The reputation, I, and the religion,
(I was about to say, and had not err'd)
Is Queene *Pecunia's*.

> (*The Staple of Newes*, II.i.38–43)

She makes good cheare, she keepes full boards,
She holds a Faire of Knights, and Lords,
A Mercat of all Offices,
And Shops of honour, more or lesse.
According to Pecunia's *Grace,*
The Bride hath beauty, blood, and place,
The Bridegroom vertue, valour, wit,
And wisedome, as he stands for it.

> (*The Staple of Newes*, IV.ii.109–116)

While the resemblances cited above are no certain proof of indebtedness, they do strongly imply that Shakespeare's *Timon of*

Athens did suggest situation, idea, phrase, to Jonson, to be imitated, expanded, perhaps transmuted into Jonsonian matter. The idea that Jonson borrowed from *Timon of Athens* is reinforced also by the fact that some more obvious borrowings, or thrusts, from perhaps a dozen of Shakespeare's plays appear almost at random throughout *The Staple of Newes*, in addition to the more concentrated Shakespearean matter in the passages involving Lickfinger, the Master Cooke.

Of the group which I have specified as "occasional lines or phrases" echoing Shakespeare, the first that should be noted is a line not actually in Shakespeare, but attributed to him by Jonson.[8] It occurs in the "Induction," being spoken by Prologue to the four Gossips, Mirth, Tatle, Expectation, and Censure, who constitute a more or less formal Chorus—one which is a very thinly disguised cross-section of the very spectators viewing *The Staple of Newes*. Says Prologue, "Cry you mercy, you never did wrong, but with just cause." Since the "Induction," aside from names and speech prefixes, is set up in italics, the line itself, not in italics, is represented as a quotation. The passage in which Jonson attributes the line to Shakespeare is well known, but should be in part reproduced here:

> I *remember*, the Players have often mentioned it as an honour to *Shakespeare*, that in his writing, (whatsoever he penn'd) hee never blotted out line. My answer hath beene, Would he had blotted a thousand.
>
> . . . .
>
> Many times hee fell into those things, could not escape laughter: As when hee said in the person of *Caesar*, one speaking to him; *Caesar, thou dost me wrong.* He replyed: *Caesar did never wrong, but with just cause.*

(Discoveries, lines 647–65)

The line was presumably once in *Julius Caesar*, and one can almost wish that it remained instead of those which probably replaced it:

> Know *Caesar* doth not wrong, nor without cause
> Will he be satisfied.

(III.i. 47, 48)

[8] For extended discussions of what may have happened in connection with this line, see De Winter, 125–28; and Herford and Simpson, XI, 231–33.

The *Discoveries* must have been written after the fire of 1623, for in the "Execration upon Vulcan" Jonson says that he lost

twice-twelve-yeares stor'd up humanitie,
With humble Gleanings in Divinitie.

One wonders, of course, whether the reference to *Julius Caesar* is recovered from the "twice-twelve-yeares stor'd up humanitie," or is produced afresh, after 1623, as a consequence of the publication of the First Folio. It is probably nothing more than coincidence that both Caesar and Peniboy Senior are deaf in one ear, but it may be worth noting in connection with the definite reference to *Julius Caesar* made in Prologue's quotation.

Of Tom the Barber, who has, while eavesdropping, heard Picklocke first admit, and then deny, that he held Peniboy Canter's estate in trust, says Picklocke, "a rat behind the hangings." The likelihood that this is an echo of the slaying of Polonius in *Hamlet* is noted by De Winter.[9] Probably a glance at the play within a play, the "Mousetrap," of *Hamlet* is intended in Mirth's comment on the courtier Fitton in the "fourth Intermeane": "*and lie so, in waite for a piece of wit like a Mousetrap.*" In the same scene, Picklocke accuses Peniboy Junior of being "Sicke of selfe-love." Herford and Simpson are reminded of Olivia's analysis, in *Twelfth Night*, of Malvolio: "O, you are sick of self-love."[10]

Three common proverbs are used by Jonson in *The Staple of Newes* and by Shakespeare. It would be rash, of course, to insist that Jonson borrowed them from Shakespeare, but it is interesting to examine in juxtaposition the manner in which they are put to work by the two writers. In *III Henry VI*, York is speaking to Queen Margaret:

It needes not, nor it bootes thee not, prowd Queene,
Vnlesse the Adage must be verify'd,
That Beggers mounted, runne their Horse to death.
(I.iv.125–27)

Shakespeare's use of the proverb is rhetorical, sententious, part of an attack on the poverty of Margaret's father, the King of Na-

[9] De Winter, ed., *The Staple of Newes*, 220.
[10] Herford and Simpson, *Ben Jonson*, X, 289.

ples. Jonson takes the formality out of his use of the proverb, giving it to Gossip Tatle in the fourth Intermeane, as a part of a foolish attack by his Chorus on his beggar, Peniboy Canter: "*I, but set a beggar on horse-backe, hee'll neuer linne till hee be a gallop.*" In *II Henry VI*, Hume is speaking in soliloquy: "They say, a craftie Knaue do's need no Broker, / Yet am I *Suffolke* and the Cardinalls Broker" (I. ii. 100, 101). Jonson's use of the same proverb is less obvious: "P.IV. A fine well-spoken family. What's thy name? / BRO. *Broker*. P.IV. Me thinks my vncle should not need thee, / Who is a crafty Knaue, enough, beleeue it" (II. v. 82–84).

Jonson's acquaintance with the three parts of *Henry VI* is shown by his attack in the Prologue to *Every Man in His Humour*;

> Or, with three rustie swords,
> And helpe of some few foot-and-halfe-foot words,
> Fight ouer *Yorke*, and *Lancasters* long Jarres.
>
> (Prologue. 9–11)

Still a third proverb is used by both men, this being Shakespeare's version in *All's Well that Ends Well*:

> *Clo.* My poore bodie Madam requires it, I am driuen onby the flesh, and hee must needes goe that the diuell driues.
>
> (I.iii.30–32)

Jonson's use of the proverb is the more sophisticated in that he expects his audience to recognize it in an exchange of repartee:

> FIT. An odde bargaine of Venison, To driue. P. SE. Will you goe in, knaue? LIC. I must needs, You see who driues me, gentlemen. ALM. Not the *diuell*.
>
> (II.iv.37–39)

The remaining group of what I have designated as "occasional lines or phrases" appears in *Troilus and Cressida*. The passages cannot, of course, be called parallels, but they come inevitably to mind to one who is familiar with both *Troilus and Cressida* and *The Staple of Newes*. Jonson had some reason from earlier days to be familiar with Shakespeare's play, for in *Poetaster* he had attacked, if not Shakespeare himself, at least the members of Shakespeare's company. The writer of a Cambridge play, 3 *Parnassus*, suggests that Shakespeare in reply to *Poetaster* had given Jonson "a purge that made him bewray his credit."[11] This purge has not been certainly identified, but perhaps the likeliest candidate for it is the portrait of Ajax in *Troilus and Cressida*, as spoken by Cressida's servant Alexander:

> This man Lady, hath rob'd many beasts of their particular additions, he is as valiant as the Lyon, churlish as the Beare, slow as the Elephant: a man into whom nature hath so crowded humors, that his valour is crusht into folly, his folly sauced with discretion: there is no man hath a vertue, that he hath not a glimpse of, nor any man an attaint, but he carries some staine of it. He is melancholy without cause, and merry against the haire, he hath the ioynts of euery thing, but euery thing so out of ioynt, that hee is a gowtie *Briareus*, many hands and no vse; or purblinded *Argus*, all eyes and no sight.
>
> (I.ii.9–31)

Later in the play Thersites, the foul-mouthed commentator, says to Ajax,

> thou hast no more braine then I haue in mine elbows:
> An Asinico may tutor thee.
>
> (II.i.47–49)

This is the first usage of *assinigo* recorded in the *New English Dictionary*. The word delights Jonson, for it provides him with a happy epithet for his collaborator and enemy, Inigo Jones: "You would be an Asinigo by your ears."[12] Jonson uses the word in *The Staple of Newes*, of Shunfield the cowardly captain:

> FIT. To be fairely knock'd o' the head.
> SHV. With a good Ieere or two. P.SE. And from your iawbone,
> *Don Assinigo?*[13]
>
> (V.v.12–14)

[11] *A Select Collection of Old English Plays*, ed. W. Carew Hazlitt (15 vols.; London, 1874), IX, 194.
[12] From "Expostulation with Inigo Jones" (Herford and Simpson, VIII, 403).
[13] Both De Winter and Herford and Simpson note Shakespeare's use of "Assinigo" in *Troilus and Cressida*.

There are two rather striking ideas in *Troilus and Cressida* which may possibly be echoed by Jonson in *The Staple of Newes*. Aeneas, ironically rebuking himself, says

> The worthiness of praise distaines his worth:
> If that he prais'd himselfe, bring the praise forth.
> (I.iii.241–42)

In *The Staple of Newes* Jonson has Peniboy Junior boast to Pecunia of his generosity in buying the clerk's place for Tom the barber. In a typical Jonsonian manner what was in effect a "sentence" in *Troilus and Cressida* is delivered as dialogue in *The Staple of Newes*:

> P.CA. He should haue spoke of that, Sir, and not
> you: Two doe not doe one Office well. P.IV. 'Tis
> true, But I am loth to lose my curtesies.
> P.CA. So are all they, that doe them, to vaine ends,
> And yet you do lose, when you pay you(r) selues.
> (III.ii.9–13)

In *Troilus and Cressida*, Hector speaks this sentence in the course of the debate over continuing the war:

> 'Tis made Idolatrie
> To make the seruice greater then the God.
> (II.ii.56,57)

The same idea is used twice in *The Staple of Newes*. The first is, characteristically, a dialogue:

> PEC. Why do you so, my Guardian? I not bid you,
> Cannot my *Grace* be gotten, and held too,
> Without your selfe-tormentings, and your watches,
> Your macerating of your body thus
> With cares, and scantings of your dyet, and rest?
> P.SE. O, no, your seruices, my *Princely Lady*,
> Cannot with too much zeale of *rites* be done,
> They are so sacred. PEC. But my Reputation
> May suffer, and the worship of my family,
> When by so seruile meanes they both are sought.
> (II.i.21–30)

The second use of the idea is in the form of a sentence spoken inevitably by Peniboy Canter:

> Superstition
> Doth violate the Deity it worships.
>
> (V.vi.23, 24)

It has been suggested earlier that Lickfinger, the Cooke, shares largely in the choric commentary, along with Peniboy Canter, and that much of the material that may be of Shakespearean origin is in those passages where he takes part in the dialogue. Yet, his function is not, as is the Canter's, primarily to show the proper use of Pecunia, but to comment on the nature of poetry and the poet. He is almost obsessed by the idea that the arts of poetry and cookery are one—and that the origin of both is in the "Kitchin." In *Neptunes Triumph* Jonson acknowledges indebtedness for this idea to the *Deipnosophistae* of Athenaeus, but he pushes Lickfinger's ideas so persistently that the Cooke becomes almost a humorous character. In those portions of the play where Lickfinger appears, or is discussed, he functions in a sense in a dual role: as the object of commentary which is, I believe, spoken in reality of Shakespeare; and, when Lickfinger himself speaks of the "mastercooke," I believe he is speaking for Jonson about Shakespeare.

The name of this philosopher of the kitchen probably came, if not out of Jonson's own fertile invention, from *Romeo and Juliet*. This is Shakespeare's use of the proverb, "It is an ill cook that cannot lick his own fingers."

> *Cap.* So many guests inuite as here are writ, Sirrah, go hire me twenty cunning Cookes.
> *Ser.* You shall haue none ill sir, for Ile trie if they can licke their fingers.
> *Cap.* How canst thou trie them so?
> *Ser.* Marrie sir, 'tis an ill Cooke that cannot licke his owne fingers: therefore he that cannot licke his fingers goes not with me.
>
> (IV.ii.1–8)

Our first introduction is to the Lickfinger who is Jonson himself —of the "mountaine Belly." Peniboy Senior inquires of Broker,

Where's *Lickfinger* my Cooke? that vnctuous rascall?
Hee'll neuer keepe his houre, that vessel of kitchinstuffe.
(II.ii.68.69)

Having arrived late by half an hour, Lickfinger excuses himself in these words:

> I haue lost two stone
> Of suet i' the seruice posting hither,
> You might haue followed me like a watering pot,
> And seene the knots I made along the street.[14]
> (II.iii. 13–16)

One is reminded on reading the passage of Prince Hal's wonderful lines about Falstaff:

> *Falstaffe* sweates to death,
> and Lards the leane earth as he walkes along.
> (*1 Henry IV*, II. ii. 115–16)

The next appearance of our unctuous cook is at the office of the Staple, where he seeks news to enliven a feast to be prepared by him and served in the Apollo room, the occasion being the entertainment of Pecunia and her train by Peniboy Junior. But what Lickfinger says of himself is, I suggest, said of Shakespeare. The essential passage is this:

> P.IV. What *Lickfinger*! wilt thou conuert the *Caniballs*,
> With spit and pan Diuinity? LIC. Sir, for that
> I will not vrge, but for the fire and zeale
> To the true cause; thus I haue vndertaken:
> With two Lay-bretheren, to my selfe, no more,
> One o' the broach, th' other o' the boyler,
> In one six months, and by plaine cookery,
> No magick to 't, but old *Iaphets* physicke,
> The father of the *European* Arts,
> To make such sauces for the Sauages,
> And cooke their meats, with those inticing steemes,

[14] Jonson is perhaps also borrowing from Jonson. These are Ursula's words in *Bartholomew Fayre*:

A poore vex'd thing I am, I feele my selfe dropping already, as fast as I can: two stone a sewet aday is my proportion.
(II. ii. 79–81)

As it would make our *Caniball-Christians*,
Forbeare the mutuall eating one another,
Which they doe doe, more cunningly, then the wilde
Anthropophagi; that snatch onely strangers,
Like my old Patrons dogs, there.

(III.ii.165–80)

The enterprise of converting the "Caniballs" is perhaps the publication of the First Folio itself. The two "Lay-bretheren" may well be Heminge and Condell, or possibly the noble Earls of Pembroke and Montgomery. The "mutuall eating" one another by "Caniball-Christians" is perhaps an echo of the passage in *The Merchant of Venice*, between Jessica and Launcelot Gobbo:

> *Jes.* I shall be sau'd by my husband, he hath made me a Christian.
> *Clow.* Truly the more to blame he, we were Christians enow
> before, e'ne as many as could wel liue, one by another: this making
> of Christians will raise the price of Hogs, if wee grow all to be
> porke-eaters, wee shall not shortlie haue a rasher on the coales for
> money.

(III.v.121–29)

The "Anthropophagi" appear, not only in *Othello* (I.iii.144), but also in *The Merry Wives of Windsor* (IV.v.9). Finally, "My old Patrons dogs there," named Block and Lollard, will in a sort of mad scene endure a very unfair trial at the hands of Peniboy Senior. One is reminded of Launce's interrogation of his dog in *The Two Gentlemen of Verona* who, like Block and Lollard, "made water against a gentlewoman's farthingale." The trial scene in *The Staple of Newes* inevitably brings to mind King Lear's mock trial of his daughters, but one must, I suppose, agree with the anguished utterance of Coleridge, "I dare not, will not think that Honest Ben had Lear in his mind in this mad scene."[15]

In the same scene, though not spoken by Lickfinger, there appears to be a glance at a pair of stage directions in *The Tempest*:

> *Solemne and strange Musicke: and Prosper on the top (inuisible:)*
> *Enter seuerall strange shapes, bringing in a Banket; and daunce*

---

15 S. T. Coleridge, *Lectures and Notes on Shakespeare and Other Dramatists*, in *The World's Classics Series* (London, 1931), 266.

about it with gentle actions of salutations, and inuiting the King, &c. to eate, they depart.

(III. iii. s.d. following 19)

He vanishes in Thunder: then (to soft Musicke.) Enter the shapes againe, and daunce (with mockes and mowes) and carrying out the Table.

(III. s.d. following 82)

The lines in *The Staple of Newes* are a part of the unsuccessful wooing of Pecunia by Cymbal, the master of the Staple:

> Your meat should be seru'd in with curious dances,
> And set vpon the boord, with virgin hands,
> Tun'd to their voices; not a dish remou'd,
> But to the *Musicke*, nor a drop of wine,
> Mixt, with his water, without *Harmony*.

(III.ii.230–34)

While we are still at the office of the Staple, there is additional discussion of Lickfinger in which comments made about him appear to be references to the work of Shakespeare:

> ALM. I was at an *Olla Podrida* of his making,
> Was a braue piece of *cookery*! at a funerall,
> But opening the pot-lid, he made vs laugh,
> Who'had wept all day! and sent vs such a tickling
> Into our nostrills, as the funerall feast
> Had bin a wedding-dinner. SHV. Gi' him allowance,
> And that but moderate, he will make a *Syren*
> Sing i' the Kettle, send in an *Arion*,
> In a braue broth, and of a watry greene,
> Iust the Sea-colour, mounted on the backe
> Of a growne *Cunger*, but, in such a posture,
> As all the world would take him for a *Dolphin*.

(III.iii.29–40)

It seems highly probable that Hamlet's lines, "The funeral baked meats / Did coldly furnish forth the marriage tables," lie behind "The funerall feast had bin a wedding-dinner." The image of Arion on the dolphin's back occurs in *Twelfth Night* (I.ii.15), or possibly Jonson had in mind the image of the "mermaid on a dolphin's back" of *Midsummer Night's Dream* (II.i.150).

The possibility that the work of Shakespeare was in Jonson's mind as he wrote the passages pointed out above suggests that the *Olla Podrida* (putrid pot) may also concern Shakespeare. It may, in view of the reference to the "funerall feast" be an assessment of *Hamlet*. But there are other possibilities. For the meaning of Olla Podrida, the *New English Dictionary* offers this interesting quotation:

> 1622 Mabbe, Sr. Aleman's *Guzeman*
> "Olla podrida, is a very great one, contayning in it divers things, as Mutton, Beefe, Hens, Capons, Sawsages, Piggs feete, Garlick, Onions, &c. It is called *Podrida*, because it is sod leisurely, til it be rotten (as we say) and ready to fall in peeces.... In English it may well beare the name of Hodge-podge."

Passages in two plays other than *Hamlet* might have inspired the epithet. The first is, naturally, the cauldron of the witches in *Macbeth*:

> Fillet of a Fenny Snake,
> In the Caldron boyle and bake:
> Eye of Newt and Toe of Frogge,
> Wooll of Bat and Tongue of Dogge:
> Adders Forke and Blinde-wormes Sting,
> Lizards legge and Howlets wing.
>   (IV.i.12–17)

A second possibility for the "Olla Podrida" is in *Titus Andronicus*, a play singled out for special attack, along with *The Spanish Tragedy*, in the "Induction" of Jonson's *Bartholomew Fayre*. In the fifth act Titus has in his power the sons of Tamora, who have ravished Lavinia, cut off her hands, and cut out her tongue:

> Harke Villaines, I will grin'd your bones to dust,
> And with your blood and it, Ile make a Paste,
> And of the Paste a Coffen I will reare,
> And make two Pasties of your shamefull Heads,
> And bid that strumpet your vnhallowed Dam,
> Like to the earth swallow her increase.
> This is the Feast, that I haue bid her to,
> And this the Banquet she shall surfet on,

For worse then *Philomel* you vsd my Daughter,
And worse then *Progne*, I will be reueng'd,
And now prepare your throats: *Lauinia* come.
Receiue the blood, and when that they are dead,
Let me goe grin'd their Bones to powder small,
And with this hateful Liquor temper it,
And in that Paste let their vil'd Heads be bakte.

(V.ii.187–201)

The "Coffen" of the third line is a pastry shell, and our friend Lickfinger uses "coffins" for his "red-Deere Pyes." The terrible banquet does indeed get served to Tamora, with Titus *"like a cooke, placing the meat on the Table."* [16]

In *Neptunes Triumph*, not performed "at the Court on the Twelfth night, 1623" (1624) there occurs this dialogue:

> COOKE
> Were you euer a *Cooke*?
> POET
> A Cooke? no surely
> COOKE
> Then you can be no good *Poet*. For a good Poet differs nothing at all from a *Master-Cooke*. Eithers Art is the wisdome of the Mind.

Shortly thereafter there follows a tribute to "a *Master-Cooke*," which appears in substantially the same form in *The Staple of Newes*, though there Lickfinger speaks of "the" master cook.

In *The Staple of Newes* the passage occurs in a dialogue between Madrigal "the Eg-chind *Laureat*," whose "wreath / Is piec'd and patch'd of dirty witherd flowers" (George Wither?) [17] and the redoubtable Lickfinger. I submit that in these lines Jonson, through Lickfinger the Cooke, speaks, as he does in the front mat-

---

[16] The "Arion" on a "Dolphin," the "Olla Podrida," and the massive military image for the Cooke's efforts, of this passage appear also in *The Bloody Brother*, by B.J.F., printed in 1639, where they are there spoken by a "Master Cooke." *The Bloody Brother* is of uncertain date and authorship, but the probability is that the images are in a passage written by John Fletcher (though frequently assigned to Jonson), imitating not *The Staple of Newes*, but identical passages in *Neptunes Triumph*.

[17] See De Winter, *The Staple of Newes*, pp. lv–lix.

ter of the Folio, of the "beloved, The AVTHOR MR. WILLIAM
SHAKESPEARE:"

A Boyler, Range, and Dresser were the *Fountaines,*
Of all the knowledge in the *uniuerse.*
And they'are the *Kitchins,* where the *Master-Cooke—*
(Thou dost not know the man, nor canst thou know him,
Till thou hast seru'd some yeeres in that deepe schoole,
That's both the *Nurse* and *Mother* of the *Arts,*
And hear'st him read, interpret, and demonstrate!)
A *Master-Cooke!* Why, he's the *man* o' men,
For a *Professor!* he designs, he drawes,
He paints, he carues, he builds, he fortifies,
Makes *Citadels* of curious fowle and fish,
Some he *dri-ditches,* some *motes* round with *broths.*
Mounts *marrowbones,* cuts *fifty-angled custards,*
Reares *bulwark* pies, and for his *outer workes*
He raiseth *Ramparts* of immortall *crust;*
And teacheth all the *Tacticks,* at one dinner;
What *Rankes,* what *Files,* to put his dishes in;
The whole *Art Military.* Then he knowes,
The influence of the *Starres* vpon his meats,
And all their seasons, tempers, qualities,
And so to fit his relishes, and sauces,
He has *Nature* in a pot, 'boue all the *Chymists,*
Or airy bretheren of the *Rosie-crosse.*
He is an *Architect,* an *Inginer,*
A *Souldiour,* a *Physician,* a *Philosopher,*
A generall *Mathematician.* MAD. It is granted.
    LIC. And that you may not doubt him, for a *Poet—*
    ALM. This *fury* shewes, if there were nothing else!
And 'tis diuine! I shall for euer, hereafter,
Admire the wisedome of a *Cooke!*
                                (IV, ii, 12–41)

There is little in the passage quoted which might be identifiable
as specific reference to Shakespeare's work. The "deepe schoole"
of line sixteen may be the First Folio. Probably the "curious fowle
and fish" are suggested by *The Tempest.* "The influence of the
Starres" may contain a glance at the star-crossed lovers of *Romeo*

and Juliet. "*Nature* in a pot" is reminiscent of these lines in "To the Memory":

> *Nature her selfe was proud of his designes,*
> *And ioy'd to weare the dressing of his lines!*

In the same poem Jonson renders great tribute to Shakespeare's art, ending the passage with a pun in military terms on Shakespeare's name: "*he seems to shake a Lance, / As brandish't at the eyes of ignorance.*" In the "Master-Cooke" passage Jonson conceives the cook's art altogether in military terms.

One who is at home with Shakespeare's plays does indeed feel that an "*Architect*" has built most of them—or perhaps that the mind of an architect has fitted the language and action to the geography of the stages of The Theater and the Globe; that an "*Inginer*" helped the "*Souldiour*" plan the military excursions; that a true "*Physician*" did indeed diagnose and prescribe for the ailments of a Lear or a Lady Macbeth; that a "*Philosopher*" asked the great questions of *King Lear* and *Hamlet*. But he is perhaps unwilling to concede that a "*Mathematician*" could have produced the confusion among the "talents" of *Timon of Athens.*

If this portrait of "the *Master-Cooke*" is indeed a tribute to Shakespeare by Jonson, perhaps one of the greatest tributes of all lies in omissions. The master cook is given no competence in law or religion—two professions which could be exemplified by Jonson in such practitioners as Voltore and Tribulation Wholesome.

Of the many parallels, echoes, or perhaps friendly thrusts, suggested above, some few are almost certainly references to the work of Shakespeare; many others may be—or may not be—concerned with Shakespeare; and very probably some of the resemblances in idea or phrase are merely fortuitous.

But I believe that in the aggregate, they offer a very strong suggestion that about 1623 Jonson renewed his knowledge of the plays of Shakespeare. Possibly his reading was done in preparation for rendering assistance in assembling the front matter of the volume. Perhaps it was done as a consequence of the loss of his own library to Vulcan. Whatever the reason, the work of Shakespeare was in the mind of Jonson as he wrote *The Staple of Newes*, to the extent, I believe, of a very noble tribute to the "*Master-Cooke.*"

INDEX

Abbott, George, Archbishop of Canterbury, 163–64

Allegory: in *CR*, 30–31, 44, 48, 57; in *SN*, 27, 44

Andrews, Launcelot, Bishop of Ely, 164

Appearance vs. reality: as key to Humourous Group, 5, 53, 58–60, 89, 112, 118; symbolic values in *BF*, 165–75

Aristophanes, 15; as source for J, 174, 179

Athenaeus: as source for J, 179, 191

Audience: J's attitude toward, 15–16, 21–24, 46, 119, 121, 168

Barish, Jonas A., cited, 72 n., 150 n.

Baum, Helena Watts, cited, 4 n., 167 n.

Berringer, Ralph W., cited, 128 n.

Bloody Brother, The, 196 n.

Braggart: as basic comic character, 59–64, 82–84. *See also* Hypocritical Man

Broker: as basic comic character, 4, 29–46, 123; as "bawd," 29–30, 33–34, 36, 38–40, 44–45, 118; as necessary comic tool, 31, 45–46; distinct from Wits, 34; not punished, 44; plays without Broker, 30–31, 40, 45; possessing humourous traits, 44–45; use of Plyant Woman, 46–48. *See also* Broker Group

Broker Group, 4–5, 29–50, 123; as satiric commentator, 29, 36–37, 38, 42–44; as dispenser of comic fates, 29; as "winderup," 29, 31–34, 36–39, 42–44, 50; not humours characters, 49; not punished, 44, 50; use of "bait," 46–49

Buckingham, George Villiers, Duke of, 66, 176

Bunyan, John, 150

Butter, Nathaniel, 21 n.

Campbell, Oscar J., cited, 180

Campion, Thomas, 152 n.

Carleton, Sir Dudley, 155

Carr, Robert: *See* Somerset, Earl of

Chamberlain, John: on Carr-Howard scandal, 155, 156–59, 163–64

Chambers, E. K., cited, 128 n., 165 n.

Chapman, George, 145, 162–63

Charles I, 176

Chaucer, Geoffrey, 161; as source for J, 179

Choric Group, 4–5, 5–29, 118, 123; 166; as dispenser of comic fates, 10, 10–11, 14, 118; as spokesman for J, 28–29, 49, 118; not humours characters, 28, 49

Chorus: as basic comic character, 4, 10–24, 123; as dispenser of comic fates, 10, 10–11, 14; as J's spokesman, 10, 12, 13, 13–14, 14, 15, 49; as mover of dramatic action, 10, 12–13, 14; as satiric commentator, 10, 11, 11–13, 14, 15, 69, 105; as semiformal chorus, 15–24; as audience: *see* "Grex," "Intermeane," "Chorus." *See also* Choric Group

Coleridge, S. T., cited, 193

Comedy of manners: The Wit, 5

Condell, Henry: as Shakespeare Folio editor, 176, 177, 193

Courtling: as basic comic character, *see* Would-Be Man

Deity: as basic comic character, 4, 24–29, 123; as dispenser of comic fates, 25, 50; as mover of action, 27; as satiric commentator, 26–27; as fallible character, 25; as allegorical figure, 27. *See also* Choric Group

Dekker, Thomas: Demetrius Fannius as, 91–92; *Satiromastix*, cited, 127–28

Devereaux, Walter Bouchier, cited, 162